TO PLUCK UP,
TO TEAR DOWN

i

INTERNATIONAL THEOLOGICAL COMMENTARY

Fredrick Carlson Holmgren and George A. F. Knight
General Editors

TO PLUCK UP, TO TEAR DOWN

A Commentary on the Book of

Jeremiah 1–25

WALTER BRUEGGEMANN

WM. B. EERDMANS PUBL. CO., GRAND RAPIDS

THE HANDSEL PRESS LTD, EDINBURGH

Copyright © 1988 by Wm. B. Eerdmans Publishing Co.
First published 1988 by William B. Eerdmans Publishing Company,
255 Jefferson Ave. S.E., Grand Rapids, Mich. 49503
and
The Handsel Press Limited
33 Montgomery Street, Edinburgh EH7 5JX

Reprinted, October 1993

Library of Congress Cataloging-in-Publication Data

Brueggemann, Walter.
To pluck up, to tear down :
a commentary on the book of Jeremiah 1-25 / Walter Brueggemann.
p.   cm. — (International theological commentary)
Bibliography: p. 220
ISBN 0-8028-0367-9
1. Bible.   O.T.   Jeremiah I-XXV — Commentaries.
2. Bible.   O.T.   Jeremiah I-XXV — Theology.   I. Title.   II. Series.
BS1525.3.B78   1988

224'.207—dc19   88-19722
                                                                          CIP

Eerdmans ISBN 0-8028-0367-9

Handsel ISBN 0 905312 87 2

CONTENTS

ABBREVIATIONS

ICC	*International Critical Commentary*
JSOT	*Journal for the Study of the Old Testament*
LXX	Septuagint
RSV	Revised Standard Version
SBL	Society of Biblical Literature

EDITORS' PREFACE

The Old Testament alive in the Church: this is the goal of the *International Theological Commentary*. Arising out of changing, unsettled times, this Scripture speaks with an authentic voice to our own troubled world. It witnesses to God's ongoing purpose and to his caring presence in the universe without ignoring those experiences of life that cause one to question his existence and love. This commentary series is written by front-rank scholars who treasure the life of faith.

Addressed to ministers and Christian educators, the *International Theological Commentary* moves beyond the usual critical-historical approach to the Bible and offers a *theological* interpretation of the Hebrew text. Thus, engaging larger textual units of the biblical writings, the authors of these volumes assist the reader in the appreciation of the theology underlying the text as well as its place in the thought of the Hebrew Scriptures. But more, since the Bible is the book of the believing community, its text has acquired ever more meaning through an ongoing interpretation. This growth of interpretation may be found both within the Bible itself and in the continuing scholarship of the Church.

Contributors to the *International Theological Commentary* are Christians—persons who affirm the witness of the New Testament concerning Jesus Christ. For Christians, the Bible is *one* Scripture containing the Old and New Testaments. For this reason, a commentary on the Old Testament may not ignore the second part of the canon, namely, the New Testament.

Since its beginning, the Church has recognized a special relationship between the two Testaments. But the precise character of this bond has been difficult to define. The diversity of views represented in these publications makes us aware that the Church is not of one mind in expressing the "how" of this relationship. The authors of this series share a developing consensus that any serious explanation of the Old Testament's relationship to the New will uphold the integrity of the Old Testament. Even though Christianity is rooted in the soil of the Hebrew Scriptures, the biblical interpreter must take care lest he "christianize" these Scriptures.

Authors writing in this commentary series will, no doubt, hold various views concerning *how* the Old Testament relates to the New. No attempt has been made to dictate one viewpoint in this matter. With the whole Church, we are convinced that the relationship between the two Testaments is real and substantial. But we recognize also the diversity of opinions among Christian scholars when they attempt to articulate fully the nature of this relationship.

In addition to the Christian Church, there exists another people for whom the Old Testament is important, namely, the Jewish community. Both Jews and Christians claim the Hebrew Bible as Scripture. Jews believe that the basic teachings of this Scripture point toward, and are developed by, the Talmud, which assumed its present form about 500 C.E. On the other hand, Christians hold that the Old Testament finds its fulfillment in the New Testament. The Hebrew Bible, therefore, belongs to both the Church and the Synagogue.

Recent studies have demonstrated how profoundly early Christianity reflects a Jewish character. This fact is not surprising because the Christian movement arose out of the context of first-century Judaism. Further, Jesus himself was Jewish, as were the first Christians. It is to be expected, therefore, that Jewish and Christian interpretations of the Hebrew Bible will reveal similarities *and* disparities. Such is the case. The authors of the *International Theological Commentary* will refer to the various Jewish traditions that they consider important for an appreciation of the Old Testament text. Such references will enrich our understanding of certain biblical passages and, as an extra gift, offer us insight into the relationship of Judaism to early Christianity.

An important second aspect of the present series is its *international* character. In the past, Western church leaders were considered to be *the* leaders of the Church—at least by those living in the West! The theology and biblical exegesis done by these scholars dominated the thinking of the Church. Most commentaries were produced in the Western world and reflected the lifestyle, needs, and thoughts of its civilization. But the Christian Church is a worldwide community. People who belong to the universal Church reflect differing thoughts, needs, and lifestyles.

Today the fastest-growing churches in the world are to be found, not in the West, but in Africa, Indonesia, South America, Korea, Taiwan, and elsewhere. By the end of the century, Christians in these areas will outnumber those who live in the West. In our age, especially, a commentary on the Bible must transcend the parochialism of Western civilization and be sensitive to issues that are the special problems of persons who live outside the "Christian" West, issues such as race relations, personal survival and fulfillment, liberation, revolution, famine, tyranny, disease, war, the poor, religion, and state. Inspired by God, the authors of the Old Testament knew what life is like on the edge of existence. They addressed themselves to everyday people who often faced more than everyday problems. Refusing to limit God to the "spiritual," they portrayed him as one who heard and knew the cries of people in pain (see Exod. 3:7-8). The contributors to the *International Theological Commentary* are persons who prize the writings of these biblical authors as a word of life to our world today. They read the Hebrew Scriptures in the contexts of ancient Israel and our modern day.

The scholars selected as contributors underscore the international aspect of the Commentary. Representing very different geographical, ideological, and ecclesiastical backgrounds, they come from over seventeen countries. Besides scholars from such traditional countries as England, Scotland, France, Italy, Switzerland, Canada, New Zealand, Australia, South Africa, and the United States, contributors from the following places are included: Israel, Indonesia, India, Thailand, Singapore, Taiwan, and countries of Eastern Europe. Such diversity makes for richness of thought. Christian scholars living in Buddhist, Muslim, or Socialist lands may be able to offer the World Church insights into the biblical message—insights to which the scholarship of the West could be blind.

The proclamation of the biblical message is the focal concern of the *International Theological Commentary*. Generally speaking, the authors of these commentaries value the historical-critical studies of past scholars, but they are convinced that these studies by themselves are not enough. The Bible is more than an object of critical study; it is the revelation of God. In the written Word, God has disclosed himself and his will to humankind. Our authors see themselves as servants of the Word which, when rightly received, brings *shalom* to both the individual and the community.

—George A. F. Knight
—Fredrick Carlson Holmgren

AUTHOR'S PREFACE

My access to the tradition of Jeremiah is through the work of my teacher, James Muilenburg. It was he who led me first to recognize the rhetorical power of that tradition, mediated through the pathos of the prophet. Unfortunately his own magisterial work on Jeremiah remains unpublished. My own work is at best an echo of what he had seen, but I am in any case glad to acknowledge my primal indebtedness to him. I am especially grateful to Fredrick Holmgren and George A. F. Knight, editors of the *International Theological Commentary* series, for their support and their critical attentiveness to the manuscript. They have pressed important issues that clarified my thought and my articulation. The other acknowledgment is to Donna Bass, who has done heroic and patient secretarial work on many drafts of the manuscript.

Columbia Theological Seminary
WALTER BRUEGGEMANN
OCTOBER 20, 1986

INTRODUCTION

HISTORICAL CONTEXT

The book of Jeremiah is reflective of and responsive to the historical crisis of the last days of Judah, culminating in the destruction of Jerusalem and the temple in 587 B.C.E. This crisis is the dominant and shaping event of the entire OT. The destruction evoked an extensive theological literature of which the book of Jeremiah is one major component.[1]

The last days of the 7th cent., the time of Jeremiah, witnessed the abrupt collapse of the Assyrian Empire and its prompt displacement by the Babylonians under the governance of Nebuchadnezzar. The Judean crisis must therefore be understood in the context of Babylonian imperial ambitions and expansionism. The power of Babylon to the north of Judah, however, was not the only foreign power with which Judah had to deal. Judah had to attend also to the Egyptians to the south, whose policy was to maintain Judah as a buffer against Babylonian pressure. Thus Judah was placed precisely and precariously between Babylon and Egypt. The Judahite kings in the years after Josiah (639-609) vacillated between Babylonian and Egyptian alliances. Finally Babylonian policy would no longer tolerate such political double-mindedness and moved against Jerusalem to end its political independence.[2]

Jehoiakim (609-598), son of Josiah, played a daring game of "in-

---

1. See Peter R. Ackroyd, *Exile and Restoration,* Old Testament Library (Philadelphia: Westminster; London: SCM, 1968), and Ralph W. Klein, *Israel in Exile,* Overtures to Biblical Theology 6 (Philadelphia: Fortress, 1979).

2. For a general review of the period, see Bustenay Oded, "Judah and the Exile," in *Israelite and Judean History,* ed. John H. Hayes and J. Maxwell Miller, Old Testament Library (Philadelphia: Westminster; London: SCM, 1977), 435-488; and Miller and Hayes, *A History of Ancient Israel and Judah* (Philadelphia: Westminster; London: SCM, 1986), 381-429.

ternational roulette" between Egypt and Babylon, eventually evoking Babylon's first incursion into Jerusalem in 598. One outcome of the events of 598 was the exile of Jehoiakim's son Jehoiachin to Babylon, where he remained for many years as titular head of the dynasty. Many prominent citizens of Judah were deported with him. For the period of 598-587, yet another son of Josiah, Zedekiah, presided over the affairs of Jerusalem but in the end had no chance for independent action in the face of Babylon. During these years, there was an intense rivalry between the community in Jerusalem (over which Zedekiah presided), and the exilic community in Babylon (in which Jehoiachin was understood as the legitimate leader).

Babylon's final decisive blow against Judah came in 587. The Babylonian Empire terminated Judah's existence as an independent political entity. Jerusalem and its environs were made part of a governorship accountable to the empire. A second and even more extensive deportation of Jerusalem's citizens occurred, as part of a general strategy for consolidating the Babylonian Empire and maintaining power. This radical displacement raised in Judah and Jerusalem a range of critical questions, moral and religious as well as political.

It is therefore possible to understand and explain the events around 587 in terms of *Realpolitik,* that is, in terms of political tensions between states and the overriding military and imperial power of Babylon. The realities of the political, military, and historical process provide convincing proof of Judah's helplessness in the face of Babylonian power, a helplessness exacerbated by the unwise and weak leadership it received from its monarchy. The Jeremiah literature is familiar with the realities of imperial politics and is conversant with those modes of thinking. However, Jeremiah does not pursue a *Realpolitik* interpretation of Judah's crisis of termination and displacement, but offers a different, alternative reading of those events. As an alternative to a political analysis, the tradition of Jeremiah proceeds on the basis of a theological perspective.

THEOLOGICAL TRADITION

The literature of Jeremiah engages in anguished poetic reflection and didactic prose explanation about the cause of Israel's end and the destiny of those deported to Babylon. Jeremiah's reading is not shaped by power politics but by the categories of Israel's covenantal traditions of faith, which concern the holy purpose and power of

Yahweh and the aches and hopes of the faithful community. As the categories of analysis and understanding shift from matters of international power to concerns of covenantal faithfulness, so also the modes of speech change. The odd result is that the great political event of 587 is discerned through passionate poetry and uncompromising theological analysis. Out of that poetry and analysis emerges a poetic anticipation of a new historical possibility for Judah—an anticipation that pushes powerfully beyond imperial permits and transcends the seeming prohibitions of the empire.

When the events of 587 are read from a theological perspective, Judah's destiny will be shaped finally not by power as the world judges power, but by the covenantal realities of Yahweh's sovereignty and power. We may identify three elements that are constitutive of this covenantal understanding of historical reality.

1. The governing paradigm for the tradition of Jeremiah is *Israel's covenant with Yahweh, rooted in the memories and mandates of the Sinai tradition*. That covenant taught that the sovereign God of Israel required obedience to covenant stipulations about social practice and power. Disobedience to those covenant stipulations would result in heavy sanctions (curses) that would be experienced as death or displacement.

When the events of 587 are read in the light of the claims of covenant, the Babylonian invasion and deportation are understood as the means of implementation of the harsh sanctions (covenant curses) already known and articulated in the Sinai tradition. The reality of Babylonian power is not denied, but is firmly subordinated to and incorporated into the intention of Yahweh. The book of Jeremiah thus mediates the reality of imperial politics through the theological claims of covenant.[3]

The mediation of political reality and covenantal faith is offered with amazing daring, in order to insist that there is a moral dimension to the termination and deportation. The destruction of Jerusalem wrought by Babylon is presented as a covenantal response of the God of Israel to Judah's refusal to adhere to covenantal requirements. Such a conclusion follows from the categories of Israel's faith, but to link the historical crisis to those categories is a bold interpretive act. Indeed, that Jeremiah's contemporaries could not discern the relation between imperial politics and covenantal theology is a central issue of the book.

---

3. See John Bright, *Covenant and Promise* (Philadelphia: Westminster, 1976), 140-170.

This governing paradigm of covenant indicates that Jeremiah is in important ways related to and derived from the traditions of Deuteronomy.[4] This connection (generally affirmed in a scholarly consensus) is important because the book of Deuteronomy gives a clear and uncompromising presentation of the covenant relation in Israel's faith. Deuteronomy makes clear that Israel's life begins in Yahweh's act of mercy and fidelity, and that Israel's proper response is obedient listening. Moreover, Deuteronomy asserts that every dimension of Israel's common life is to be brought under the rubric of covenant obedience. Indeed, it articulates a strategy for making public life fully covenantal.[5] Finally, Deuteronomy most clearly presents the potential curses that will come upon Israel for disobedience. The convergence of Deuteronomy and Jeremiah is clear not only in terms of theological substance, but also in matters of style and forms of articulation. Jeremiah's proclamation and the entire book of Jeremiah operate on theological assumptions that are most clearly presented in Deuteronomy. The tradition of Jeremiah is not closed and reductionistic, but it is clear about the claims of covenant.

2. The book of Jeremiah, however, cannot be completely understood by simple reference to a notion of covenant violation and covenant curse, the central assumptions of Deuteronomic theology.[6] Along with the paradigm of covenant, the book of Jeremiah affirms another theological claim, *the pathos of Yahweh*. In spite of Israel's obduracy and recalcitrance, Yahweh nonetheless wills a continuing relation with Israel. This will is rooted in nothing other than God's in-

---

4. For summary statements from the older criticism, see John Bright, "The Date of the Prose Sermons of Jeremiah," in *A Prophet to the Nations,* ed. Leo G. Perdue and Brian W. Kovacs (Winona Lake, Ind.: Eisenbrauns, 1984), 193-212; and J. Philip Hyatt, "The Deuteronomic Edition of Jeremiah," *ibid.,* 247-267. The Deuteronomic dimension of Jeremiah has been most programmatically argued by Robert P. Carroll, *From Chaos to Covenant* (New York: Crossroad; London: SCM, 1981).

5. Norbert Lohfink ("Distribution of the Functions of Power," *Great Themes from the Old Testament* [Edinburgh: T. & T. Clark, 1982], 55-75) has argued that in Deut. 16–18, one can discern a proposed "constitution" for organizing and authorizing a particular mode of public life.

6. The simple structure of violation and curse is also central to the "prophetic lawsuit" of indictment and sentence; see Claus Westermann, *Basic Forms of Prophetic Speech* (Philadelphia: Westminster; London: Lutterworth, 1967). But the language of Jeremiah is closer to that of Deuteronomy (e.g., Deut. 28).

explicable yearning, which is articulated in Jeremiah as God's pathos, presented in turn through the pathos of the poet.[7]

Thus the severity of covenant sanctions and the power of God's yearning pathos are set in deep tension. This deep tension forms the central interest, theological significance, and literary power of the book of Jeremiah. This yearning pathos that is presented as God's fundamental inclination toward Judah is a departure from and critique of the primary inclination of Deuteronomic theology.[8]

The juxtaposition of covenant claim and pathos makes clear that God is, in the life of Judah, more complex, free, and less controllable than a simple scheme of retribution would suggest. It is this greater complexity in the character of God that the rich rhetoric of the book of Jeremiah seeks to articulate. The theological richness of Yahweh's character evokes and requires a subtle rhetoric that is full of ambiguity, passion, and incongruity. The book of Jeremiah is so powerful and compelling because it has a mode of expression appropriate to its astonishing subject.

The mediation of the claims of covenant through the surprising power of Yahweh's pathos permits the book of Jeremiah to move beyond the crisis of exile and death in the 7th and 6th cents. to envision a newness that is wrought out of God's gracious resolve and powerful will. The move beyond covenantal sanction is unwarranted, but that move is possible because of God's magisterial freedom, through which God can and does act beyond warrants. Jeremiah's discernment and articulation of the freedom and pathos of Yahweh enables the poet to break out of the tight categories of covenantal sanctions and move to an articulation of hope.

3. The third constituent element necessary to understand the theology of the book of Jeremiah is the *royal-temple ideology of Jerusalem.* This ideology articulated in the Jerusalem establishment, fostered by

---

7. See Abraham J. Heschel, *The Prophets* (New York and London: Harper & Row, 1962), 103-139, 221-278.

8. It is worth noting that in Deut. 7:7, a classic text on the election, the verb *hashaq* is used: "The LORD set his love upon you." The RSV translation, "set his love on," is an anemic one. The verb suggests a passionate, craving physical grasping of another in powerful embrace. It is this dimension of passionate craving that is articulated in Jeremiah's vivid imagery, and that gives his poetry such power and poignancy. In this, the poetry of Jeremiah runs well beyond the restrained articulations of Deuteronomy. While the tradition of Jeremiah may be informed in this regard by Deuteronomy, the theme is much more fully utilized, so much more so that it amounts to an important departure from the tradition of Deuteronomy.

the king and articulated by temple priests, claimed that the God of Israel had made irrevocable promises to the temple and the monarchy, had taken up permanent residence in Jerusalem, and was for all time a patron and guarantor of the Jerusalem establishment. Jeremiah's work only makes sense as an antithetical response to that ideology.

The royal-temple ideology, embodied in temple liturgy and royal claims of legitimacy, asserted and imagined that it was an indispensable vehicle for God's way and blessing in the world. It was therefore assumed that the royal-temple apparatus was immune to covenant sanctions and to God's judgment. This ideology was the official religion of Jerusalem and no doubt was popularly embraced. The tradition of Jeremiah articulates a sustained challenge to the royal-temple ideology, insisting on the centrality of covenant commandment and dismissing the notion of immunity from judgment. The counterclaim of the tradition of Jeremiah is rooted in the old radical theological tradition of Sinai and was, as events materialized, vindicated by the actual end of Jerusalem. History showed that, indeed, Jerusalem was not immune to judgment.

The painful experiences around 587 made clear the inadequacy of both the old covenant theology and the royal-temple theology. While the sympathies of the Jeremiah literature are clearly with the former, neither tradition had the resources to provide the way out of the despair of exile. The new circumstances around 587 required a new theological assertion.[9] In his rereading of the events around Jerusalem in his moment of proclamation, Jeremiah therefore used various elements of already existing interpretation models. These models, however, are handled in ways that are freshly discerning and astonishingly imaginative. The outcome is that Jeremiah's rendering of Jerusalem's experience and destiny is a wholly new one that belongs peculiarly to this literature.

In arriving at this imaginative, subtle, and bold rereading, the book of Jeremiah:

(1) reinterprets the events of *Realpolitik* through the categories of covenantal obligation and covenantal sanctions,

(2) disrupts the claims of the covenantal (Deuteronomic) pattern of obligation and sanction by a disclosure of the pathos of God that will not be contained in the tradition of covenant, and

---

9. See Gerhard von Rad, *Old Testament Theology,* 2 (New York: Harper & Row; Edinburgh: Oliver & Boyd, 1965), 263-277.

(3) utilizes the combination of covenantal motifs and divine pathos to critique and reject the claims of the royal-temple ideology.

By such creative transformation of the available traditions, Jeremiah asserts that the city will be dismantled by the will and power of Yahweh (and not by the decision of Babylon), and that a new community of covenantal possibility will emerge after the dismantling, as a free gift of Yahweh.

THE BOOK

The book of Jeremiah is a complicated literary composition that has evoked much scholarly attention. During the last century, an approximate consensus has been reached among critical scholars that the book contains three layers of literature reflecting three layers of redactional activity: (1) the poetic utterances of the prophet Jeremiah, (2) the narrative accounts of Baruch, and (3) the theological overlay of Deuteronomic theologians.[10] This consensus reflects a scholarly view that the literature has emerged through identifiable stages of editorial activity. There is not agreement, however, among scholars about the precise extent of each of these layers of literature, nor the process by which they came to be a part of the book.

That three-source critical consensus, however, is now open to serious doubts because scholars are no longer agreed that the character of the book can be understood according to such a mechanical literary process. The literary formation of the book is much more dynamic and processive than such a three-document proposal would allow. Moreover, the new stress on the canonical shape of the literature may diminish the pertinence of these older historical-critical questions. Nonetheless, the residue of the old scholarly consensus includes two important points to which scholars give general and broad assent.

First, there is a core of material that originated with the historical person of Jeremiah. Second, an extended process of editorial work has transformed and perhaps made beyond recovery the original work of the prophet. What we now have is a literature decisively shaped by a later traditioning process. Beyond the general conclusion that the book contains *material from Jeremiah* and *subsequent editorial activity,* there is no discernable agreement among scholars.

---

10. For a review of scholarship, see Brevard S. Childs, *Introduction to the Old Testament as Scripture* (Philadelphia: Fortress; London: SCM, 1979), 342-344.

Attempts to refine or advance beyond the "three-source critical consensus" may be grouped in three scholarly positions.

1. The more conservative critical position, perhaps standing in closest continuity to the older critical scholarship, is represented by William L. Holladay[11] and by the well established commentary of John Bright.[12] This approach seeks to determine the date and exact historical setting of each textual unit. It asks specific historical questions of each passage. Moreover, this approach is inclined to maximize the role of the actual person Jeremiah by assigning as much material as possible to the prophet. The work of Holladay and Bright, therefore, is inclined to accept whenever possible the claim of the book of Jeremiah itself, that the materials do indeed stem from the work of the prophet.

2. In sharp contrast to this first approach is the dominant tendency of recent British scholarship, articulated especially by Robert P. Carroll,[13] but also by Peter R. Ackroyd[14] and Ernest W. Nicholson.[15] This scholarly position focuses on the Deuteronomic editing of the book of Jeremiah in the Exile, a generation or two after the person of Jeremiah. The canonical text of Jeremiah is understood to be the work of exilic editors and redactors who have recast and transformed the older material for the sake of the community in exile, under the influence of the tradition of Deuteronomy. This approach focuses on the constructive pastoral and theological intention of the community in exile that construed the tradition of Jeremiah in fresh directions in order to meet fresh religious needs. As a result of the exilic community's theological mediation of the Jeremiah tradition, we cannot recover with any certitude any of the actual words of Jeremiah. Indeed, we have no access to the person of Jeremiah or his words, except as mediated by the community, and to pose such an historical question is both futile and irrelevant. From this scholarly perspective, the book of Jeremiah is seen to have no interest in the person of Jeremiah, and thus neither should we. Pursuit

---

11. William L. Holladay, *Jeremiah: Spokesman Out of Time* (Philadelphia: United Church, 1974), and now *Jeremiah 1,* Hermeneia (Philadelphia: Fortress; London: SCM, 1986).

12. John Bright, *Jeremiah,* 2nd ed., Anchor Bible 21 (Garden City: Doubleday, 1978).

13. *From Chaos to Covenant.*

14. "The Book of Jeremiah—Some Recent Studies," *Journal for the Study of the Old Testament* 28 (1984): 47-59.

15. Ernest W. Nicholson, *Preaching to the Exiles* (Oxford: Blackwell, 1970).

of such historical questions about the person or the words of the prophet should be abandoned.

We are at an especially fortuitous time in Jeremiah studies, because in 1986, both Holladay and Carroll published commentaries that provide a sustained presentation of their quite contrasting arguments.[16] These two commentaries represent the major literary-critical developments in Jeremiah studies since the older three-source critical consensus. They are likely to determine the shape and parameters of scholarly conversation for a long time to come.

The two perspectives of Holladay and Carroll stand in sharp contrast to each other. Holladay is inclined to assign to the prophet Jeremiah as much as possible, whereas Carroll believes that the work of the original prophet is beyond identification or recovery, so weighty is the exilic recasting of the corpus. Despite the sharp contrasts of their literary assumptions, however, it is important to note that Holladay and Carroll proceed with quite parallel concerns. Both ask primarily historical questions, and both are singularly concerned to identify the historical location of the text. Whereas Holladay is concerned in some way with "the quest for the historical Jeremiah," Carroll, so to speak, is engaged in a "quest for the Deuteronomic Jeremiah." Much is to be learned from both enterprises, but both leave matters of interpretation incomplete. There is a tendency to focus so much on questions of historicity and redaction that literary and theological questions of the text as it stands do not receive as much attention as might be desired.

3. A third perspective has been adumbrated by Brevard S. Childs, who proposes to subordinate historical questions to the canonical shape of the literature.[17] Childs recognizes and seeks to value both the "original Jeremiah" and the "Deuteronomic editor." He has taken the uncontested literary judgment that the "original Jeremiah" has been recast by Deuteronomists in exile and has shown how that editorial/canonical combination of "original" and "exilic" materials

---

16. Holladay, *Jeremiah 1,* Hermeneia; Carroll, *Jeremiah,* Old Testament Library (Philadelphia: Westminster; London: SCM, 1986). Also published in this remarkable year in Jeremiah studies was William McKane, *Jeremiah,* 1, International Critical Commentary (Edinburgh: T. & T. Clark). The commentaries of Holladay and Carroll likely represent the extreme parameters of current discussion. McKane's is a close and technical study filling the long lamentable void in the ICC series. None of these commentaries was available in time for me to benefit in my work on chs. 1–25.

17. *Old Testament as Scripture,* 345-354.

articulates the theological claim of God's judgment against recalcitrant Jerusalem and God's promissory act of newness.[18] The canonical shape of the book thus makes clear that God "watches over" the
sovereign word of God, first to pluck up and tear down, then to plant
and to build (Jer. 1:10; 31:27-30). The initial word of Jeremiah was
a word of judgment, of plucking up and tearing down. A quite distinct second word of hope has been imposed upon the judgment of
planting and building. The dual theme of judgment and promise is
reflected in the editorial shaping of the canonical text.[19] The intent
and effect of Childs's work is to free the double theological assertion
and function of the text from its particular historical locus in the 7th
and 6th centuries. Childs does not seek a Jeremiah dating with Holladay, nor an exilic placement with Carroll. He brackets out such historical questions for the sake of the text's twofold theological intention. A study of Childs' proposal shows the extent to which Holladay
and Carroll, while drawing opposite conclusions, are in fact addressing very similar questions, the very questions Childs critiques.

There is at present no scholarly consensus about these three quite
different perspectives. It is not the interest of the present commentary
to advance this critical conversation, nor to adjudicate between these
several alternatives. It is perhaps enough to conclude that the theological tradition of the book of Jeremiah continues to be lively and
energizing long after the end of the work of the prophet Jeremiah.

THE PERSON OF JEREMIAH

In light of the preceding statement concerning the work of Holladay
and Carroll, it is not surprising that the question of the "person of
Jeremiah" is exceedingly difficult.[20] A more conservative view (Hol-

---

18. In a general way the "original work" of Jeremiah presents a statement of God's judgment and the "exilic material" articulates God's promissory work. Childs, however, is interested in the double theological intention, not in the historical placement of the various texts.

19. On the general structure of judgment and promise in the prophets,
see Ronald E. Clements, "Patterns in the Prophetic Canon," in *Canon and
Authority,* ed. George W. Coats and Burke O. Long (Philadelphia:
Fortress, 1977), 42-55. The structure of the book of Jeremiah provides
evidence for Clements's general notion.

20. See David Jobling, "The Quest of the Historical Jeremiah: Hermeneutical Implications of Recent Literature," in *A Prophet to the Nations,*
ed. Perdue and Kovacs, 285-297; and Timothy Polk, *The Prophetic Persona,*
JSOT Supplement 32 (Sheffield: University of Sheffield Press, 1984).

laday and Bright) assumes that one can in some way reach close to the person of Jeremiah and reconstruct that historical person from the data. At the other extreme, Carroll concludes that the materials have been so completely reshaped that they provide no clues to the historical person and that there is no access. It may well be, however, that these alternatives put the question wrongly.

Every historical presentation of a personality is a mediation and a construction.[21] What we have of the person of Jeremiah in the book of Jeremiah is more like a "portrait" that reflects the taste and interest of the artist, rather than an objective report that is factually precise. At the same time, as Timothy Polk has argued, it can hardly be denied that in the midst of this complicated Jeremiah literature there is an anchoring reference to a powerful personality about which the editors had some knowledge and some conviction.[22] That knowledge and conviction of the historical person, however, are given to us in ways that reflect the interests and faith of those who give us the data.

Thus I have no difficulty in speaking of the person of Jeremiah, while being aware that the only "person" of Jeremiah about which we can know anything is given us through an intentional construction. I have characteristically spoken in my exposition of "the poet," "the prophet," or "Jeremiah" as the agent behind and within the text. Such a reference is not naively historical. To speak of "Jeremiah" is to refer to the constructed *persona* of the prophet that is no doubt rooted in the actual reality, and that equally without doubt is mediated and constructed for us in a particular way. Such a reference is in

---

21. Roy Shafer, *Language and Insight* (New Haven: Yale University Press, 1978), 8-18, argues that every personal presentation of a historical self is a "construction." He concludes that this is so even when a person presents himself or herself. That being so in our self-presentation, it is obviously so when any literary effort is made to "present" an historical person. Thus there can be little doubt that Jeremiah as given us in the book of Jeremiah is a "construction." See Walter Brueggemann, "The Book of Jeremiah: Portrait of the Prophet," *Interpretation,* 37 (1983): 130-145.

22. Polk has argued well the delicate interaction between the constructive tradition and the person of the prophet. Finally he comes down on the side of the "persona" as a purposed paradigm for the reading community: "In my opinion, it violates the integrity of the text, *qua* poetry, to replace the given literary context with the conjectured historical occasion of the writing process and so to construe the text as referring to authorial circumstances rather than to the subject as it is literarily defined" (*The Prophetic Persona,* 165).

part an expository convenience, for clearly there is an agent who is evoker and actor in the text. But such a reference to "Jeremiah" is also a recognition that there is a coherence in the text in some way reflective of and witness to concrete historical experience and faith. The determination whether such evidences point to a discernible historical figure or an imaginative literary construct is not required for this exposition, and finally adjudication of the matter is impossible. We know enough about tradition, context, and style to recognize "the voice" at work in the text, even if we name that voice with full recognition of the ambiguity, complexity, and uncertainty surrounding that portrayed person.[23]

AN INTERPRETIVE PERSPECTIVE

In my interpretation I have paid special attention to two emerging methods in Scripture study.

1. *Sociological analysis* has recently become important in Scripture study.[24] In this method, one pays attention to the interests, ideologies, and constructions of reality that are operative in the formation and transmission of the text.[25] The biblical text is understood as neither neutral nor objective, but as located in, reflective of, and concerned for a particular social context that is determinative of its shape and focus. This approach is distinct from the older historical-critical approach because it does not seek specific historical placement but, rather, a placement within various social voices or dynamic forces. Interpretation requires attention both to the particular voice in the text and to the other voices in the situation with which this voice may be in dispute, tension, or agreement.

The use of sociological analysis in the reading of Jeremiah is com-

---

23. Robert M. Polzin, *Moses and the Deuteronomist* (New York: Seabury, 1980), has utilized the notice of conflicting "voices" in the text to good advantage. His work is informed by the critical theory of V. N. Voloshinov.

24. See Robert R. Wilson, *Sociological Approaches to the Old Testament*, Guides to Biblical Scholarship (Philadelphia: Fortress, 1984). While Wilson well articulates the method, a much more substantive and influential use of the method is by Norman K. Gottwald, *The Tribes of Yahweh* (Maryknoll, N.Y.: Orbis, 1979). Gottwald's sociological analysis has been instructive for me in understanding Jeremiah's radical critique of the urban establishment of Jerusalem.

25. On such social construction, see Peter L. Berger and Thomas Luckmann, *The Social Construction of Reality* (Garden City: Doubleday, 1966).

plicated because the world of the text permits the sounding of many voices. We may surmise voices present in the situation of the text representing the old covenant tradition, the memory of hurt from Hosea, the legitimacy of the monarchy, the high temple theology of the priesthood, pro-Babylonian and pro-Egyptian political preferences, and the powerful families of nobility that are in tension with the royal family and may represent the old claims of rural elders. In reading Jeremiah one asks how these various voices interact with each other, which ones are allied against what other ones, and how they are variously presented as reflective of or resistant to the will of Yahweh. In a later generation of the Jeremiah tradition, we likely contend with pastoral voices among exiles, with the claims of the community that remained in Judah, and again with pro-Egyptian voices. It is not nearly so important to date passages as it is to attend to the interaction of these several forces that vied for influence and legitimacy.

The interaction of these different voices in Jeremiah tend to coalesce around one central issue. The text of Jeremiah articulates a dispute (reflective of a conversation in Jerusalem) about who rightly understands historical events and who rightly discerns the relation between faith, morality, and political power. The tradition of Jeremiah articulates a covenant-torah view of reality that stands in deep tension with the royal-priestly ideology of the Jerusalem establishment. The Jeremiah tradition insists that covenant fidelity is the clue to public well-being, and a violation of such fidelity will bring death to the community. The tradition of Jeremiah assumes and argues that the historical process in Judah is rightly perceived not by those in the temple establishment, but by the voice of covenant fidelity that is clearly marginal. The book of Jeremiah is nearly unambiguous in its conviction that the Jerusalem ideology is a mistaken, fraudulent notion of public life that can only lead to death. This central tension between perceptions of reality, reflective of a deep social conflict, is present in many—if not all—parts of the book of Jeremiah.

The use of sociological analysis enables the interpreter to place the dispute between covenantal and noncovenantal notions of life and community into the particular social life setting of the divided Jerusalem community. The articulation of the social forces at work in this dispute permits the ongoing power and pertinence of the Jeremiah tradition in subsequent generations and new social settings. The claims of the royal-priestly ideology repeatedly are embodied, generation after generation, in monopolistic centers of domination in every sphere of human life. These centers imagine they are immune from the risks and responsibilities of the historical process. Conversely, a passionate commitment to covenant stands in every generation and every circumstance as a critical alternative to such domination.

The text requires very little explicit "application" to see that centers of domination still lead to exile and death, and that covenantal alternatives, mediated by God's sovereign graciousness, continue to be a fragile offer of life. The text continues its authoritative claim in new situations because the same social realities recur, and because the same witness to the same sovereign God is pertinent in new situations.

2. *Literary analysis* (which does not refer to the old source analysis) is equally important in present Scripture study.[26] In this method, one pays attention to the power of language to propose an imaginative world that is an alternative to the one that seems to be at hand—alternative to the one in which the reader or listener thinks herself or himself enmeshed. Literature then is not regarded as descriptive of what is, but as evocative and constructive of another life world.[27] In this method, one takes the "world" offered in the text as a possible alternative world without excessive reference to external historical factors and without excessive interest in questions of authorship. This approach permits literature to be enormously daring and bold,

---

26. Among the better representatives of this approach in an expanding literature are the books of Robert Alter, *The Art of Biblical Narrative* (New York: Basic Books; London: Allen & Unwin, 1981), and *The Art of Biblical Poetry* (New York: Basic Books, 1985); Meir Sternberg, *The Poetics of Biblical Narrative* (Bloomington: Indiana University Press, 1985); Phyllis Trible, *God and the Rhetoric of Sexuality,* Overtures to Biblical Theology 2 (Philadelphia: Fortress, 1978), and *Texts of Terror,* Overtures to Biblical Theology 13 (Philadelphia: Fortress, 1984); and David M. Gunn, *The Story of King David,* JSOT Supplement 6 (1978), and *The Fate of King Saul,* JSOT Supplement 14 (1980). For the delicate relation between literary theory and literary method, see John Barton, *Reading the Old Testament* (Philadelphia: Westminster; London: Darton, Longman & Todd, 1984).

27. This perspective on biblical literature is especially derived from the work of Paul Ricoeur, *Essays on Biblical Interpretation* (Philadelphia: Fortress; London: SPCK, 1980). See the helpful introductory article by Lewis S. Mudge in that volume ("Paul Ricouer on Biblical Interpretation," 1-40). More directly, the work of Amos N. Wilder has best considered the cruciality of language for its evocative, imaginative power. See Wilder, "The Word as Address and the Word as Meaning," in *The New Hermeneutic,* ed. James M. Robinson and John B. Cobb, Jr. (New York and London: Harper & Row, 1964), 198-218.

and often abrasive and subversive in the face of the presumed world of the listener. It places the listener in crisis, but also presents the listener with a new zone for fresh hope, changed conduct, and fresh historical possibility.

The conviction that literature is evocative and not merely descriptive has significance only as that conviction receives specific implementation. This requires a careful "close reading" of the text in which one pays attention to the use, repetition, and arrangement of words, shifts in voices, deliberate verbal strategies that cause breaks, surprises, contrasts, comparisons, ambiguities, and open-ended wonderment in the text. The interpreter focuses on the action and voice of the text itself and is not led away from the actual work of the text by any external reference or hypothesis.

This method of literary analysis is useful in the study of Jeremiah in three ways. First, one notices the powerful and provocative use of metaphor and image. One must follow the daring use of the specific language of the text if one is to sense the intention of the text.[28] One becomes aware that the language is carefully and artistically crafted so that the text can never be summarized but only "followed" in its portrayal of a fresh reality that takes its life from the powerful, passionate speech of the concrete text.[29] It becomes clear then that *what is said* is congruous with and dependent upon *how it is said.*[30]

---

28. James Muilenburg, "The Terminology of Adversity in Jeremiah," in *Translating & Understanding the Old Testament,* ed. Harry Thomas Frank and William L. Reed (New York: Abingdon, 1970), 42-63, has made an important beginning on these matters in the book of Jeremiah. Unfortunately, Muilenburg's acute and discerning analysis of the rhetoric of Jeremiah remains unpublished. For an appreciative assessment of his work that centered in Jeremiah, see Bernhard W. Anderson, "Introduction: The New Frontier of Rhetorical Criticism," in *Rhetorical Criticism: Essays in Honor of James Muilenburg,* ed. Jared J. Jackson and Martin Kessler, Pittsburgh Theological Monograph 1 (Pittsburgh: Pickwick, 1974), ix-xviii; repr. in *Hearing and Speaking the Word,* ed. Thomas F. Best (Chico, Calif.: Scholars Press, 1984), 14-23.

29. On the notion of "following" the text, see W. B. Gallie, "The Historical Understanding," in *History and Theory,* ed. George H. Nadel (1965; repr. Middletown, Conn.: Wesleyan University Press, 1977), 149-202. Gallie's treatment concerns narrative, but the same posture applies to all texts that have such passionate concrete historical intentionality.

30. On the profound connection between what is said and how it is said, see the careful analysis of Gail R. O'Day, *Revelation in the Fourth Gospel: Narrative Mode and Theological Claim* (Philadelphia: Fortress, 1986).

Through its concrete language the text of Jeremiah can variously evoke a sense of creation that has massively regressed to chaos (4:23-26), an awareness of God's grief and sickness at Judah's obduracy (8:18–9:3), or the resumption of wedding parties in a land where all such social rejoicing had stopped (33:11; cf. 7:34; 16:9; 25:10). The boldness of the metaphors witnesses to and evokes radical endings and astonishing beginnings in the social process.

The concreteness and imaginative power of such speech invites a different discernment and experience of the world of Jerusalem and Babylon. In turn, it summons the listener to reject the ideological discernment of the world by the royal-temple establishment, which is shown to be false and which will only lead to death. The language of the text means to penetrate and expose the counterinterpretations of the "establishment" for what they are: misleading, misinformed notions that lead away from the power and possibilities of historical reality as an arena of God's rule and purpose. The "establishment" assumed a kind of political, moral, intellectual autonomy that the Jeremiah tradition critiques as false and deathly.

Second, it is crucial to our interpretation that Jeremiah's proposal of the world is indeed an imaginative construct, not a description of what is nor a prediction of what will be. Jeremiah is attentive to the data all around him, but the text itself is not intended as descriptive account, nor can it be assessed as such. It invites the listener to participate in the proposed world so that one can imagine a terminated royal world while that world still exists, and one can receive in imaginative prospect a new community of covenant faith where none has yet emerged. The text leads the listener out beyond presently discerned reality to new reality formed in the moment of speaking and hearing. [31]

Third, if the context of Jeremiah's work is the royal-priestly ideology of the Jerusalem establishment (as my sociological presentation above suggests), then the alternative imaginative portrayal of a covenant community is juxtaposed to that royal-priestly ideology. The text offers imaginative alternatives to established ideology in the conviction that God is at work to *create a new alternative community* ("to plant and to build"; 31:27-30). The freedom of liberated, faithful speech anticipates and evokes new public reality.

Thus the two methods of sociological and literary analysis, when

---

31. See for example Bernhard W. Anderson, "'The Lord Has Created Something New': A Stylistic Study of Jer. 31:15-22," in *A Prophet to the Nations,* ed. Perdue and Kovacs, 367-380.

utilized in Jeremiah, yield respectively *a critique of ideology* and a *practice of liberated imagination*. These two methods enable us to take a fresh look at critical theological issues in the Jeremiah tradition. A sociological analysis helps us see how the covenantal perspectives of the prophetic tradition stand over against royal ideology. A literary analysis helps us see how Judah is invited to act faithfully, even if that faithfulness is against the presumed interest and "truth" of the Jerusalem establishment.

When the text is read and heard as a critique of ideology and as a practice of alternative imagination, the text continues to have power and pertinence in many subsequent contexts, including our own.[32] Indeed, the text has the powerful capacity to cause us to rediscern our own situation, to experience our situation in quite new ways, and to participate in our own historical situation with new liberty and fresh passion—liberty and passion that arise in and with faithfulness. Such a text, when read critically, characteristically assaults every "structure of domination" with its self-serving and misrepresenting propaganda, including our own military, technological, consumer-oriented establishment. Such a text, when read imaginatively, issues a forceful invitation to an alternative community of covenant, including a risky invitation in our own time to practices of justice, risks of compassion, and sufferings for peace.

This text does not require "interpretation" or "application" so that it can be brought near our experience and circumstance. Rather, the text is so powerful and compelling, so passionate and uncompromising in its anguish and hope, that it requires we submit our experience to it and thereby reenter our experience on new terms, namely the terms of the text. The text does not need to be *applied* to our situation. Rather, our situation needs to be *submitted* to the text for a fresh discernment. It is our situation, not the text, that requires a new interpretation. In every generation, this text subverts all our old readings of reality and forces us to a new, dangerous, obedient reading.[33]

---

32. James A. Sanders ("Hermeneutics," in *The Interpreter's Dictionary of the Bible,* Supplement, ed. Keith R. Crim [Nashville: Abingdon, 1976], 406), has rightly suggested that "dynamic analogy" is a helpful way to interpret the text. He stresses that the analogy must be "dynamic," that is, one that emerges out of one's own interpretation and experience. Thus I have not pressed analogies in my interpretation, but invite the reader to make those connections out of experience and interpretation.

33. David Tracy (*The Analogical Imagination* [New York: Crossroad; London: SCM, 1981], chs. 3 and 4), has shown how a "classic" must have continued, ongoing, and developing interpretation in order to be timely

If such a subversive reading of reality appears to us unreal, too dangerous, and too costly, we must recognize that for most in the 7th and 6th cents. it was rejected for exactly the same reasons.

Indeed, everything depends on our reading and hearing this text. If we fail to hear this text, we may succumb to a fraudulent discernment of our situation. Like ancient Jerusalem, we shall imagine that the present is decided by the policies of the empire and not by the pathos of the holy, faithful God. Like ancient exiles, we may imagine that our situation is occupied only by despair and alienation, that God's arm is shortened and there is none to comfort. We shall miss the summons home, the faint beginnings of new laughter in Jerusalem, and shall still be submitting to the empire when we could be on our way rejoicing. Everything depends on the text, for without this transformative, critical, liberating, subversive speech, we shall live in a speechless, textless world that is always misunderstood. Without the text we are at the mercy of powerful ideology, of misrepresenting propaganda, of anxieties that make us conformist, and despair that drives us to brutality. It is precisely the text in its odd offer of holiness and pathos, of rending and healing, that dismisses ideology, exposes propaganda, overrides anxiety, and offers forgiveness in the place of brutality.

A commentary as this one must focus on what the text of Jeremiah meant in its ancient speaking and hearing. But that ancient speaking and hearing keeps pushing into our present. What it "meant" has incredible power to "mean" now.[34] It meant then that Yahweh would work a powerful, savage, pathos-filled purpose with that people, and it still means that that purpose is at work among us. It meant that Yahweh could grieve a terrible ending, and it still means we face terrible endings over which Yahweh grieves. It meant that Yahweh had the resilient power to work a newness among the displaced, and it still means that Yahweh's resilient power is at work in such displacements. It meant and means that

---

as well as timeless. Jeremiah is just such a tradition that is both timely and timeless, kept timely by repeated interpretation.

34. The split of "what it meant" and "what it means" has been championed by Krister Stendahl ("Biblical Theology, Contemporary," in *The Interpreter's Dictionary of the Bible,* ed. George A. Buttrick [Nashville: Abingdon, 1962] 1:418-420), but in retrospect seems clearly to have been a misperception. See the criticism of Stendahl by James Barr, "Biblical Theology," in *IDB, Supplement,* 106. In this commentary it is assumed that what "meant" inescapably "means," and both the writer and the reader are engaged in that interpretive transaction.

the prideful empire, the pitiful royal leadership, the self-serving religionists, the cynical forces in society, cannot have their way, for history with Yahweh is about another intention. To be sure, the meaning we receive from the text is nuanced very differently from its early "meant." Our meaning is transmitted through our Enlightenment modes of scientific and rational autonomy. We cannot so easily ascribe the shape of the historical process to a single agent. My comments intend not to be reductionist or blindly supernaturalist. We can only interpret in our own situation when we know the historical process admits of no easy interpretation. Nonetheless, this textual tradition in its anguish and in its buoyancy witnesses to an inescapable hovering of God that is oddly sovereign in ways that outdistance our desperate modernity. Poetic anguish, lyrical expectation, metaphorical openness, and imaginative ambiguity are ways in which sovereign hurt and fidelity are mediated to us. This powerful mediating shocks our intellectual self-confidence and invites us to reengage life with courage, awe, and submissiveness. This commentary is about that other holy, passionate, powerful intention that plucks up and tears down, that plants and builds, that subverts and amazes.

THE WORD
THROUGH JEREMIAH
Jeremiah 1

EDITOR'S PREFACE (1:1-3)

These verses are an editor's preface to the book of Jeremiah, with parallels in other prophetic books (Isa. 1:1; Hos. 1:1; Amos 1:1). The formula reminds us that the present book of Jeremiah is the result of a long, complicated editorial process. These verses appear simply to provide historical data about the setting of the book, but in fact this introduction addresses issues more serious than historical placement.[1]

The unit identifies Jeremiah in a double way, historically as rooted in the priestly traditions of Anathoth (likely derived from the conservative covenantal traditions of Abiathar; 1 Kgs. 2:26-27) and theologically as recipient of Yahweh's invasive sovereign word. These introductory sentences intend to identify and authorize Jeremiah as a vehicle for Yahweh's governing word spoken at a specific time and place.

1:2-3 These verses make clear, however, that the editor does not linger long over the person of Jeremiah. What is of interest is "the word of the LORD," mentioned twice. The word of the LORD is not identified with the words of Jeremiah, nor with the book of Jeremiah. There are here two levels of word, that of Yahweh and that of Jeremiah. This preface makes no judgment about their relation to each other. It is enough to recognize that the words of this book stand in some special connection to the word of Yahweh. The theological claim of these verses is that the life of Jeremiah and this text sound the sovereign voice of Yahweh.

The word of the LORD is not a romantic or floating spiritual notion. It can be precisely linked to a chronological process. The arena

---

1. See Gene M. Tucker, "Prophetic Superscriptions and the Growth of a Canon," in *Canon and Authority*, ed. George W. Coats and Burke O. Long (Philadelphia: Fortress, 1977), 56-70.

of Yahweh's governing word is lodged in the reigns of Josiah (626-609 B.C.E.), Jehoiakim (609-598), and Zedekiah (598-587). The word of Yahweh is borne by the prophet, but it impinges upon the royal reality. It intrudes into the neat chronology of the kings to give us early notice that another governance is here that will unsettle the neat, fixed chronology. The word opens royal reality to another governance.

The phrase "until the captivity of Jerusalem" provides the terminus toward which the book of Jeremiah moves. This is more than a chronological reference. It is an awesome and dreadful formula. It is a clue to the intent of Yahweh's word and a signal about the nature of the book of Jeremiah. No doubt the book contains passages after 587, and there are evidently elements of hope; but the canonical scheme announces that the end point of this prophetic tradition coincides with the end point of historical Judah and of viable Jerusalem. Nothing more, it is suggested in these verses, can be said or need be said after that terrible moment. The word is on the move toward exile. Nothing the kings can do will alter that massive bent to the historical process of God's people. The kings, alleged managers of the historical process, stand helpless and exposed in the face of that disposition of Yahweh. It is a theme we will encounter repeatedly.

As the book of Jeremiah now stands, these verses on exile (*golah*) have as their counterpart Jer. 52:27-34. These together form an envelope at beginning and end of the book, in order to assert that this entire literary tradition is preoccupied with exile, with its source in Yahweh and its embodiment in Israel, Yahweh's people. The working out of Yahweh's word as Jeremiah's word has as its purpose and intent the ending of Jerusalem, the dismantling of that royal world, the termination of the recital of kings in Jerusalem. It is as though in this terse preface we are given the entire plot to the book of Jeremiah. The whole book as it stands is a literary-theological disclosure of the unraveling of a royal world, of the disintegration of a stable universe of public order and public confidence. The man Jeremiah is thrust into the middle of that dismantling to bring the deathliness of Jerusalem to speech. It is as though the die is cast even before the person of the prophet appears. The kings are named who are the helpless, unwitting recipients of this terminating action. Most importantly, however, it is the speech of Yahweh that evokes the end. The known world is not ending in spite of Yahweh's governance, as though Yahweh were weak. Rather, it is ending precisely because of Yahweh's governance. What may appear to be weakness and failure on the part of Yahweh is in fact Yahweh's policy.

The book of Jeremiah is thus an unwelcome offer. If we enter, we are invited to accompany the painful, genuinely unthinkable process whereby the Holy City is denied its special character and is handed over, by the intent of Yahweh, to the ruthlessness of Babylon. Kings, of course, never believe history works that way. Kings imagine that royal decisions can shape public life. But this literary piece asserts otherwise. Because of Yahweh, the historical process is headed toward exile. That is where disobedient history finally leads. No escape is available. Here, such escape is not even hoped for, for that would be hope against the sovereign policy decision of Yahweh. There are chronological difficulties in this scheme, but those difficulties are modest compared to the overriding assertion that an ending is willed that is now brought to speech. And when it is spoken, the ending will not go away. We only wait and watch for the ending to materialize. The book of Jeremiah is a witness to that long torturous watch.

JEREMIAH'S CALL (1:4-19)

The book of Jeremiah "redescribes" the historical process by which God's people *go into exile* and surprisingly, come *out of exile*. That redescription hinges on the powerful presence of Yahweh in the historical process through Yahweh's word that has its own free say, without reference to human strategies and calculations. The tradition of Jeremiah is a stunning reflection on the power of Yahweh's word to order historical events (on which see Isa. 14:24-27; 55:8-9). That decisive say of Yahweh, inscrutable as it is, is borne through the human agency of Jeremiah, whose spoken word turns out to be the governing word of Yahweh. This strange convergence of human agent and sovereign word is a fundamental assumption of the prophetic tradition, which is made without embarrassment. The text offers no explanation about how the prophetic word is a sovereign word of Yahweh. Human words turn out, often to our dismay, to be the governing word of Yahweh. The speech of Jeremiah is presented as decisive both for entry into exile and return from it.

1:4-10 These verses are commonly regarded as a "call narrative" of the prophet Jeremiah. The words reflect common stylized features of such a call.[2] Those standard and predictable features include:

---

2. See Norman Habel, "The Form and Significance of the Call Narratives," *Zeitschrift für die alttestamentlichen Wissenschaft* 77 (1965): 297-323.

    divine initiative (v. 5)
    human resistance (v. 6)
    rebuke and reassurance (vv. 7-8)
    physical act of commissioning (v. 9a) and
    substance of commission (vv. 9b-10).

Three understandings of the narrative are available to us.

1. The text reports the actual personal experience of Jeremiah. This has been the conventional interpretation, especially among those who are interested in the personality and "spiritual experience" of the prophet. On this reading, the text tells about how this known person received authority.

2. Because the sequence is so stylized, it is suggested that this is a liturgical report of something like an ordination service.[3] This interpretation lessens the personal intensity of the first view, but has the merit of lodging the authority of the prophet more decisively in the institutional life and social fabric of the community. The prophet does not receive authority as primitive "raw data," but authority is mediated through a community that acknowledges the authority claimed for the prophet. The authority of the prophet then is a much more public authorization and might illuminate why Jeremiah has as much access as he had to public officials. These verses suggest that in the liturgy he has been publicly recognized to have this special vocation.

3. It has also been suggested that the text reflects neither personal nor liturgic experience but is an editorial construction, according to literary convention, to give authorization to the text that follows this chapter.[4] While this may sound odd to us, such a judgment reflects the turn of contemporary scholarship away from the person of Jeremiah to the book of Jeremiah. From this perspective, the intent of this narrative is to affirm that the text which follows is not merely a human construction, but is in fact the purposeful governing assertion of Yahweh, who will have history move as Yahweh asserts it.

According to this canonical interpretation, the personal response

---

3. See Henning Graf Reventlow, *Liturgie und prophetisches Ich bei Jeremia* (Gütersloh: Gerd Mohn, 1963), 24-77.

4. See Robert P. Carroll, *From Chaos to Covenant* (New York: Crossroad; London: SCM, 1981), 49-58. Carroll takes the call narrative as a literary device wrought by the Deuteronomic editors. Brevard S. Childs (*Introduction to the Old Testament as Scripture* [Philadelphia: Fortress; London: SCM, 1979], 348-350), relates the biographical material to the shaping of the canonical tradition.

of Jeremiah is rather incidental. There may be fear because Yahweh's word is a hard, dangerous word to speak. It is a sovereign word that changes the historical process, and finally that purpose can be resisted neither by the prophet nor by the king. If this third interpretation is a serious one (as I judge it to be), then the accent falls not on the personal struggle of the man, but on the substantive sovereign word of v. 10. At the most, the prophet is a bearer of this word that will decide the future of the city, the temple, the dynasty and, indeed, the nation. Interpretive interest is immediately shifted away from the person of the prophet toward the prophetic text. It is this shift away from the personal to the canonical that permits the speech of Jeremiah to have continuing interest and power for us.

The six verbs of v. 10—"pluck up" and "break down," "destroy" and "overthrow," "build" and "plant"—are a pointed statement of God's way with the nations. The first four verbs are negative. They assert that no historical structure, political policy, or defense scheme can secure a community against Yahweh when that community is under the judgment of Yahweh. The last two positive verbs, "build" and "plant," assert in parallel fashion that God can work newness, create historical possibilities *ex nihilo,* precisely in situations that seem hopeless and closed. God works in freedom without respect either to the enduring structures so evident, or to the powerless despair when structures are gone. God alone has the capacity to bring endings and new beginnings in the historical process (cf. Deut. 32:39; Isa. 45:7; 113:7-9).

It may be suggested that this range of six verbs provides the essential shape of the book of Jeremiah in its present form (cf. Jer. 18:7-10; 24:6; 31:27-28; 42:10; 45:4).[5] The book of Jeremiah in its main thrust concerns *the ending of beloved Jerusalem,* an ending wrought by the purposes of Yahweh in the face of every kind of human resistance, and *the formation of a new beloved Jerusalem* wrought by the creative power of Yahweh against all the data and in the face of massive despair. Indeed, the coming and going of Jerusalem (and by inference any historical structure) is not according to its own capacity for life and survival, but only according to the sovereign inclination of Yahweh. The prophet (prophetic person,

---

5. See the discerning analysis of Prescott H. Williams, Jr., "Living Toward the Acts of the Savior-Judge," *Austin Seminary Bulletin* 94 (1978): 130-139; and the canonical reflections of Ronald E. Clements, "Patterns in the Prophetic Canon," in Coats and Long, *Canon and Authority,* 42-55.

prophetic text) authorized to carry this word is derivative from and subordinated to the irresistible purposes of Yahweh. Thus the text makes a sweeping claim for God's free governance.

In the NT one can see how this same bold way of thinking is applied to the claims made for Jesus. In John 2:19 the verbs "destroy" and "raise up" appear. They are used with reference to the Jerusalem establishment, specifically the temple. But an important interpretive move is made so that the intent is to speak of the crucifixion and resurrection of Jesus. The value of observing this analogy is to see that, in those early claims for Jesus, the early Church derives its understanding of the historical process from prophetic faith, and perhaps precisely from Jeremiah. In both cases, Jeremiah and Jesus, the text invites one to reckon with the reality of discontinuity in the historical process out of which God can work a powerful newness, utterly inexplicable.

The conversations with and about the prophet in Jer. 1:5-9 are aimed toward God's magisterial governance expressed in v. 10. It is no wonder that the prophet resists, for who wants to bear such a burdensome and unwelcome word! But the word overrules its bearer. The message requires the messenger. What follows in the book of Jeremiah is a study of how this word of harsh endings and amazing beginnings has its way with specificity. We must not be unduly preoccupied with the person of the prophet who here is the way of God's specificity. In this unit the person of the prophet is not a subject but an object of God's overriding verbs. As the person of the prophet is subject to God's sovereign action, so also is the history of Jerusalem, of Judah, and finally of Babylon. That sovereign action, to which v. 3 has already given notice, revolves around the inescapable reality of exile. Because there is this particular exile into which and out of which God's people must go and come, there must be this prophet to speak Judah into exile and out again.

1:11-16 In this passage are reports of two "visions" that support the claim of Yahweh in vv. 4-10. The first of these (vv. 11-12) concerns a play on words: *shaqed* ("almond") and *shoqed* ("watching"). We need not linger over the question of the phenomenon of vision.[6]

---

6. On the phenomenological issues, see C. Johannes Lindblom, *Prophecy in Ancient Israel* (Philadelphia: Muhlenberg; Oxford: Blackwell, 1962), esp. ch. 3; and the disciplined reflections of Susan Niditch, *The Symbolic Vision in Biblical Tradition* (Chico, Calif.: Scholars Press, 1983).

The prophets obviously saw things others did not see and made connections that others missed. We do not have data about the experiential factors in such occurrences, and it is idle to speculate. In this text the point is not the almond tree, which must have been obvious to anyone who could look at bushes. The point is the *watching* that Yahweh does, and that was not so obvious to every observer. It is asserted that Yahweh's purpose (i.e., plucking up and tearing down, planting and building) has been unleashed in history. That purpose is a power at work in the midst of public life. While invisible, Yahweh attends to that resolve, guarantees it, and will see that it comes to fruition. The "watching" that Yahweh does is not unlike the patient, concentrated, intense watching in ambush of a leopard ready to spring (see 5:6 with the same word for "watch").

Elsewhere it is claimed that the watch of Yahweh has two stages (31:28), one negative and one positive. Both stages are guarded and vouchsafed by Yahweh until fruition. For the people of God this means it is ordained that there will be a painful ending and a stunning beginning. Such a way of thinking is alien to our positivistic modes which assume that all of history is made by human decision. That, of course, is what the kings in ancient Jerusalem thought as well. They took their own decisions too seriously. They imagined they were unfettered to do whatever they pleased as long as it worked. But this "watching" of Yahweh asserts that there is a shape, a flow, and an intentionality to history that cannot be nullified or evaded. That intentionality overrides all human posturing. That certitude is the basis of human hope, and it is the basis of judgment against human pretension. Interpretation of the book of Jeremiah must at the outset face this odd view of the course of persons and nations.[7] Another governance is at work that finally must be honored and that will not be mocked. The prophet bears this awesome disclosure that makes all human governance provisional. For that reason, the disclosure is never welcome, for it jeopardizes the pretense of human management.

The second vision (1:13-16) becomes more concrete in implementing the mandate of v. 10. The word to be announced also becomes unambiguously negative. Verse 10 contains four negative and two positive verbs. For much of the text of Jeremiah, however, the two positives are kept in abeyance. The main claim of the text (and

---

7. Klaus Koch refers to this understanding of the historical process as "suprahistory" and "metahistory" (*The Prophets,* vol. 1: *The Assyrian Period* [Philadelphia: Fortress; London: SCM, 1982], 144-156).

of the prophet) is the harsh ending now to come. In this vision the text becomes more specific about Yahweh's purpose against Judah. The occasion for the vision (which quickly becomes an oracle) is a stove that apparently faces south, suggesting a "hot threat" from the north. Again, it is not the vision but the construal of the vision that interests the text and us.

a. The vision concerns the coming of an unnamed, awesome, and dreaded nation that will invade from the north and occupy Judah and Jerusalem. The words are deliberately vague and imprecise. This is not political analysis, but poetic vision. The very vagueness makes it even more ominous, for there is no defense against such a hovering. What is undoubted is that Judah is thrust into the map of international reality. That entire map is governed and managed by Yahweh. Judah now must cope with the changing configurations of international power. It is beyond the interest of the text here that we speculate about the identity of the nations. Surely this is a veiled allusion to the massive expansion of the Babylonian Empire, which came out of nowhere in the lifetime of the prophet. Indeed, for the Jeremian analysis of world history, Babylon looms as the central fact, central save one other factor. That other factor is Yahweh's sovereignty. Nations rise and fall, come and go, according to Yahweh's magisterial purpose. These nations are "summoned" by Yahweh. They are, knowingly or not, simply agents of Yahweh's way among the nations. The great theological-political judgment of the book of Jeremiah is to see, assert, and establish a congruity between the purposes of Yahweh and the reality of Babylon. Kings in Jerusalem noticed Babylon but missed Yahweh's sovereignty. In the end, they missed everything.

b. The trigger for the historical process of "plucking up and tearing down" is not political or economic. It is theological and moral. Judah has done evil (v. 16; RSV "wickedness"). It is important to render the word as "evil," because the "evil" of the nations (v. 14) is a response to the "evil" of Judah.[8] The decisive evil of Judah, which will lead to the end of all old arrangements of power and security, is the abandonment of Yahweh. Everything hangs on the First Commandment concerning exclusive loyalty to Yahweh (Exod. 20:3). The burning of incense and worshipping other gods is not a critique

---

8. Patrick D. Miller, Jr., has shown how the prophetic notion of punishment corresponds with some precision to the affront (*Sin and Judgment in the Prophets*, SBL Monograph 27 [Chico, Calif.: Scholars Press, 1982]). In this case "evil" will be punished with "evil."

of "religious behavior." It is, rather, a critique of a fundamental shift in social practice and loyalty. Appeal to "other gods" is Jerusalem's attempt to secure its own existence by mobilizing divine power without submitting to Yahweh's sovereignty. Judah has preferred to trust in "the works of their own hands." In that way, Judah imagines it can have security while retaining control over its own destiny. The prophetic alternative insists that security only comes by submission, which entails yielding control.

The sin of Judah is an effort at theological, political, historical autonomy, the nullification of Yahweh's governance of public life. That problem of social autonomy is a contemporary issue, but it is not only a problem of modernity. It is a recurring temptation for every concentration of power to imagine itself self-sufficient and therefore free to order its life for its own purposes without the requirements of Yahweh (cf. Isa. 10:13-14; 47:8; Ezek. 28:2,9; 29:3).[9] As we shall see, in Jeremiah it is the disregard and nullification of Yahweh's sovereign will (expressed in social practice, religious activity, and policy formation) that regularly evoke the dismantling to come.

1:17-19 The oracle that derives from the second vision (v. 13) continues, but we treat these verses distinctly because of the major rhetorical break that is evident. Verses 14-16 concern the public intention of Yahweh. Verses 17-19, by contrast, are concerned with the particular destiny of the person of Jeremiah, who must bear this unbearable word against an unresponsive people. The rhetorical shift is marked by "but you" (v. 17). The God of this oracle is not indiscriminate. This God does not flatten the judgment so that everyone is treated in the same way. An important distinction is made between the majority, who are unresponsive and so under threat, and this minority voice (Jeremiah), who holds faithfully to the purpose of Yahweh. In a quite practical way, there are hints of a notion of a faithful remnant.

In 45:5 the same rhetorical move is made with reference to faithful Baruch. In both cases, specific faithfulness is acknowledged against the main inclination of Israel. Indeed, these two "but you" speeches in 1:17-19 and 45:5 may at one time have formed an envelope for the entire text. These two promises may provide a clue to the editorial history of the book of Jeremiah. That editorial work was done by those who came after Jeremiah, who lived in the Exile, and

---

9. See Donald E. Gowan, *When Man Becomes God,* Pittsburgh Theological Monograph 6 (Pittsburgh: Pickwick, 1975).

who took the text seriously. These faithful people understood themselves to be recipients of the same "but you" assurances. These two "exceptions" to the general judgment against Jerusalem may open a way to hope in Israel. For hope of "planting and building" is carried in this situation only by the true faithful remnant who took seriously that Yahweh did watch over the historical process in the face of massive empires and in the face of massive hard-heartedness in Judah. (See the same minority of two who open the future in Num. 14:30.) The specific oracle to Jeremiah echoes the initial summons of Jer. 1:4-10.

a. The prophet is summoned to dress for combat. As he speaks the truth about Yahweh and Jerusalem, he inevitably collides with the dominant ideology of king and temple. This combat is reinforced by the "againstness" in which Jeremiah is set and that is rhetorically so heavy in these verses. He must be ready and so "girded" for his dangerous role.

b. The prophet is provided an assurance that consists only in Yahweh's promise of solidarity. Indeed, it is not even promised that Yahweh will do anything, only that Yahweh will be there. Thus, the unequal quarrel is established that juxtaposes God's sovereign word against the mistaken ideology of the Jerusalem establishment. Jeremiah and the prophetic tradition of passion and poignancy carry that sovereign word; the mistaken ideology of the holy city has plenty of advocates and spokespersons. God promises to Jeremiah God's personal solidarity in the face of massive public resistance. The man Jeremiah, the book Jeremiah, the community gathered around this text, are located precisely in this unequal quarrel.

The issue turns on whether Yahweh really governs, because that governance is always slow, always invisible, always capable of other explanation. The question surfaces in the midst of the well-being of Jerusalem: will the city come to exile (cf. 1:3)? Or will it be safe, as the ideology claimed, because of reliance on old conventional promises? Will those traditional promises override the commission of "pluck up and tear down" as Hananiah urged (ch. 28)? The answer is not known in advance. The question is posed, and answered, at deep cost to Jeremiah, who must articulate the risky problem of Yahweh's governance. The promise of solidarity in the midst of such a quarrel strikes one as a weak resource. It struck Jeremiah so as well. But it is all that is ever offered Jeremiah, save capitulation to the ideology. And it is all that is offered to the community around the text. The assurances provided the "truth-speakers" against ideology are always thin and precarious, because the managers of the ideology seem to monopolize all the big, powerful promises. The unequal quarrel is underway in the text, hardly a fair fight.

We read the call narrative as a clue to the person of the prophet. But we read it also as a clue to the editing community that in subsequent time understood itself as heir to the harsh mandate and the thin promise. In some sense we dare to read it as a clue to the contemporary interpreting community that also struggles with the mandate and counts on the promise. Our exposition cannot easily sort out the distinctions of prophetic person, editing community, and interpreting community. They come together for us because at the outset we trust the canonical judgment of 1:1-3 in seeing the convergence between the specific words of Jeremiah and the overriding sovereign word of Yahweh. If we are to have either, we will have to submit ourselves to both the text and the governing word of Yahweh, which asserts exile, promises homecoming, and assures solidarity.

THE WILD VINE

Jeremiah 2

This chapter contains some of the most poignant and richly imaged poetry of Jeremiah. It is marked by only two major speech formularies (vv. 1-2a, 4-5a), and the structure of the poetry is not easy to determine. Despite these stylistic difficulties, the intent of the poetry seems clear enough. The poetry is an assault on Judah's imagination, requiring Judah to see its actual situation differently, to understand the causes of that situation and its inevitable outcome. The dominant theme is evident and redundantly stated: Israel has been unfaithful to Yahweh and stands under harsh judgment. There will be a temptation in interpretation to summarize and reduce, and one must have the patience to stay with the poetic nuance and detail in order to hear fully the word given through the poem.

2:1-3a These verses are marked off as a separate poem by the rhetorical formulae, "The word of the LORD . . ." and "says the LORD." They function as a historical retrospect, providing a basis for what follows. These verses employ two distinct metaphors. First, Judah's relation with Yahweh is like a marriage. The honeymoon period in the wilderness is remembered and celebrated (cf. Deut. 8:2-4). This positive reading of the early covenantal period is in contrast to Ezekiel, who reads the entire history as one of estrangement. The language of the poet is covenantal: "devotion" *(hesed)*, "love" *(ahab)*, "following after" *(halak)*. In those days of manna, Israel was totally dependent on Yahweh and glad to be so. As we shall see, this metaphor of marriage is taken up in the subsequent poetry to make a different point. One who has sworn such fidelity and loyalty is bound and belongs with and to the partner. One who has made such a bonding is not free to disregard or pervert it, which is what has happened in Judah.

This poetic reading of the relation of Yahweh and Judah is continued in Jer. 2:2b-3 with a very different metaphor, that of a harvest offering. The first produce of the season, the tenderest, is offered to Yahweh as acknowledgment that because the land is Yahweh's (cf.

Lev. 25:23; Deut. 26:2-10) Yahweh is entitled to the early produce.
Yahweh is entitled to Israel because Israel belongs to Yahweh. The
governing word is "holy." Israel is completely devoted to Yahweh,
existing for no other reason and available for no other use. This
metaphor is congenial to the marriage imagery, where Judah is also
totally devoted to Yahweh. That relation is also exclusive. Both Israel
and Yahweh delight in it. As wife and as firstfruits, Israel belongs exclusively to Yahweh, and exists for no other purpose. This motif of
belonging exclusively is central to the covenant between Yahweh and
Israel (Exod. 19:6; Deut. 7:6).

The positive metaphors provide the context for the harsh and unexpected turn in Jer. 2:3b. Whoever eats this produce is guilty and
receives evil. To eat (use) what belongs only to Yahweh is to pervert
its proper use and distort this relationship. The interpretive link between vv. 2-3a and v. 3b is left unspoken. We are not told how the
totally devoted bride/offering becomes a source of guilt. But clearly
these two words, "guilt" (indictment) and "evil" (sentence), provide
the structure for what is to follow.[1] The poet contrasts the present
sorry situation of violation, fickleness, and brokenness with what
was and what could be. The language is elusive as is so much of the
poetry in Jeremiah. but its claim is not obscure. Not only is the
honeymoon over—the whole relationship is deeply distorted. What
had been a happy marriage and a joyous offering is now deeply perverted, seemingly beyond recall.

2:4-13   Scholars conventionally present this section as a clear example of a prophetic lawsuit[2] that expresses the disastrous incongruity between faithful Yahweh and fickle Israel. The skeletal structure
of these verses is therefore that of the lawsuit, but the meaning of
these verses will be fully grasped only when one attends to the way
in which poetic imagery and rhetorical delicacy give flesh and life to
this skeleton. The lawsuit form ensures that this is not undisciplined,
rambling poetry, while at the same time the poetry imbues the conventional form with new power. It is the way of the poem to require
a fresh discernment of reality that calls Israel to accountability for its

---

1. On the lawsuit form, see Claus Westermann, *Basic Forms of Prophetic
Speech* (Philadelphia: Westminster; London: Lutterworth, 1967).

2. See Herbert B. Huffmon, "The Covenant Lawsuit in the Prophets,"
Journal of Biblical Literature 78 (1959): 285-295; Prescott H. Williams,
Jr., "The Fatal and Foolish Exchange: Living Water for 'Nothing,'" *Austin
Seminary Bulletin* 81 (1965): 3-59.

distorted relation with Yahweh. The text "spills a whole kaleido-scope of metaphorical false identities for Israel."[3]

2:4-8   Here is Jeremiah's classic indictment, asserting that Israel has forfeited its relationship with Yahweh. After the broad summons to indictment (v. 4), v. 5 functions as a general critique of Israel. The tone of the initial question is like the hurt of a wounded lover. The opening question, "What wrong did your fathers find?" is a legal defense of Yahweh in divorce proceedings. It asserts that there was nothing wrong with Yahweh. It follows, therefore, that the fault must lie with Israel. What was to be intimate has become distant. The dominant verb is "went after" *(halak)*. In v. 2, the same verb ("follow") is used for fidelity. Now it suggests infidelity. The critique is that Israel went after other gods who are "nothing." And since one takes on the character of the god one follows, Israel predictably has become a "no thing" as well (cf. Hos. 9:10; Ps. 115:8). Loyalty one has toward any god is decisive for the shaping of human life. We become like the god we serve. Pursue a bubble and become a bubble.[4] The object of love determines the quality of love.

In Jer. 2:6, 8 we are told what Israel did wrong. "They did not say . . ." The recital of Yahweh's story was no longer on their lips. They disregarded their shaping memory. Where the story of Yahweh is forgotten, Israel disregards its peculiar covenantal way in the world, and soon loses its reason for being. Verses 6-7 recite the credo that they "did not say," that has been forgotten. That credo is dominated by the word "land": land of Egypt, land of deserts and pits, land of drought and darkness, land that none passes through, plentiful land, defiled land, heritage. Israel's whole life is about land.[5] Yahweh's primal gift is land. Jeremiah is concerned with the sure-coming destruction, exile, and land loss. This passage suggests that

---

3. William L. Holladay, *The Architecture of Jeremiah 1–20* (Lewisburg, Pa.: Bucknell University Press, 1976), 45.

4. The Hebrew word *hebel* is the same as used in Ecclesiastes and there is regularly rendered "vanity." It bespeaks vapor or unreality, an appearance that has no real substance.

5. On the theme of land in Jeremiah, see Walter Brueggemann, "Israel's Sense of Place in Jeremiah," in *Rhetorical Criticism*, ed. Jared J. Jackson and Martin Kessler, Pittsburgh Theological Monograph 1 (Pittsburgh: Pickwick, 1974), 149-165; and, more recently, Walther Zimmerli, "The 'Land' in the Pre-exilic and Early Post-exilic Prophets," in *Understanding the Word*, ed. James T. Butler, Edgar W. Conrad, and Ben Ollenberger, JSOT Supplement 37 (1985), 252-255.

where the story of the land is lost, the loss of the land itself will soon follow.

When the phrase "did not say" is repeated a second time (v. 8), we are given evidence of the result of such forgetting. Where there is such amnesia, one is not surprised that derivative requirements of humanness erode. Where the creed is distorted, public life becomes skewed. The entire leadership structure of the community is included in the indictment: priests, judges, rulers, prophets—civic and religious leadership. To "know Yahweh" (v. 8; cf. 22:16) is to practice justice. Where Yahweh is not known, justice is not embraced. The poet is not engaged in moralizing. Rather, he discerned the collapse of public institutions. Priests no longer provide serious leadership. Judges forget their central commitment to justice. Rulers forget that power is a trust from Yahweh. Prophets forget that God has summoned them. The indictment ends with a third "go after," so that 2:8 forms an inclusion with the same verb in v. 5. The community is unfaithful. It has lost its foundational point of reference.

2:9-13   From this massive critique follows the prophetic "therefore." The unavoidable outcome is that Yahweh will take Israel to court to establish Israel's fickleness. Israel went after other gods (vv. 5-8), instead of after Yahweh (v. 2). Yahweh does not want simply to terminate the relation, but is willing to struggle, perhaps to fix blame, perhaps also to recover the relationship. Either way, court adjudication becomes a crucial metaphor. Indeed, the whole of Israel's history is now read as a lawsuit. The events of exile and/or destruction so near at hand are the implementation of that judgment which God has already decreed.

In vv. 10-11 the situation is ludicrous. Israel has this utterly faithful God for a partner, yet engages in "partner swapping." It is ludicrous because other people—Cyprus to the west, Kedar to the east—have lesser, unreliable gods and do not change. References to Cyprus and Kedar are inclusive: look everywhere from west to east! But Israel, in its recalcitrance, exchanges the only true God for the gods of Canaan, who cannot profit (v. 8). Israel has distorted things at the foundation, not being able to sort out what is real and unreal, what is true and false, what is life-giving and death dealing (Rom. 1:20-25). Adam C. Welch suggests that Israel trades gods because this one is too demanding.

> But the grace which gave much asked much; it demanded self-surrender. And without self surrender on the part of those who

received it, grace became an empty word. No other nation changed its god, non-entity though that was. The reason for the constancy was that it all meant so little. There was no cause to forsake such gods, because it involved so little to follow them. Israel forsook Yahweh, because the relation to Him was full of ethical content. . . . Yahwism had this iron core in it. The iron core was that Israel could only have Yahweh on His own terms. . . . Yahwism was no colorless faith which was simply the expression of the people's pride in itself and its destiny. It laid a curb on men, it had a yoke and bonds. The bonds were those of love, but love's bonds are the most enduring and the most exacting.[6]

It is no wonder that the great cosmic powers, heaven and earth, observe this sorry situation and are stunned (Jer. 2:12). Heaven and earth in this poem (cf. Isa. 1:2) function as witnesses who guarantee oaths and who observe patterns of faithfulness and fickleness. Because heaven and earth know Yahweh to be the true God (cf. Ps. 96:11), Israel's shabby response to Yahweh is exposed for what it is. In this cosmic court there is no doubt about the guilty party.

Jeremiah 2:13 functions as a reprise that reiterates the main point. Israel has forsaken an initial commitment to Yahweh. The poem introduces the metaphor of living water and empty cisterns. Yahweh is the living water that originates as gift outside of Israel (cf. John 4:10). Israel need not generate its own water or conjure its own life. It is freely given by this gracious partner of a God who is owner and husband. But Israel has rejected such a free gift that embodies its very life, and wants to be its own source of life—which of course leads only to death. The metaphor is water, but behind it lies the metaphor of marriage. "Forsake" is better understood in terms of marriage. The wrong that brings judgment is to abandon a true and faithful lover for a life of fickleness. It is as destructive as it is stupid (contrast Isa. 54:6-8, when God is the one who abandons, but not to perpetuity).

The metaphor of broken marriage is intimate and domestic, but its importance is public and historical. Israel's life is a gift of this covenant partner. The metaphor of firstfruits concerns an initial uncompromising claim of Yahweh to use and enjoy. But that uncompromising claim has been compromised. Where the gift is rejected and the partner is abandoned, life cannot continue. The metaphors

---

6. Adam C. Welch, *Jeremiah, His Time and His Work* (1928; repr. Oxford: Blackwell, 1951), 183.

serve the programmatic statement of Jer. 1:10. There will surely be a plucking up and a tearing down of one so faithless, who in this poem is none other than Jerusalem.

2:14-37 This longer unit is not a poem with a clear literary structure. Rather, it weaves together a variety of themes and metaphors in subtle and intricate ways. Rhetorically it may function as Yahweh's court testimony against Israel, anticipated in v. 9. The effect of the poem is to show that Israel's attempt to live outside a relation with Yahweh and to find other life-support systems is sure to fail and end in exile. Here as much as anywhere in Jeremiah, we must let the poetry have its own say without holding too precisely or too closely to a sustained argument.

2:14-19 Verse 14 puts a rhetorical question that assumes the answer: no, Israel is not a slave or a servant. Israel has not become a prey to the nations because it was fated for that by a bad birth. Israel is, rather, a much-loved heir and did not need to have this happen. The destruction has not happened for reasons of destiny, but for reasons of Israel's choice (vv. 15-16). Israel (i.e., Jerusalem) finds itself at the mercy of ruthless foreigners. The double use of the verb "forsake" in vv. 17,19 provides the reason (we have already seen the verb in v. 13). This trouble of a historical kind has happened because Israel has forsaken and abandoned Yahweh, has refused the marriage relation of v. 2, has refused the exclusive belonging of v. 3a, has refused to be the Israel God intended. Such a refusal may seem like freedom, but in fact it is death.

2:20-28 The foundational rejection of covenant with Yahweh is given in v. 20. Israel refused to be Yahweh's covenant partner, thinking autonomy was preferable. The poetry then presents a variety of perverted identities, with each one imagined to be proper and true. These verses attribute false assertions of identity to Judah:

> You said, "I will not serve" (v. 20).
> You say, "I am not defiled, I have not gone after the Baals" (v. 23).
> You said, "It is hopeless . . ." (v. 25).
> You say to a tree, "You are my father," and to a stone, "You gave me birth" (v. 27).
> They say, "Arise and save us" (v. 27).

Everything Judah says is false. Judah distorts reality and leads to destruction. Reality is the very opposite of what Judah says in these five assertions. Judah must accept its identity as Yahweh's covenant partner and vassal or die (v. 20). Judah is indeed defiled, a violation of the holiness of v. 3 (v. 23). Judah's relation with Yahweh is not hopeless but could be restored (v. 25). Judah trusts a tree and a stone, but they are neither Judah's future hope nor root progenitor (v. 27). Judah appeals to false gods, but they will not save (v. 27). The poetic strategy is to let Judah condemn itself out of its very own mouth.

Around these five false statements the poet has employed various images of distortion. In v. 21 the choice vine has become wild (cf. Isa. 5:1-7). In Jer. 2:23-24 Judah was to be a loyal partner but has become like a wild animal in heat, desperate to find any partner. In v. 26 Judah is like a thief who is exposed for mistaken action. By v. 28 Yahweh is prepared to leave Judah to its own hopeless resources.

2:29-37 As vv. 20-28 state the indictment, so vv. 29-37 now lead to the sentence. They begin in vv. 29-30a with Yahweh's self-vindication of innocence of wrongdoing. Yahweh has not betrayed Judah. No, it is the other way around. Judah has forgotten Yahweh (v. 32). The image of bridal ornaments serves to speak about something especially treasured and also to refer to the initial image of vv. 1-2. What is most treasured has been readily abandoned. By a distorted marriage relation, wickedness leads to judgment. The wickedness (v. 33) is infidelity that includes exploitation of the poor (v. 34). The result is that Egypt and Assyria will abuse Judah. That, however, is not simply the working of international policies. It is rooted in Yahweh's final rejection of Israel as the covenant partner (v. 37).

Jeremiah dares to say that Yahweh's connection to Judah is not unconditional. There are limits beyond which this fidelity will not go, and Judah has now reached the limit. Yahweh is prepared to give Judah over to the consequences of its own choices. The outcome is the termination of the relation so celebrated in vv. 1-2. This relation with God is not a guaranteed state, but a relation that depends on responsiveness. When the relation is neglected and grows cold, Yahweh will terminate. What courage, what nerve it must have taken to recite such a poem which announces that Judah's status as Yahweh's partner is now over!

The convergence of religious fickleness, political whoredom, and covenantal disregard shows that the poet is engaged in an acute critical analysis. Yahweh is not a God who is slotted in religious categories, but Yahweh is always related to a social system of values, policies, and conduct. When Yahweh is rejected, covenantal values disintegrate and life becomes a frantic pursuit of self-securing. Judah is therefore on a course to death. That death may ostensibly come at the hands of the empire, but in fact it is Yahweh who will finally relinquish his precious partner. There are limits. Yahweh has tried and tried (v. 30), but now it is enough. The God of high hopes (v. 21) is now the God of pained disillusionment.

The poet struggles here, as frequently, with the incredible obtuseness of this people. Not only is there an abandonment of God, but covenantal sensitivities have so collapsed that Israel is unable to recognize the quality and shape of its actions. In the face of the data, so clear to the poet, Judah continues to maintain innocence (vv. 23,35). It is as though Judah lives in a land of pretense in which its actions are not connected to anything, in which actions have no outcomes.

The rich play of metaphors of vine, camel, wild ass, thief, lover— all of this constitutes an invitation to Judah to see reality differently. The words press Judah's awareness in a variety of directions. The decisive metaphor is that of marriage and infidelity (thus the words, "forget, forsake, rebel, reject"), which ends in harlotry and harsh judgment. Yahweh speaks as a chagrined lover, a stern judge, a companion who wants to be on the way with Israel. But Israel is on *another way* (vv. 16-18), a way that can only lead to death. Life is given only in relationship with Yahweh, nowhere else. Nonetheless, Judah chooses another way.

Notice that the concern of the poem is properly theological—not moral, not political. The overriding issue is the refusal to have Yahweh as God. The consequences of Israel's great refusal are implemented in history. Israel is exposed to ruthless imperial powers. Jeremiah's discernment of the historical process never permits religious issues to be isolated from real public issues. Yahweh's governance appears in the dangerous realities of power politics. Jeremiah's theological discernment occurs in the midst of astonishing imperial politics. The rule of Yahweh, acted out among the emperors, brings death to a faithless partner.

RETURN TO ME

Jeremiah 3:1–4:4

This remarkable poem resumes the metaphor of marriage introduced in ch. 2. The long section of 3:1–4:4 has a complex redactional history.[1] The basic intention of the unit is an indictment of
Judah (Jerusalem) and a stern invitation to return to Yahweh. The
poetic elements address this issue. The language of "house of Israel"
(3:20) likely is a reference to the covenanted community and is
politically undifferentiated. That is, it simply refers to the community of faith and could as well apply to Judah and Jerusalem as the
northern community. It is also not impossible, however, that the
poetry originally was addressed to the north, also called Israel, but
then is reused with reference to the south. The poetry provides no
direct clues with which to resolve this issue.

In the prose of vv. 6-11, however, the language is much more precise and differentiated. There Judah—the same Judah addressed in
the poetry—is contrasted negatively with northern Israel. In the next
prose section (vv. 15-18) a return of Judah to Jerusalem after exile is
envisioned, as well as a gathering of northern Israel to Jerusalem. It
is not necessary or possible to trace the details of redactional development. It is possible, however, to see in these three layers of the text
a sequenced reflection on Judah and Jerusalem, first addressed as the
community of faith; second, as a community more fickle than the
north; and third, as the restored community. Each element reflects a
particular historical moment. They are joined together in 3:1–4:4 to
provide a sustained reflection that encompasses the course of Judah's
life with Yahweh, a life reflected upon throughout the tradition of
Jeremiah.

We have seen the positive assertion of the marriage metaphor
(2:1-2), and its negation in the triple use of the word "forsake." This
poem seems to begin with an allusion to the torah teaching of Deut.

---

1. See John Bright, *Jeremiah*, 2nd ed., Anchor Bible 21 (Garden City,
N.Y.: Doubleday, 1978), 25-27.

24:1-4.[2] In the torah text it is prohibited that a twice-married woman may return to the first husband when rejected by the second husband. For our purposes, the three important phrases in Deut. 24:4 are:

(1) "may not take her again,"
(2) "she has been defiled,"
(3) "bring guilt upon the land."

The first phrase prohibits the return to the first husband. The return is prohibited even if both parties want to reestablish the relationship. The second phrase asserts that the woman is "defiled" by the second husband, that is, rendered unacceptable to the first husband. The third phrase, in characteristic Deuteronomic fashion, links the defilement of the woman to the defilement of the land, so that both the woman and the land are contaminated.[3]

The torah teaching only provides the beginning point for the present poem. The poet exercises imagination and carries the metaphor in quite new and inventive directions. Yahweh is the first husband; "other lovers" (false gods, false alliances) are the second husband for whom Judah has forsaken Yahweh. Judah is the faithless wife of Yahweh. The designation of husband-wife established in the poem of Jer. 2 is assumed in the poem of chs. 3–4. Now the question in ch. 3 is: what can happen next? The crisis turns on the capacity of Yahweh, the first husband, to take back the wife, Judah, after defilement by a second relationship. Yahweh's capacity to take back is clearly precluded by the torah. Yahweh, in spite of the torah, nonetheless yearns for the return of Judah to the covenant. This yearning on the part of Yahweh violates the torah, yet Yahweh's great love for Israel is sufficient to risk God's own violation of the torah. The yearning also violates common sense and pride. No husband, so it may be assumed from social convention as well as the torah teaching, would be so vulnerable as to take back such a fickle wife.

---

2. On the relation between Deut. 24:1-4 and Jer. 3:1, see Michael Fishbane, *Biblical Interpretation in Ancient Israel* (New York and Oxford: Oxford University Press, 1985), 307-312; Trevor R. Hobbs, "Jeremiah 3:1-5 and Deuteronomy 24:1-4," *Zeitschrift für die alttestamentliche Wissenschaft* 86 (1974): 23-29.

3. On the relation between treatment of land and treatment of women, see the discerning comments of Wendell Berry, *Recollected Essays 1965-1980* (San Francisco: North Point, 1981), 191, 215; and my expository comments on his thesis in "Land, Fertility, and Justice," in *Theology of the Land,* ed. Bernard F. Evans and Gregory D. Cusack (Collegeville, Minn.: Liturgical Press, 1987), 41-68.

Such violation of the torah, however, is the stunning point of the poem. Against all expectations which should lead to final rejection, Yahweh, the God of Israel, will risk humiliation and defilement.[4] Jeremiah here echoes the insight of Hosea on the vulnerable, risky love of Yahweh for Israel. God is unlike every human analogy (cf. Hos. 11:8-9: Yahweh is God, not "man"). John Calvin says it well: "But we have seen at the beginning of the chapter that there is a difference between God and husbands. As then God did not deal, as he might justly have done, with the Israelites, and did not execute a capital punishment, as he might rightly have done, and what was usually done."[5] The central point of Jer. 3:1–4:4 is that God is not like human analogies, but will take the fickle partner back. The remainder of this section is an invitation, a yearning, and an urging for "return."

3:1 Verse 1 takes up the torah teaching in three rhetorical questions. The answer to the first is clearly "no." No, Yahweh will not return to Judah. This "no" is supported by the second question, which asserts land pollution. The third question is in fact an indictment for adultery with "lovers." It implies that Israel cannot return to Yahweh. The action of Judah makes return impossible, both on grounds of torah restrictions as well as common sense. Such betrayal precludes reconciliation.

3:2-5 These verses extend the theme with a series of indictments and sentences. The savage indictment likens lustful Israel to an ambushing Arab. The irony is intense. One would expect a lone woman on the road to be ambushed. But, shamelessly, the woman assumes the role of ambusher, so desperate is she for any lover. Parallel to the torah provision, such an action pollutes the land, so that not only are

---

4. On the capacity of God to violate God's own torah, see W. Sibley Towner, *Daniel,* Interpretation (Atlanta: John Knox, 1984), 89, in his comment on Daniel 6:

The corollary question is whether God is trapped by the immutability of his own law. One is sometimes stunned at the intensity with which the psalmist reminds God of his own commitments to crush the wicked and to slay the psalmist's own opponents. . . . We also have words to Israel that God is capable of transcending his own law. God's law is immutability, and yet God himself can suspend it if compassion so demands.

5. John Calvin, *Commentaries on the Book of the Prophet Jeremiah and the Lamentations,* vol. 1 (repr. Grand Rapids: Baker, 1979), 167.

the people of Judah unclean but the land is also unclean. (This theme
is utilized by Ezekiel to assert that God cannot stay in such a polluted
place [Ezek. 8:6].) Thus, the defilement of land anticipates not only
the exile of Judah but also the departure of Yahweh, the decisive absence of God from Jerusalem. The concern of the poet is never only
the two covenant partners, but also the land. It is betrayal and abuse
of the land that requires exile from off the land.

The result of the pollution is conveyed through the "therefore" of
Jer. 3:3: the pollution has caused drought (cf. Lev. 26:19 and, by contrast, Ezek. 34:26). Yet even in the face of such data, Israel is incredibly recalcitrant, refusing to blush (cf. Jer. 8:12). Judah is not
only wayward, but ignorant. As a faithless wife she is so eroded in
sensitivity that she is not even embarrassed over her action. Jer. 3:4
implies that Israel has attempted to restore relation with Yahweh by
uttering an address of covenant loyalty, "father." The disjunctive "behold" of v. 5 tells Israel, however, that the evil actions override any
verbal repentance. Israel's actions are so loud and decisive that verbal
repentance is regarded as frivolous. Yahweh yearns for reconciliation,
but it will be on Yahweh's terms—and that requires a real change, not
merely a verbal gesture. So the waiting continues. The grieving
husband waits with expectation, but not without requirement.

3:6-10   These verses pursue the same general theme, but are prose
and are generally reckoned as a later addition. Judah is contrasted
with Israel, the northern kingdom, and is found to be even worse
(cf. Ezek. 23:4-11).[6] Judah is portrayed as even more calloused than
Israel. The reference to Josiah may link this judgment to the failure
of the Reform of 621 B.C.E. It is as though Yahweh believes that if
the degradation to which Yahweh subjects Judah is deep enough, it
will move Judah to change. But Judah is not moved and does not
change. Instead the pathos of Yahweh is intensified, for Yahweh still
expects a return. In such gestures as Jer. 3:4-5 Judah makes a move,
but it is a false move *(sheqer)*. This false move appears regularly in
Jeremiah as a motif for dishonest covenant.[7] Even in its ostensible

---

6. While this prose element may indeed be a later interpolation, the
contrast between north and south is not unthinkable in the tradition of
Jeremiah. Notice that in 7:12-15 a comparison is established. In that case
the south is said to be like the north, not worse than the north as here.

7. See James Muilenburg, "The Terminology of Adversity in
Jeremiah," in *Translating & Understanding the Old Testament,* ed. Harry
Thomas Frank and William L. Reed (Nashville: Abingdon, 1970), 42-63.

return, Judah continues to act out the very alienation that is at the root of the problem.

3:11-13 The poem resumes (after the contrasts made in vv. 6-10) with an intense urging to return to the relationship. Israel, the northern community, is invited back by Yahweh. This invitation likely reflects a Josianic appeal to the north. That is, the religious appeal is related to a political recovery of northern territory by Josiah. The appeal is the voice of an offended husband seeking his wife back, even against the torah, even in the face of humiliation. The ground for repentance is a threefold statement about Yahweh, for the basis of new possibility is only in Yahweh, not in Israel. Yahweh will not be angry (cf. Ps. 103:9). Yahweh is "merciful" (the term is again *hesed,* on which see Jer. 2:2). The third statement on Yahweh is an answer posed to the question in 3:5. Even this yearning husband does not envision return without condition. To come home the ex-wife must acknowledge her promiscuity (v. 13). The poet struggles to articulate the anguish of Yahweh, who on the one hand wants the relation and on the other hand will not relinquish his own self-regard. The tension so felt and spoken by the poet tears at the heart of God, who yearns, but who will not be mocked, trivialized, or used.

3:14-20 The poetic verses of this unit (vv. 14,19-20) offer a second invitation to return. They affirm again that the covenant people have been fickle, but also that Yahweh will cause a homecoming. The emphasis in vv. 19-20, however, is not on the summons or the possible return but on the grief of Yahweh, who is variously an affronted parent or a betrayed husband. The poetry moves easily from one metaphor of familial relationship to the other. Verse 19 is a reflective soliloquy on the high hopes God had for a relationship of trust and intimacy, how God had planned to give over to this beloved child the best of the land. But all those keen hopes have been destroyed by the fickleness of Israel, who preferred other lovers. Thus the basic form is a summons to return, but the substance pushes against the form to articulate the grief of God. According to the nuance of the rhetoric, the grief may not yet be completely hopeless about a restored future, but it is well on its way to hopelessness. The poet presents a profound conflict, in which the heart of God yearns in hope for Israel but also grieves over Israel's betrayal. In this moment the relationship could be resolved in either direction.

Verse 19 is among the most poignant in Jeremiah. The poet has taken the anguish of a parent as his medium (cf. Hos. 11:1-9). The poet portrays for us a parent who has labored and dreamed for the glorious day when the child will be old enough, responsible enough, and responsive enough to receive all that has been saved for the child from the beginning. The father wants to give the child this inheritance even more than the child wants to receive it. But the moment of gift never comes, because the child neither knows nor cares. The wounded father is left with the shambles of hard work and broken dreams and knows the bitter combination of deep hurt and heavy resentment.[8]

The intervening prose of Jer. 3:15-18 is thought by most scholars to be later, echoing motifs from Ezekiel. The promise of a new shepherd (v. 15) is closely linked to Ezek. 34. The transformation of Israel in Jerusalem sounds like the restoration of Jerusalem in later Ezekiel. The unity of Judah and Israel here articulated is either an echo or anticipation of Ezek. 37:15-23. These verses seem attached to Jer. 3:14 (which appears to be earlier poetry) concerning a return to Zion.

In their present location vv. 15-18 form an important counterpoint to the poetry of alienation. The poetry announces the fickleness of Judah and the pathos of God. The prose articulates God's resolve in spite of the fickleness. The dramatic contrast between fickleness and pathos is crucial for the canonical assertion of the text. The poem is clearly heavy with judgment, but the canonical form finally focuses on the restoration. The present shape of the text is arranged to hold in tension the motifs of Israel's fickleness and Yahweh's pathos. The prose indictment of Israel's fickleness is flat, direct, and unambiguous. But the countertheme of Yahweh's yearning pathos is a dramatic surprise. The fickleness of Israel should evoke Yahweh's anger, and indeed it does. But along with anger is Yahweh's relentless yearning for a restored relationship. Both prose and poetry are necessary to articulate this powerful surprise. The two inclinations are dramatically juxtaposed as poetry and prose, though we do not yet know which way the issue will be settled. In these verses filled with hope the completed tradition asserts that God's yearning for a relation is so powerful and so resilient that in the end there is a new relation wrought, not out of Judah's repentance, but out of Yahweh's resolve. But the restoration is only "in those days." The prose of hope does not cancel out the poetry of hurt, but it

---

8. On the pathos of this relationship, see James Muilenburg, "Father and Son," in *Hearing and Speaking the Word,* ed. Thomas F. Best (Chico, Calif.: Scholars Press, 1984), 283-293.

comes after and presumes the painful alienation. The juxtaposition is not unlike the poetic articulation of Isa. 54:7-8, in which both abandonment and restoration are governed by the same God.

We are now in a position to consider the canonical shape of this unit. Judah stands under indictment as a fickle wife (Jer. 3:2-5). Judah is more faithless than is Israel (vv. 6-10). Israel is also guilty, but less guilty and is invited to return (vv. 11-13). The first thirteen verses establish the failure of both north and south, Israel and Judah. But both communities are invited to return (in violation of the torah prohibition of Deut. 24:1-4). Israel is invited back (Jer. 3:12,14), and Judah is assured return (vv. 14-15). Both Israel and Judah are restored to well-being and relationship (v. 18). The passage thus moves from utter faithlessness to astonishing restoration. The shift from faithlessness to restoration is accomplished because of Yahweh's resilient fidelity, fidelity in the face of fickleness, fidelity that is rooted in God's deep pathos (vv. 19-20). On the basis of *faithlessness* become *restoration* through *pathos,* a new possibility is envisioned for Israel and the nations (3:17; 4:2), grounded in "truth, in justice, and in uprightness." The marks of truth, justice, and uprightness now to be implemented are contrasted with the present condition of falseness, injustice, and perverseness. There is hope now grounded in God's passion, but it is hope that looks failure honestly in the face and moves beyond it.

3:21-25 A third element of the summons to return now follows after 12-14 and 19-20. The invitation is offered in v. 22, a summons plus an assurance that God will heal. It is not clear if this summons is to be taken at face value, or if this is a mocking at Israel's too-easy presumption upon Yahweh. In any case, vv. 21,22b,23 are an articulation of repentance, an acknowledgement of guilt, and a recognition that trust in other gods has been an exercise in futility. It is affirmed, ironically or not, that only Yahweh can be Israel's deliverer.

The concluding verses, vv. 24-25 (prose), are in the form of a confession of sin. The poetic verses initiated the repentance, but the confession here is much more serious. It contains a judgment on the history of Israel. Jeremiah 2:2 affirmed that there was a honeymoon period of fidelity, but here the infidelity is "from our youth" (cf. Gen. 8:21). That is, through the entire history of the covenant there never was a time of faithfulness. From the very beginning Israel has been seeking alternatives. The "shame" and "dishonor" of Jer. 3:25 continues the metaphor of the shamed woman, now twice rejected— first by Yahweh her husband and then by her subsequent lovers as well. She is therefore left scandalized and without a place of belonging. Her own actions have caused her to be utterly displaced, abandoned with none to welcome her to safety. Through her own stupid actions, Judah is rejected. Her life, apart from the intervention of Yahweh as her advocate, is in profound jeopardy.

4:1-4 It may surprise us that in the face of such a history of infidelity there is still a chance to return to Yahweh. That in itself is an astonishing possibility. In this concluding section God issues yet another invitation, but that invitation comes neither easily nor cheaply. Yahweh's invitation is demanding and rigorous as Yahweh now sets conditions for return. The conditions are introduced by "if" three times in the RSV (twice in Hebrew):

> if you return
> if you remove
> if you swear
> *then* . . . (only then . . .).

The conditions are that Judah must cast off all other loyalties and reclaim Yahweh as sovereign LORD. The last line of the condition recalls Judah to the great themes of covenantal faith: truth, justice, righteousness. The last pair of words ("justice" and "righteousness") is a classic prophetic formulation (cf. Amos 5:7,24; 6:12; Isa. 5:7; 9:7; Jer. 22:3,15). The price of return to Yahweh is to order human life according to covenantal norms. The third element, "truth," reflects a peculiarly Jeremianic focus on the sense of falseness (cf. 9:3) that permeates the life of Judah.[9] Covenant with Yahweh requires the reconstruction of all of life with a new orientation. Yahweh yearns for a renewed relationship, but it is not a shapeless, desperate yearning. It is yearning for a relation in which Yahweh's sovereign will is taken seriously. Because Yahweh is finally sovereign, no other kind of relationship is thinkable or workable.

The "then" (consequence) of repentance and reorientation of life is the implementation of God's promise to Abraham (Gen. 12:3; 18:18;[10] 22:18; 26:4; 28:14). The restoration of covenant thus will

---

9. See Thomas W. Overholt, *The Threat of Falsehood: A Study in the Theology of the Book of Jeremiah,* Studies in Biblical Theology, 2nd series 16 (London: SCM; Naperville: Allenson, 1970).

10. On the crucial theological placement of this text, see Jose P. Miranda, *Marx and the Bible* (Maryknoll, N.Y.: Orbis, 1974), 94-97.

benefit not only Judah but the other nations that derive new life from that covenant.[11]

Jeremiah 4:3-4 reiterates the requirements of return with three new imperatives. The two imperatives of v. 3 ("break up and sow") seem to draw upon Hos. 10:12, using images drawn from agricultural practices. The imperative "circumcise" seems to appeal to the imagery of Deuteronomy (Deut. 10:16; 30:6), which is the most demanding tradition of covenant. Indeed, this summons mobilizes the best memories of Israel to make an appeal to the contemporaries of the poet.

It is clear that this extended unit (Jer. 3:1–4:4) is a subtle and complex literary whole. In rough sketch, the movement of the poem is as follows.

(1) Appeal to the torah, only to move beyond the permit of torah (3:1a);

(2) Application of torah teaching in order to convict wayward Israel (vv. 1b-5);

(3) Contrast with Israel, showing Judah more unfaithful (vv. 6-10);

(4) First appeal for return (vv. 11-13);

(5) Second appeal for return (vv. 14-20);

(6) Third appeal for return (vv. 21-25);

(7) Fourth appeal for return (4:1-4).

This poem is a meditation on the theme of return. The torah of Deuteronomy explicitly states that the wife shall not return. The connections to Deut. 24:1-4 make clear that the dominant concern is neither spiritual repentance nor a moral reconstruction. It is about a relationship that has been violated beyond recall. Yahweh, the first husband, has been deeply affronted. Judah, the wayward wife, is now rejected, scandalized, and exposed. The second lover has clearly failed. According to torah, it is impossible to go back to Yahweh, the first lover. Yet this is a meditation precisely on the unheard-of possibility of such a return. The return is possible because both the need of Judah and the yearning of Yahweh fly in the face of the torah. The torah establishes that Judah has no right to return. The torah estab-

---

11. On the continuing concern for justice and righteousness as it concerns a blessing to the nations (and not only to Israel), see Hans Walter Wolff, "The Kerygma of the Yahwist," in *The Vitality of Old Testament Traditions,* ed. Walter Brueggemann and Hans Walter Wolff (Atlanta: John Knox, 1975), 41-66.

lishes that Yahweh has no obligation to take her back. The themes of guilt and betrayal are stated with overriding power and clarity.

None of that quite touches the central affirmation of the poem, however. The truth of the matter is that, after the requirements of torah are acknowledged, there is the unfinished business of the relationship that the torah cannot contain. That unfinished business is to see how, in what ways, under what circumstances, a reestablished first marriage is possible. It is clear from 3:1b-5 that Judah has no case to make for herself. This is reinforced by vv. 6-10,24-25. Yet it is also clear in vv. 15-18 that Yahweh can do a new promissory act, even in the face of the torah. But neither of these touch the real issue. The real issue is that *Yahweh is hurt* and filled with humiliated indignation. Nonetheless, *Yahweh is open* to restoration. It is as though the poet cannot clearly come down on one side or the other, because the God known to the poet is in God's own heart unclear. The yearning and indignation are locked in deep tension. The repentance of 3:4 seems to signal the hoped-for intimacy of v. 19, but it is not serious repentance. The outcome of this poem is that repentance which restores relationship is demanding and costly, very likely more demanding and more costly that this partner can handle.

Notice how this poem stays at the level of relational imagery. There is no connection here to actual historical content. Nor is there any explicit ethical requirement made beyond the generalities of 4:1-4. This is indeed a poetic reflection that leaves everything open beyond the hurt, pathos, and yearning of the relationship. How the future of the relation is to be actualized is left open. The poem does not deal with political or ethical reality. It cuts underneath that to the wounded hope of God. What counts now is not fox-hole repentance in order to survive. What counts now is the reality of this husband, who with bitter yearning and affronted loyalty, still is open to a relation, even against the wisdom of the torah. If perchance the relation can be resumed, it will be outside the righteousness of the torah. It will be the odd righteousness of the first husband (Yahweh) who violates the torah for the sake of the relationship (cf. Ps. 143:1-2). Yahweh's powerful yearning risks defilement for the sake of covenant (cf. Luke 7:34-35)!

TERROR ON EVERY SIDE
Jeremiah 4:5–6:30

The preceding poetic unit has portrayed God for us as a wounded, betrayed lover and husband yearning for a return. Even at the end of the unit there is still the hope that Israel will "come home." The mood is starkly different as this next section begins. Now there is no such yearning. Now there is darkness and harshness. This is a very different voice of God, who has reached the limit of yearning and the far edge of compassion. John Calvin draws this conclusion: "God now shews that he was not, as it were, at liberty to forgive the people; 'Even if I would,' he says, 'I could not.'"[1] We see the other side of God's inclination, which is that, for all of God's considerable passion and compassion, God will not be mocked.

This long section includes some of the most poignant poetry of the prophet. It is largely lacking in explicit historical allusion. It offers an open-ended poetic reading of reality that could be heard in more than one historical context, which is what gives it such enduring power.[2] Most scholars believe this poetry comes from the early period of Jeremiah's poetry, but that is not important for our purposes. It is a miscellaneous collection without a clear ordering or structure, but one may identify at least four recurring themes.

(1) Anticipations of an invading army dispatched by Yahweh;
(2) Prophetic ruminations on personal grief and judgment;
(3) Harsh visions of the end of the human, historical process;

---

1. *Commentaries on the Book of the Prophet Jeremiah and the Lamentations,* vol. 1 (repr. Grand Rapids: Baker, 1976), 252.

2. That the text is not so closely tied to historical placement enhances its enduring canonical power for the community. On the process of textualization and the resulting authority, see Werner H. Kelber, *The Oral and the Written Gospel* (Philadelphia: Fortress, 1983). While Kelber's work concerns the Gospels, the point is valid for the tradition of Jeremiah as well. This methodological awareness makes questions of historical reference less important.

(4) Statements of guilt and punishment, which follow standard prophetic motifs.

4:5-8 This is the first of the poems in which Jeremiah characterizes an invading threat sent by Yahweh from the north (cf. 1:13-15). There has been much scholarly speculation on the identity of this enemy.[3] Older scholarship identified it as the Scythians, based on enigmatic references in the ancient historian Herodotus. A judgment closer to the actual concern may suggest that it is the Babylonian armies who did indeed come against Jerusalem in 598 and 597 B.C.E. To try to specify an historical referent, however, is to miss the point. This is not an historically descriptive narrative. Rather, it is an act of poetic imagination that does not depend on historical referent. Its purpose is, rather, to evoke in the listening community an awareness and a sense that this religious, political enterprise (Jerusalem) which has seemed so secure is in fact under massive assault, and that any complacency or "ease in Zion" (cf. Amos 6:1) is misplaced and ill-informed. The poet does not want his listeners to make a political analysis, but to let the dangerous reality—that the world of Jerusalem is not what they thought it was—play upon their perception and imagination.

The erroneous perception of Jeremiah's audience has been deliberately misinformed by a royal-temple ideology that screened out covenantal reality and permitted self-deception.[4] The poetry

---

3. John Skinner, *Prophecy and Religion: Studies in the Life of Jeremiah* (1922; repr. Cambridge and New York: Cambridge University Press, 1955), 37-45, offers a review of the problem and the possibilities of historical identification of the "foe from the north." Concerning historical identification, he concludes: "The conclusion is very uncertain; but we shall lose nothing if we take the Scythian poems to be in the main imaginative anticipations of future calamities, always shooting ahead of the accomplished fact, but at the same time following more or less the development of a grave national crisis which was as real to the prophet's countrymen as it was to himself" (44).

4. The "royal-temple ideology" is rooted in the Davidic oracle of 2 Sam. 7 and the temple dedication of Solomon in 1 Kgs. 8. In these two events of oracle and dedication, the family of David and the temple establishment were able to claim for themselves the patronage of and alliance with Yahweh as the God who had made an abiding commitment to that enterprise. While the establishment of temple and dynasty was a gift of God's graciousness, that gift became distorted so that the eternal purposes of God came to be identified with the policies and purposes of the urban

seeks to penetrate that ideology with a harsh and eloquent dose of reality. Jeremiah 4:5-6 sounds the bugle of warning trumpeted by a sentry to the north. The enemy has been spotted. His listeners, however, do not hear any such warning, for they have been lulled into imagining there was no threat. The poet anticipates, long before the actual fact of invasion; but the poet shrewdly does not identify, for that would flatten the poetic invitation into a description without power. Were the enemy named, then a debate could ensue about how to meet the threat. But the poet wants no such debate. He only wants his listeners to notice.

In Jer. 4:7 the metaphor of a lion is used to characterize the invader, a metaphor used by Hosea (Hos. 5:14-15) for Yahweh. In our poem the lion is the enemy people, but in Jer. 4:8 this is linked to the irresistible anger of Yahweh. The poet does not urge any specific response beyond formal grieving. There is no suggestion that any repentance is possible or desirable. Now the die is cast. Mobilization has begun and will not be averted. Judah is at war. Jerusalem is under attack. The army may be Babylonian, but the real agent is Yahweh. That of course makes the danger massive, ominous, inescapable. Yahweh is now engaged in a dread military exercise against God's own beloved Jerusalem. The wounded warrior has become invading army. Judah is left only to grieve the death that is now sure. In the lyrical maneuver of this war poem the poet has deftly overwhelmed the Jerusalem establishment and its claim to immunity from attack.

4:9-10 This small unit is a prophetic reflection on the preceding poem. It is as though Jeremiah articulates both sides of a conversation. First he announces the massive threat as a speaker for Yahweh (v. 9). Then he responds to the threat as though its weight only now sinks in (v. 10). Persistently the poet carries on a critique against the leadership that he regards as self-serving. In v. 9 he names them, king/princes/priests/prophets. All of them are inade-

---

establishment. This gave excessive legitimacy to the economic-political enterprise of the city and made its policies immune from criticism because of religious legitimacy. The outcome is the establishment of a self-serving, self-deceiving ideology that nullified every ethical demand and every historical ambiguity. Clearly the prophetic tradition in general and Jeremiah in particular stand in harsh criticism of this ideology. On the tension between the royal-temple ideology and a prophetic alternative, see Walter Brueggemann, "The Epistemological Crisis of Israel's Two Histories (Jer. 9:22-23)," in *Israelite Wisdom*, ed. John G. Gammie (Missoula, Mont.: Scholars Press, 1978), 85-105.

quate for the real crisis that they did not believe would come. These lines either reiterate the chagrin of the leaders or mock their now-shaken self-confidence. When all forms of official leadership have failed, only Jeremiah remains to provide shape to public life. He now undertakes to do the one thing still pertinent. He prays. In v. 8 he had urged lament. Now in v. 10 he utters Judah's complaint for them. (The prayer is paralleled in Ezek. 11:13, where that prophet also grieves the end of the beloved people of God.)

The prayer of Jeremiah in Jer. 4:10 may contain some irony. There has been talk of well-being *(shalom)*, when the historical reality is destruction (sword). The official line was, "It can't happen here," but it can, because it is. There is a deep incongruity between what is recited as official cant and what is taking place. The possible irony is that Jeremiah blames Yahweh for the cover-up, as though Yahweh were the source of the self-deceiving ideology of the Jerusalem establishment. There has indeed been deception, but it cannot be blamed on Yahweh. Surely it is not Yahweh who said "Peace, peace" (cf. 6:14; 8:11). Rather, it was the royal leadership, precisely those named in 4:9. Thus these verses that are cast as lament are in fact an assault on the official royal ideology that has refused to face reality. The reality, according to this poet, is that Jerusalem is ending. The poet has discerned and articulated what the official leadership is unwilling and unable to see. The poetry has the effect of delegitimating the public leadership that has refused to face reality. Nothing remains to be done except to hold the funeral. Leadership that ultimately deceives will finally bring destruction.

4:11-18 After an introduction in vv. 11-12 that utilizes the images of wind and winnowing as metaphors for harsh judgment of the invading army, the poetry is resumed. The language in v. 13 is hyperbole, wanting to assert that this people (still unnamed) is massive, awesome, irresistible. This invader is so overwhelming that Judah is reduced to funeral songs, to sing of its own death. For one brief moment (v. 14) it is suggested that the washing of repentance might still permit rescue (cf. Isa. 1:16; Ps. 51:7). The poet clings to that thin possibility, but nothing comes of it. It is as though the hope for repentance is only an instant of wistfulness that the poet cannot in fact believe or entertain. There is a chance, but that slight chance is soon abandoned in the rush of the poetry. Jeremiah 4:15 returns to the dramatic characterization. The guards in the north, in Dan and in the tribe of Ephraim, send signals ahead. They warn Jerusalem by a series of communications that Jerusalem is next in line; nothing can slow down the terror and pace of this coming enemy. (On the role of the sentries in the north, see the contrasting function in Isa. 40:9-11; 52:7-10.) The juggernaut is under way and none can slow it.

In Jer. 4:17b-18 it is asserted that this invasion is not arbitrary, but is in fact the consequence of Israel's own disobedient life. We should not miss the massive and bold act of imagination that stands at the center of this poetic claim. The poet links the *internal failure* of social life in Judah and the *external threat* of Babylonian expansionism. They are linked as cause and effect, as sin and judgment. Judah has failed to trust Yahweh; *therefore* Babylon invades Judah. One could offer political and geopolitical explanations about the coming of the Babylonians, but the poet has no interest in such knowing analysis. It is the work of the poet to focus with single-minded passion on one aspect of reality to the disregard of all else. The poet here focuses on the failure and fickleness of Judah in response to the covenant expectation of Yahweh, who is variously father, husband, judge. Shameless and unlimited transgression finally will bring the downfall.

History is a process over which Yahweh is sovereign and through which that sovereignty is worked out. The rule of Yahweh is not done "supernaturally," but through historical agents—in this case, the coming of this unnamed but awesome army that will not be resisted. Surely this poem is not a scientific description of an actual army. It is a poetic invitation. It does not want to change political postures in Judah, for that is not the work of the poet, but to penetrate the religious indifference and covenantal recalcitrance from which policy comes. Thus the language is bold and daring, without responsibility for being factually precise. The prophet wants to bring the imagination of Judah into touch with the theological reality of judgment. The visible threat of the Babylonian army is only an occasion for speaking of covenantal realities. The real threat from the north (or from wherever) is in fact the inescapable and uncompromising rule of Yahweh.[5]

DISASTER FOLLOWS DISASTER (4:19-31)

This extended poetic unit shows the power of Jeremiah's prophetic

---

5. On Yahweh's rule in history, see the comments of Klaus Koch, *The Prophets,* vol. 2: *The Babylonian and Persian Periods* (Philadelphia: Fortress; London: SCM, 1984), 25-32. Koch appeals to the metaphor of Jeremiah, "the way of Yahweh" as the form of Yahweh's governance.

poetry in an unmistakable way. In this unit five distinct metaphors are employed in rapid succession. There is a sharp discontinuity as the poem moves from one metaphor to the next, because no logical coherence is intended. The five metaphors are:

(1) Personal anguish and disruption because of an invading army (vv. 19-22);

(2) A scenario of the dismantling of all of creation (vv. 23-28);

(3) A scene of frantic escape (v. 29);

(4) The futility of a prostitute whose allure is empty and ineffective (v. 30);

(5) The death cry of a woman in labor, vulnerable to murderers (v. 31).

The extreme images all point to the stunning assertion that death is coming in Jerusalem soon. The metaphors are to be understood with powerful concreteness, yet they all point beyond themselves to this overriding fact of the historical crisis of Jerusalem.

4:19-22   As the text is now arranged, this portion of poetry (like vv. 9-10 after vv. 5-8) is a personal response to the public disclosure of vv. 11-18. No doubt Jeremiah constructed both pieces, the public warning and the personal response. Dramatically, the two poetic pieces are to engage each other, so that the rawness of the situation for both Judah and for the poet is clear. This piece (vv. 19-22) is presented not as public proclamation, but as a scenario of the prophet at home. But even there, apart from his public responsibility, he is intensely troubled. He is troubled so that his stomach churns. His bowels twist in agitation, so deep is his alarm and his anxiety. He is anxious, unsettled, frightened, to the point of heart palpitations. The reason is the bugle, the approaching army, the enmity of Yahweh, the collapse of his world.

The poet has had a vision of a chain of disasters as the invading army moves toward the beloved city. Suddenly the threat is here, here in Jerusalem, here in his very bedroom. The poem is a fantasy of how close the coming destruction is, as close as his bedroom, as close as the innards of his body. He takes his listener inside his very own person as an attempt to pierce their numbed indifference. He dares to suggest that his wild anxiety is more real than their cynical self-confidence. The invasion dispatched by Yahweh is a real threat. The poet tries to enact the threat in the most intimate language he can express. He moves between the personal language about bodily sensations (v. 19) and the language of military plunder (v. 20). Then in v. 21 he speaks a lament. The poet sees the enemy flag. It is closer than he and his contemporaries ever thought it would be. He knows it bespeaks death for him, for the others, for the city. It is death as dramatic as a soldier pulling back the drapery of his bedroom (v. 20).

Then v. 22 breaks off the agitated portrayal of invasion as judgment. This verse, not integrally related to the preceding scene, is an impatient denunciation of his listeners. They are so casual, so indifferent, because they do not notice; they do not believe the poem. They cannot participate in its vivid images, because they do not think a destructive judgment can happen here. Their reaction is contrasted with the pathos of the poetry. As they are unmoved by the theological reality of Yahweh, as they are unmoved by the political realities all around them, so now they are unmoved by the poetry. The verse speaks of "my people." The first person pronoun is likely spoken by Yahweh. It is Yahweh who sees that the covenant partner is obtuse about everything that is important. The language is not unlike 8:7 and Isa. 1:3, both of which appeal to animals that are wiser than is Israel. The Israelites are not even termed guilty, simply stupid and foolish. They are so stupid that they do not notice the world of God's life-giving governance made available only by the poem.

This indictment of stupidity has a sadness to it. The poetry uses the word "know" twice, once with Yahweh as its object and once with doing good (that is, covenantal acts) as its object. Jeremiah 22:16 makes the same connection between knowing Yahweh and knowing to do good. Covenantal acknowledgement of Yahweh and covenantal obedience are intimately linked.[6] Israel knows about neither, and therefore Israel knows nothing about its own identity and proper role in history. Israel knows many things the world values—political cunning, military planning, theological propriety—but lacks the covenantal awareness that saves. Ignorance of covenant leads to invasion and destruction. The others may not yet

---

6. On knowing as covenantal obedience, see Herbert B. Huffmon, "The Treaty Background of Hebrew *Yada‘*," *Bulletin of the American Schools of Oriental Research* 181 (1966): 31-37; and Huffmon and Simon B. Parker, "A Further Note on the Treaty Background of Hebrew *Yada‘*," *Bulletin of the American Schools of Oriental Research* 184 (1966): 36-38. What is now clear in terms of ancient Near Eastern parallels had already been articulated by John Calvin, *Institutes of Christian Religion*, I, vi, 2 (Library of Christian Classics [Philadelphia: Westminster; London: SCM, 1960]), 72: "But not only faith, perfect and in every way complete, but all right knowledge of God is born of obedience."

know, but Jeremiah already has this knowledge tearing at his very person, even as it must tear at Yahweh.

4:23-28 In these verses the tone of the rhetoric escalates. Heretofore the poetry has focused on historical-political destructions. With these verses the picture becomes cosmic in scope. The fourfold "I looked" is a staggering study of creation run amok, creation reverted to chaos. The Creator waits for the world to become the world hoped for. Yahweh waits for Israel to become fully God's people. But each time the poet looks at the world, he sees more and more of creation being nullified, regressing to the murky condition of Gen. 1:2. Israel refused to embrace the ways of the Creator. Covenantal Israel held the staggering notion that human conduct matters for the well-being of creation (cf. Hos. 4:1-3). Working from that notion, the picture of this poem is grim. Since there has not been obedience, there will be no viable creation. Disobedience finally leads to chaos for the entire creation.

This poem is a step-by-step rhetorical dismantling of creation. Jeremiah 4:23 utilizes the words of Gen. 1:2, "formless and void," to express the resurgence of chaos and disorder that is experienced by the poet at every dimension of life.[7] Then in quick succession the poet characterizes the loss of "light" (sun, moon, stars), the failure of even mountains and hills to embody stability, the disappearance of humanity and the absence of birds, and finally the end of fertile land and functioning city. Wholesale dismantling follows massive disobedience. The power of chaos is so dominant, it is as though creation never happened. This sad turn of events is the result of Yahweh's action, for Yahweh's patience has finally been exhausted.

The form of Jer. 4:27-28 differs from the symmetry of vv. 23-26. In its main claims v. 27 seems to be a confirmation of the devastation that has just been pictured. The whole world comes unglued when Israel is disobedient long enough. The nullification is total, comprehensive, and without qualification (cf. 45:4). But the last clause, "yet I will not make a full end," comes as a surprise. The line seems to qualify and contradict what has preceded. Two scholarly ex-

---

7. The poets of the Exile are able to use the old traditions of chaos as a way of speaking about exile. The historical experience of exile is akin to the cosmic sense of disorder given in the old myths of chaos. See Isa. 45:18-19; 54:9-10; and Walter Brueggemann, "Weariness, Exile and Chaos (A Motif in Royal Theology)," *Catholic Biblical Quarterly* 34 (1972): 19-38.

planations can be made. First, it has been held that the line is a late intrusion intended to soften the harshness.[8] Second, the negative "not a full end" can be textually amended to read, "I will make a full end of it."[9] However, such explanations seem contrived. A different reading is offered by John Calvin. Calvin interprets the line in terms of its harshness, "I have not made an end yet to the devastation," meaning God has yet more destruction to do.[10]

As an interpretive principle, we must seek to understand the text in its wholeness. This expression, "not a full end," is a serious counterpoint to its context, either for Jeremiah or for Yahweh. Thus we may best take it as an expression of uncertainty on Yahweh's part, wrought out of Yahweh's yearning not to destroy. Yahweh has been provoked to a harsh resolve from which Yahweh momentarily draws back. As we shall see elsewhere, it is this reluctance on Yahweh's part that becomes the ground for hope in the midst of exile, for the yearning on God's part persists, even in the face of the relentless devastation in this poetry. It is as though the very poetry of harshness moves God to new awareness of how precious Israel is in God's eyes, as though God cannot fully accept God's own poetic rendition of judgment.

Verse 28 returns to the devastation of vv. 23-27a. It characterizes both heaven and earth as engaged in deep mourning. Frequently the prophets use the metaphor of the earth mourning to refer to drought. The poem concludes with powerful resolve on Yahweh's part to persist until the old creation has been fully nullified. The life-giving functions of the earth will come to an end. The whole earth is now weak and diminished. Such a poem serves to delegitimate the regime, because it recalls that the only purpose and legitimation of the royal-temple apparatus is to ensure and implement the full effective function of creation. The grief (drought) bespeaks the ultimate failure of the regime to maintain the earth.

We may ask about the function of this dangerous poem. We must stress that it is a poem. It is not a blueprint for the future. It is not a

---

8. See George Adam Smith, *Jeremiah* (London: Hodder & Stoughton and New York: Harper, 1923), 116. Cf. Robert P. Carroll, *From Chaos to Covenant* (London: SCM; New York: Crossroad, 1981), 76-77, esp. n. 38.

9. See John Bright, *Jeremiah,* 2nd ed. Anchor Bible 21(Garden City, N.Y.: Doubleday, 1978), 33; and Wilhelm Rudolph, *Jeremia,* 3rd ed., Handbuch zum Alten Testamentum 12(Tübingen: J. C. B. Mohr [Paul Siebeck], 1968), 32.

10. Calvin, *Commentaries,* 1:240-242.

prediction. It is not an act of theology that seeks to scare into repentance. It is, rather, a rhetorical attempt to engage this numbed, unaware community in an imaginative embrace of what is happening. The world is becoming unglued. The poet has the awesome burden of helping his people sense that their presumed world is in jeopardy, because God's holy patience is fully ended. When that patience is exhausted, creation is not permitted to continue its disobedient course. The verdict of initial creation was, "It is very good" (Gen. 1:31). Here the verdict is "It is very evil." Such evil finally must be answered for.

4:29-31 These verses continue the imagery of an invading army (cf. vv. 13-17), but with the poignant use of three additional metaphors, the last two of which are abrasive and quite unexpected. Verse 29 creates a scene in which the citizens of Jerusalem scramble for safety in the face of the invader. All poise and dignity are lost as they run for cover (cf. Isa. 2:10, 19, 21). Then in Jer. 4:30 the poem abruptly introduces the metaphor of a prostitute. The scene is ludicrous: the army comes, frightened people hide, but this desolate Jerusalem is so insensitive and brazen that she has not sense enough to hide. Rather, she dresses like any conventional street prostitute— red dress, gaudy jewelry, heavy makeup. Because Judah has been a harlot, the image of harlotry fittingly explicates the poetic indictment and does not surprise. This is Yahweh's partner, shamelessly acting out her fickle identity. What does surprise us, however, is that this unacceptable behavior continues in the face of the army. Any prudent prostitute would know that such troops are dangerous, not to be seduced but to be feared, because they work violence. Judah the whore continues to misunderstand her true situation of danger, continues to misjudge the real threat of invasion, confiscation, and seizure. Instead she stands idly in front of the mirror, preoccupied only with appearance, not with the reality of death on the move.

In v. 31 the metaphor is again dramatically shifted. Out of the resolve of Yahweh, the army still approaches, but now Judah is not an alluring prostitute. Now Jerusalem is cast in a new role as a helpless, exposed woman in labor. What catches the ear of the poet (and any who will hear) is the cry of pain. The cry sounds like a labor pain, only labor pains are to give birth, the work of newness. The poet listens more carefully. The cry of the city is in fact a cry for help, a death cry, for the invaders (sent by Yahweh) are about the predictable business of rape and murder. The metaphor belongs in the same trajectory with the image utilized in 2:2 as bride, in 3:1 as faithless wife, in 4:30 as prostitute. Jerusalem is a street woman who gives birth and is overwhelmed by the army in what should have been a moment of joy. The poet presses to find a metaphor raw enough to carry the truth. Jerusalem is under judgment, about to be done in. Jerusalem may not know it, but the city is as shameful as a prostitute, as helpless as a woman in labor, exposed and endangered now because the betrayed husband has had enough of fickleness and will tolerate no more. Death must come. No one stands with Jerusalem to grieve, or to rescue.

5:1-6 This part of the poem is structured in a standard way for a lawsuit speech. It consists in two indictments, first against the poor (vv. 2-4) and then against the powerful (v. 5), followed by a concluding sentence (v. 6). The prophet is called (much like Diogenes) to search for one responsible citizen of Jerusalem who will fulfill Yahweh's expectation for justice and fidelity. A close parallel may be in Gen. 18:22-32, where the search is to find enough righteous people so that the city may be saved. Yahweh's opening offer in our text is that one such citizen will permit the city to be saved and forgiven. Thus less is required in this poem than was required of Sodom. In Gen. 18 Abraham had to find ten such persons. Jerusalem is so degenerate that Yahweh will now settle for one. Only a hint of covenantal responsiveness will be sufficient for the rescue, but no hint of such responsiveness can be found.

No trace of obedience is found among the poor (Jer. 5:4). As a consequence, pardon is not possible. They are calloused and cynical, stubborn in their ways and will not turn (v. 3). What God seeks is reliability *(emunah)*, but everything among the poor is mendacity *(sheqer)*. The poor do not know the torah. It is no different among the powerful, however (v. 5). The poet expects them to do better because they are schooled in the torah. They have had a chance to learn the way of obedience and are therefore without excuse. Yet they, too, are engaged in self-assertion and self-sufficiency (cf. 2:20), and refuse to acknowledge or live according to the covenant that gives life. Forgiveness of Jerusalem is no more possible because of the great than because of the poor. Indeed, forgiveness is not possible because the necessary trace of obedience cannot be found.

The city has refused in all parts of the citizenry to accept its proper vocation as Yahweh's covenant partner destined for submission and obedience. The hoped-for obedience is not onerous, but it is nonetheless rejected. There is a fundamental misorientation in the life of the city. The poet works two themes. First, pardon is gracious, but it is not cheap. Forgiveness still requires coming to terms with Yahweh. Second, the pathology of the community is massive and pervasive. The community practices autonomy so much that Yahweh's proper summons to accountability is simply ignored.

After these indictments v. 6 is not unexpected, though its harshness is surprising. The "therefore" means judgment. The language of the judgment is in the metaphors of ferocious animals who will attack, rend, and tear: lion (cf. Hos. 5:14-15), wolf, and leopard. The metaphors may point to the devastation of an invading army. Or perhaps the images refer directly to the coming of Yahweh. Either way, juridical language has been transposed into the law of the jungle. Disobedient Jerusalem is at the mercy of beasts of viciousness (cf. Lev. 26:22). The most interesting of the three metaphors for animals is the third, the leopard. It is depicted as an animal crouching in wait, ready to spring on any who try to escape. Observe that the judgment, as conveyed through this metaphor, is not exile but death. The leopard is "watching," the same word used in Jer. 1:12. Yahweh is ready to spring from a crouch to complete the judgment that is due and imminent against Jerusalem.

5:7-13 This section of the poem continues the language of the lawsuit. It is largely an indictment characterizing the sin of Judah, but vv. 9 and 10 allude to judgment, which inevitably follows the sin just described.

The beginning point is a question, either whimsical or pained. It looks back to v. 1. Yahweh is desperately seeking a way of forgiveness. Yahweh is ready, willing, and yearning to forgive, but Yahweh will not engage in cheap grace. There must be a hint of a turn, a gesture of obedience. There is not a single sign of it to be found, which makes forgiveness impossible and nullifies Yahweh's positive intent. The governing word for the unit is *'azab* (v. 7), to "forsake" or "abandon," the same word we have seen in 2:13,17,19, with its primary allusion to marital fickleness as in 3:1. This metaphor continually reappears in the poetry, indicating the center of Jeremiah's interest.

The acting out of this abandonment is detailed in a variety of ways. It includes false worship (note the contrast with 5:2). The people swear by other than Yahweh, even in the face of Yahweh's blessing. The tradition knows that when Israel is satiated and full, it is vulnerable to temptations to displace Yahweh as partner (cf. Deut. 8:7-10,11-17; 32:15-18). The spin-off and seemingly inevitable effect of such satiation is moral disorientation in human relations. The image of "lusty stallions" surely alludes to sexual infidelity and perversion, but it is also a metaphor for shameless self-assertion. Judah is too full of self. "Horses" in the OT are regularly found only among those who, like kings, assert their own power and seize initiative for their own lives.[11] This same fullness of self-sufficiency, which leads to moral disorientation, also leads to religious self-destruction through the mocking of God (Jer. 5:12-13). Yahweh is now trivialized so that Yahweh may be mocked (cf. Zeph. 1:12). Jerusalem imagines that it is immune from Yahweh's governance or threat. Indeed, Israel imagines that there finally is no accountability in the historical process because Yahweh is not an active agent. The prophets who are to bear witness to the initiative of Yahweh have neglected the message and so have forfeited their authority. Jerusalem has become a city without reference to God or to God's torah.

It is no wonder that God asks in indignation, "Shall I not punish?" (Jer. 5:9). This question is the other side of the question, "How can I pardon you?" (v. 7). God shall now punish. This God was disposed to forgiveness, but forgiveness in such a city would be a mockery. It would make Yahweh appear to be a docile beggar and a helpless patron. Yahweh is neither a beggar nor a patron. This city has lost its chance for forgiveness and now stands under judgment. There is a harvest of judgment that must be worked (v. 10).

In v. 10 we have a qualifying remark (as in 4:27). This may be read as Yahweh's struggle to decide how to act toward Jerusalem. The data calls for destruction, yet for a moment in the poetry Yahweh resists the necessary conclusion. Yahweh's inclination toward forgiveness—even if it is for a remnant, even if the text is late—is powerful against the need for God's self-vindication. The dilemma is real for God.[12] It is real for Jerusalem. It is real in the situation. In that dilemma of Yahweh's struggle between vengeance and forgiveness hangs the destiny of Jerusalem. The poem resolutely makes the case for destruction, with no evidence presented on behalf of the city. The only impediment against such an act is found in Yahweh's inclination. The hope of saving rests only in Yahweh, not in Jerusalem. That salvation, against the overwhelming evidence, is

---

11. On the sociological function of horses and a critique of their social function, see Walter Brueggemann, *Revelation and Violence: A Study in Contextualization* (Milwaukee: Marquette University Press, 1986).

12. On the reality of the struggle for God, see J. Gerald Janzen, "Metaphor and Reality in Hosea 11," *Semeia* 24 (1982): 7-44. This one text from Hosea is characteristically true for the prophetic texts of God's pathos.

a thin, scarcely articulated possibility. The community and its religious leaders have made light of Yahweh, have collapsed God's sovereignty, have reduced and trivialized God's majestic distance in an effort to eliminate judgment from the historical process. Such trivialization of God will not be effective, however. Almost as though in response to the mocking reductionism, the verdict is given in 5:13: Yahweh will do it!

5:14-17 This brief section resumes the theme of the invading army. It is futile for us to try to identify the specific army from the general description, because the language is not descriptive but imaginative characterization. Its purpose is not to communicate information but to create a sense in the listening community of what it is like to be on the receiving end of such an army. The poetic scenario invites Jerusalem to receive God's judgment ahead of the fact of military invasion.

This coming army is an old established power (v. 15). The coming army is ominous because its language is alien. Its coming is not a happening contained in Judah's categories of business as usual. It is a nation of giants whom Judah cannot resist (v. 16; cf. Num. 13:28,33). It is not the identity of the army but what it does that is important. The marauding action of the army is caught in the fourfold "eat" in Jer. 5:17. (The same verb is used in v. 14 to describe the fire that "devours.") The army will "consume/consume/consume/consume": harvest and food, sons and daughters, flocks and herds, vines and fig trees. The items listed here for confiscation by an occupying army are closely paralleled to those listed in 1 Sam. 8:11-17 concerning "the ways of a king." The occupying army may accomplish this seizure in a wild orgy of takeover, and the devouring will be barbaric. The parallel in 1 Sam. 8, which concerns the confiscating power of the governing agent, however, suggests another reading. The "devouring" could mean that the occupying nation will deny economic freedom and impose such a tariff that this feeble people will be taxed to death, like they would under the king in 1 Sam. 8. The threat may be of sustained occupation rather than a sudden invasion.

In whatever form the usurpation occurs, the central threat is the destruction of the fortified cities. The end of these cities means the end of organized life and the exposure of urban life to a variety of threats that the walls currently stave off. Urban life is under assault and is sure to end, bringing down with it all institutional and structural supports for public life. With the destruction of the walls, the coming of social chaos is not far behind. In Amos's oracles against the nations, the burning of the fortresses is targeted (Amos 1:7,10,12,14; 2:2,5). In the savage announcement of Hos. 2:9-13 there is an end to the public activities of an ordered community. Israel, like every community, has trusted in its social order, but that social order is now jeopardized as God unleashes judgment against the covenant-breaking community. The world as it is experienced in Jerusalem is under threat and sure to end, gobbled up ruthlessly by the greedy invader said to be an agent of Yahweh.

5:18-19 These verses provide slight but not reassuring relief from the poetry of devastation. In v. 18 the curious assurance that the destruction will not be total appears for the third time (cf. 4:27; 5:10). Yahweh's words here are curious precisely because the surrounding poetry sounds so final. Again the statement reflects indecision on Yahweh's part or, we may say, a debate in the community concerning continuity and discontinuity in the midst of devastation. No doubt some viewed this invasion as the real end. Others (e.g., Hananiah) regarded it as an interlude after which normalcy would be resumed.

But if Yahweh will not make a "full end," what then? Jeremiah 5:19 offers an answer. The single verse justifies Yahweh's judgment, and at the same time asserts that the sentence is not death but exile. First, we have again the word "abandon" *('azab)*. Israel's abandonment of Yahweh is the cause of the judgment and the justification for it. As a result of Israel's abandonment, Yahweh is within Yahweh's rights to terminate and destroy. But the remarkable word pattern in this verse concerns foreign gods and strangers in "a land not yours." Foreign *(nkr)* gods have been served. Life will be lived in a strange *(zar)* land. The use of the two words yields a pattern of disobedience/exile:

> serve *strange god*—therefore live in *strange land*
> serve *alien god*—then live in *alien land*.

The Exile is derived from and linked to the service of other gods. The presence of the word "abandon" helps to connect the whole image to the marriage metaphor. This attention to a "second lover" (cf. 3:1) leads to life in a "second land," which is a land without promise. History has a theological dimension because Yahweh's severe sovereignty finally will prevail. This history ends inevitably in exile.

5:20-31 The remainder of this chapter consists in a variety of poetic images that pursue the general prophetic motifs of judgment and sentence. What is of interest is the way in which these general themes receive particular poetic articulation.

The accusation against the house of Judah surfaces in the introductory summons of vv. 20-21. The governing word is "hear." The vocative addresses a people who are incapable of response, who are "without heart" (RSV "senseless"), who see not, who hear not (cf. Isa. 6:9-10). The envelope of Jer. 5:21 moves from *shema'* to *shema'*: "Hear . . . you who will not hear." Because "hear" is the foundational word for covenant responsiveness, this poem both summons to covenant accountability and acknowledges that it cannot happen (cf. Matt. 11:15).[13]

Jeremiah 5:22-24 combines a doxology about God's power and greatness with Israel's rejection of that great God. God's self-assertion in the doxology has motifs like those of 2 Isaiah (cf. Isa. 40:12-17; 44:21-28) and Job (5:8-15; 9:5-10), though the first person form used in Jeremiah is more forceful. The praise of Yahweh does not concern the history of Israel, but God's power in creation, the taming of chaos (Jer. 5:22), and the governance of the rain (v. 24). Yahweh is sovereign over all creation, but Israel will not acknowledge Yahweh's sovereignty even in its own life.

This countertheme of Israel's failure to acknowledge Yahweh is expressed in the question of v. 22. The question is a rhetorical one, however, because it implies the answer: Israel neither fears (cf. v. 24) nor trembles. In v. 24 Israel does not recite the credo of doxology (cf. 2:6-8). Where Israel does not say, think, or recite the sovereignty of God, Israel soon imagines it is autonomous, self-sufficient, and indeed, self-invented (cf. Deut. 8:17). The rhetoric of Jer. 5:22-24 focuses on the heart of Israel. The traditional call to Israel is to love and serve Yahweh with its whole heart, but here we meet the opposite.

> This is a people without heart (senseless) (v. 21).
> This people has a stubborn, rebellious heart (v. 23).
> They do not say in their heart (v. 24).

---

13. On "listening" as decisive in the Deuteronomic tradition that informs Jeremiah, see S. Dean McBride, Jr., "The Yoke of the Kingdom," *Interpretation* 27 (1973): 273-306; and Patrick D. Miller, Jr., "The Most Important Word: The Yoke of the Kingdom," *Iliff Review* 41 (1984): 17-29.

Israel's heart, the organ of covenant (cf. 4:4), has become alienated from Yahweh.

In 5:25-28 the poet traces what happens to a community with a disoriented heart.[14] The moral failure of Israel derives from its "practical atheism" (v. 21).[15] Israel is indicted for iniquity, sins (v. 25), wickedness (v. 26), treachery (v. 27). The result is that they are great/rich/fat/sleek, that is, satiated and self-sufficient (vv. 27-28). Israel exploits and abuses. The particularity of the offense is that they judge unjustly (cf. Deut. 16:18), they exploit orphans and fail to defend needy people (Jer. 5:28). The problem is systemic. The neglect is social. The outcome of Israel's infidelity is a society of rapacious exploitation, supported and legitimated by institutional structures. This poem points Israel back to the marginal ones for whom Yahweh has special regard. This affirmation about Yahweh is crucial and nonnegotiable for prophetic faith.

The structure of these verses conveys the close relation between the dysfunction of Israel's faith and the disorder in Israel's life:

theological disorientation (vv. 22-24),
general indictment (vv. 25-26),
self-sufficient satiation as the outcome (vv. 27-28),
abusive social practice (v. 28).

Where covenant with Yahweh is betrayed, covenant values in social relationships cannot be sustained. Interpretation of the poem must show the dialectical relation between the basic disorientation and its manifestation among "the least." Caring ethics without a core covenantal commitment is not possible.

Verse 29 asserts Yahweh's indignation and the necessity of judgment on Yahweh's part (cf. v. 9). God's yearning to forgive has turned to harshness. Verses 30-31 serve as a reprise to sound again the main theme of disobedience and judgment. The land has been defiled (cf. 2:7; 3:1-2). The leadership to whom the people turn is corrupt and self-serving (cf. Hos. 4:9). The last line of Jer. 5:31 contains an ominous question. It might be freely rendered, "What do you think will happen next?" No answer is given, but hints are everywhere in the poetry. The double use of *shema'* in v. 21 has suggested

---

14. On the cruciality of the heart, see Martin Buber, *Right and Wrong* (London: SCM, 1952), 34-52, and his comments on Ps. 73.

15. On the notion of "practical atheism," see Gerhard von Rad, *Wisdom in Israel* (Nashville: Abingdon; London: SCM, 1972), 65 and *passim*.

the two poles about which Israel must decide. The choice is stark without any ambiguity or maneuverability. One option is to listen, which might lead to a renewed people. The other option is to die. If the heart fails, as it has for Israel, the city will fail, too. The end is no longer negotiable.

6:1-8   This unit reiterates the warning of an invading army. The threat comes from the north as it characteristically does for Jeremiah, though of course it is again unnamed. The invitation to escape the coming devastation is perhaps premised on the traditional notion that some are given a permit and safe conduct to be exempted from the general destruction (e.g., Josh. 6:22-25).[16] Such a provision in the practice of war provides a basis for a remnant who may survive. The faithful are warned to escape. The poetic strategy is to indicate that most are unfaithful, most will not heed, most will not escape.

The poem mentions two results of this invasion. First, the urban elite is destroyed (Jer. 6:2). The prophets, who seem to harbor great resentment against the urban elite, delight in mocking and caricaturing the women who are the quintessence of such self-indulgent well-being (cf. Isa. 3:16-24; 47:1; Amos 4:1). Second, the city of Jerusalem will become so desolate that it will be a place for grazing, inhabited by shepherds who represent the lowest social class (Jer. 6:3; cf. Mic. 3:12, cited in Jer. 26:18). Thus, 6:2-3 provides a sharp contrast between well-bred urban women and low-grade shepherds. The one will be displaced by the other, as the city loses its role as a center of cultural refinement and economic monopoly. This is a concrete case in which first become last and last become first.

Verses 4-5 offer three quotes allegedly from the principals in the battle to come. The alleged statements are from the mouth of the invading army, designed to escalate and dramatize the sense of danger and threat. It is as though the poet takes us into the commander's tent to hear the specific strategy. The second of the three quotes shows the chagrin the successful army has at the setting of the sun, for it means the end of the battle for the day (v. 4b). The winners

---

16. On the genre of the invitation to flee, see Robert Bach, *Die Auf-forderungen zur Flucht und zum Kampf im alttestamentlichen Propheten-spruch,* Wissenschaftliche Monographien zum Alten und Neuen Testament 9 (Neukirchen-Vluyn: Neukirchener Verlag, 1962); and Patrick D. Miller, Jr., "The Divine Council and the Prophetic Call to War," *Vetus Testamentum* 18 (1968): 100-107.

never want the darkness to come (cf. Josh. 10:12-13, on the extension of the day so that God's people may win). In Jer. 6:6 the commands are in the mouth of Yahweh, who, according to the poem, is the one who fights the battle against Jerusalem. It is Yahweh who directs the siege instruments. We are not told in vv. 4-5 who is speaking, but in v. 6 the speaker—and the leader of the battle—is identified. The army is not the real threat, but is only an agent of Yahweh, who is the real threat.

Verses 6b-7 contain the indictment that is the motivation for the invasion. Six terms are used: "oppression," "wickedness," "violence," "destruction," "sickness," "wounds." The term "wicked" is quite general, as is "destruction." The more specific terms "oppression" and "violence" are perhaps the most important.[17] Congruent with 5:27-28, these terms suggest a social system in which the strong exploit the weak. The royal-temple system is under poetic assault because it sanctions systematic abuses that are practiced both by the king (cf. 22:13, 17; cf. Ps. 72) and in relation to the temple (Jer. 7:8-10). The last two terms, "sickness" and "wounds," state the consequences of exploitation: a society that does not function is immobilized and under judgment (cf. Isa. 1:5-6).

The concluding element of this unit (Jer. 6:8) is related to Yahweh's words of indecision and assurance, which we have noted elsewhere in the opening chapters of Jeremiah. A chance still remains, because Yahweh has not finally decided. The RSV rendering "be warned" is somewhat misleading. A more accurate translation would be "take correction" (*ysr*). The imperative is not a warning or a threat, but articulates the hard discipline of serious nurture (cf. Deut. 8:5). The verb suggests that Israel may still be reshaped to avert judgment. It may not yet be too late, although the double "lest" of the verse indicates the real danger. The danger is that Yahweh may leave Jerusalem, and then the city would be utterly vulnerable. As a result the land becomes desolate. It is remarkable that, in the face of intense poetic rhetoric and imagery characterizing the scope of the invasion, an alternative to "the full end" still seems available. This uncertain yet possible alternative is reflective of Yahweh's anguish and pathos over the decision that cannot much longer be averted.

6:9-15 These verses reiterate the now familiar themes of judg-

---

17. On the semantic field of this vocabulary, see Thomas D. Hanks, *God So Loved the Third World* (Maryknoll, N.Y.: Orbis, 1983).

ment and sentence. Verse 9 begins the unit with a statement of gleaning, a figure that has come to stand for judgment.[18] The general indictment of v. 10 (cf. 5:21) is that Israel's ears are uncircumcised. Israel is not capable of paying attention. They mock and despise the word of Yahweh. They are unresponsive as covenant partners. This poetic unit, like others we have considered, begins with a quite general theological point of disorientation and disobedience, and then proceeds to particulars.

The general sentence for this failure to hear is given in 6:11-12. The failure occasions the full, powerful release of Yahweh's wrath against every part of the city. This passage, unlike others that indict the leadership, includes all in the scope of disobedience—children, young men, husbands, wives, old folk (v. 11).

The judgment is that property will be reassigned, notably houses, fields, wives. The triad is the same as is stated in the commandment against coveting (Deut. 5:21). The reference to wrath in Jer. 6:11 is answered at the conclusion of this poetic unit (v. 12) with reference to the outstretched hand. The outstretched hand was positive intervention in the Exodus (cf. Deut. 26:8), but now it is negative intervention that brings destruction. The rhetoric of wrath is filled with passion and a lack of restraint. Language about the wrath of God is difficult for us to hear. We are wont to think that the love of God overrides such anger, but that surely is not the case in this portrayal of God. This powerful language has its theological rootage in the metaphor of a betrayed father and an abandoned husband. The wrath of God in Jeremiah is not that of an indifferent sovereign who crassly retaliates, but is that of one who is intimate in covenantal relation and therefore is wounded by infidelity and rejection. The yearning for return and restoration, which we have considered, feeds the hurt, which is then turned to anger. This poet does not flinch from the emergence of this enraged love, which will not be softened or compromised. The poet is willing to let God respond fully in

---

18. The metaphor has become familiar to us in the crusading hymn of faith, "The Battle Hymn of the Republic," in the lines,

Mine eyes have seen the glory of the coming of the LORD;
He is tramping out the vintage where the grapes of wrath are stored;
He has loosed the fateful lightening of his terrible swift sword;
His truth is marching on.

John Steinbeck, in *The Grapes of Wrath* (New York: Viking; London: Heinemann, 1939), has used the same metaphor to characterize a very different social crisis.

God's hurt.[19] While such an outburst may not be congenial to popular theology, it is indeed congruent with the metaphor of hurt turned to vigorous rejection. The God whose outstretched arm saved now outstretches the same arm to terminate.

Jeremiah 6:13-15a makes the general indictment of v. 10 more specific. All persons, but especially the religious leaders, are indicted for their unprincipled economics. All—the least and the greatest—are greedy and deal falsely.[20] When one does not listen to the word of God the result is destructive social policy (v. 10). This community has lost every norm by which to evaluate and assess its rapacious and exploitative greed. That destructive social practice includes recitation of the royal-temple ideology which covers over the real issues and engages in massive denial and propaganda (v. 14).[21] The poet has already suggested the profound problems and unresolved issues facing this society. The regnant ideology, however, dares to speak of well-being (*shalom*) when the realities are otherwise. The official claims are plain lies, because social reality does not correspond to its ideology. The worst part of this ideological recitation (v. 14) is that the citizens of Jerusalem themselves believe it and are persuaded by it. They have lost their capacity for critical analysis and have a sense of shame about their own wrongdoing. It is precisely the royal ideology that precludes moral sensitivity and covenantal anguish over failure. It intends to keep critical questions muted, so that establishment policy may advance unchecked. This unit concludes in v. 15b (in correspondence to vv. 11-12) with an account of the destruction that is to be wrought by the hand of God.

6:16-21   The themes of critique and judgment in these verses do not come as a sustained argument, but as a rapid sequence of changing images. Verse 16 begins with a summons to return to the ancient ways.[22] This could mean a return to the torah (cf. v. 19) or

---

19. On God's hurt, see Terence E. Fretheim, *The Suffering of God* (Philadelphia: Fortress, 1984).

20. The merism of v. 13 ("from the least to greatest") corresponds to the detailed listing of v. 11.

21. On the power of propaganda to create official reality that denies human suffering and hope, see Jacques Ellul, *Propaganda: The Formation of Men's Attitudes* (New York: Knopf, 1965).

22. On the genre of recall to "ancient paths," see Norman C. Habel, "Appeal to Ancient Tradition as a Literary Form," *Zeitschrift für die alttestamentliche Wissenschaft* 88 (1976): 253-272.

traditional teaching, even sapiential instruction.[23] It is, in effect, inviting Jerusalem back to the old Yahwistic teaching that has not been contaminated by the operative royal ideology. There are older traditions—likely theological, certainly ethical—which will help Judah reorder its life. This return to ancient paths is not a nostalgic return to "old-time religion" or "the good old days," but a return to a more radical and dangerous memory that serves to end all present complacency and to subvert all present certitudes. The summons is rejected, however, in the very same verse: "we will not walk in it." To walk on the ancient paths would mean to walk away from unbridled royal power, shamelessly exploitative temple postures, and economic practice that nourish the lives of the sleek and fat.[24] Israel rejects such a walk, because it clashes with the dominant values to which they are committed. This rejection is a rejection of Israel's primal identity.

In vv. 17-19 the speech revolves around the theme of "heed" *(q-sh-b):*

> give heed (v. 17),
> we will not give heed (v. 17),
> because they have not given heed (v. 19).

The first use is an invitation to obedience. The second is an indictment for disobedience. The third use is the ground for punishment. Israel does not listen because it imagines itself to be self-sufficient. The first "give heed" was to heed the warning of the trumpet of judgment. The third and most important is to heed "my words," "my torah." Israel has become a torah-less community, unfocused, disoriented (cf. 2 Sam. 12:9). The nations of the earth are called to witness against this torahless people bound for death. It is the torah that gives life (Ps. 19:7-9). When Israel gives up torah, it gives up Yahweh, which means giving up the chance for life.

In place of the torah, Israel has substituted cultic action (Jer. 6:20-21): frankincense, cane, sacrifices. Israel has devised a form of religion that reflects affluence, which can be safely administered, and

---

23. On "the way" as a central metaphor for the substance of Israel's faith, see James Muilenburg, *The Way of Israel* (New York: Harper & Row, 1961; London: Routledge & Kegan Paul, 1962). On "the way" as a metaphor for the contemporary possibility of serious theology, see Paul M. Van Buren, *Discerning the Way* (New York: Seabury, 1980), 1-9 and *passim.*

24. On the double use of the metaphor of way, in "going after" and "going from," see the use in 2:2 (positively) and 2:5 (negatively).

which brackets out all questions of obedience. Jeremiah, along with the entire covenantal tradition, is clear that an obedient religion does not require or prefer cultic actions of self-serving (cf. Hos. 6:6; 1 Sam. 15:22-23; Amos 5:21-24; Matt. 9:13; 12:7). Right cult is always in the service of obedience to Yahweh. This unit concludes in Jer. 6:21 with a sentence introduced by the characteristic "therefore." The stumbling block to which the poet refers is not identified, but clearly is an impediment to life (cf. Hos. 4:5).

The passage is constructed around two pairs of motifs that are the inverse of one another. The first pair, ancient paths (Jer. 6:16) and true obedience (vv. 17-19), leads to life. The second pair, ritual activity (v. 20) and stumbling blocks (v. 21), leads to death. The juxtaposition of paths and stumbling blocks is telling. The first invites to an obedient walk. The latter promises a danger when Israel decides to be on the way, whether in the ancient path or not. The internal juxtaposition contrasts torah words, which give life, and cultic actions, which are rejected as unacceptable. The poet skillfully contrasts the reliable elements of covenantal faith with the current practices that are self-indulgent. The prophetic critique asserts that Jerusalem religion has become a narcotic which precludes faithful criticism of destructive policy.

6:22-26 This is the final poetic treatment of the invading army.[25] Verses 22-23 describe the powerful coming of this unnamed threat authorized by God. The coming enemy is ruthless, shows no mercy, and is aimed precisely at Zion.

Verses 24-26 describe the reaction of frightened Jerusalem to the invading army. Israel hears the report of the coming army and is terrified and paralyzed by fear. It is not the action of the invading army, but simply reports of it that reduce Israel to trembling. Again the image of the pain of a woman in labor is used (cf. 4:31). The concluding line of 6:25, "terror on every side," is a special formula in the tradition of Jeremiah, and we shall comment on it later in more detail. It is sufficient here to note that the anticipated army puts Judah in profound jeopardy. The reaction of terror is appropriate. The terror felt by the city is articulated as grief (v. 26), an intense

---

25. Other references to an invading army occur in subsequent texts. This poem, however, is the last in the group of poems commonly regarded as a distinct corpus, referred to by scholars as "the Scythian songs." We are not interested in the historical identity of the army characterized here, but in the sustained literary power of the reference.

grief like the grief of the loss of an only begotten son. The grief is over the death of the whole people and the entire religious apparatus that legitimates the community. The ending of the city envisioned by this scenario is pathos-filled. "Terror on every side" refers to the enmity of God, behind and before, from which Judah has no route of escape.

6:27-30   This passage is a personal word to Jeremiah concerning his vocation.[26] The metaphor used identifies Jeremiah as the one who is authorized to separate precious metal from dross (cf. Isa. 1:22). Jeremiah will separate out according to the uncompromising categories of covenant obedience and disobedience. The metaphor serves to articulate one more lawsuit speech. The indictment is in Jer. 6:28: stubbornness/rebellion/corruption. The sentence is in vv. 29-30, which threatens fire and ends with the verdict "reject" (cf. Hos. 4:6). Israel is all dross, so the smelter must retain none of it. There is here no allowance for remnant or for exile. The metaphor declares a decisive end. The smelter finds Jerusalem to be all dross, without value, and so it is to be discarded. The metaphor thus comprehends both the prophetic office of Jeremiah and the destiny of the city. One is as rigorous as the other is ominous.

The long poetic unit of Jer. 4:5–6:30 utilizes a rich variety of metaphors in a most imaginative fashion to present the persistent theme of judgment. The theme is articulated with these metaphors, each of which suggests another dimension to the reality of coming judgment:

(1) The announcement of an invading army as the judgment of Yahweh who will destroy (4:5-8,11-18,29-31; 5:14-17; 6:1-8,22-26),

(2) Visions of the end (4:23-28; 5:6,18-19) that show uncertainty about the finality of the end,

(3) Articulation of disobedience and punishment in lawsuit speeches (5:1-6,7-13,20-31; 6:9-15,16-21),

(4) Personal protests and responses of the poet (4:9-10,19-22; 6:27-30).

In various ways these poems announce that, because of covenantal

---

26. These verses function, according to much scholarly opinion, as the conclusion to an extended rhetorical unit, perhaps beginning in 2:2-3 or more precisely in 4:5. See William L. Holladay, *The Architecture of Jeremiah 1–20* (Lewisburg, Pa.: Bucknell University Press, 1976), 57-97.

failure, the trusted, legitimated Jerusalem establishment is about to end. In this section the prospect of repentance, of averting judgment, is sparse. In a very general way 3:1–4:4 and 4:5–6:30 function complementarily. The former is a grudging, pathos-filled summons to repent. The latter is largely a threat because the time for repentance is exhausted. Both themes are crucial for the prophet and for Israel. Clearly, it is the latter theme of judgment that finally matters in the tradition. Israel did not heed the summons of 3:1–4:4. The judgment of 4:5–6:30 comes to fruition. Through the move from 3:1–4:4 to 4:5–6:30, the poet articulates this covenantal God who moves back and forth between *pained hope,* like a grieving father, and *enraged judgment,* like an indignant sovereign. Yahweh can never be detached and indifferent. That the people of Jerusalem could be detached and indifferent indicates how little they sense either who Yahweh is or what is happening among them. The poetic scenario in this poetry is a bold act of "tearing down and plucking up."

JEREMIAH'S TEMPLE SERMON
Jeremiah 7:1–8:3

This unit presents Jeremiah's so-called "temple sermon," perhaps the clearest and most formidable statement we have of the basic themes of the Jeremiah tradition. In its present form the words of the prophet are cast in prose that may suggest a Deuteronomic redaction. Scholars who tend to date materials around the person of the prophet date this sermon (on the basis of 26:1) to 609 B.C.E., early in the reign of Jehoiakim. Other scholars believe the text is heavily redacted and reflects theologians of the exilic period who want to justify the destruction of the temple. In either case, this text seems decisive for understanding the tradition of Jeremiah and for discerning the social context, tensions, and possibilities that belong to this theological tradition.

The temple sermon shows the prophet in profound conflict with the dominant temple ideology on which the state relied. The position taken here by the prophet could only be treated as treason by the state, because it destroyed the ideological underpinnings of the establishment (cf. 26:11). That dominant theology claimed that Jerusalem was inviolate because God had made unconditional promises. This royal tradition, albeit now distorted, is rooted in the temple and royal claims of David and Solomon. It was substantiated in the words of Isaiah a century earlier (Isa. 37:33-35),[1] and was regularly celebrated in the hymnic tradition of the Psalms (cf. e.g., Ps. 132:6-10). This ideology claimed that the unconditional promises carried by the temple establishment limited God's judgment in response to Israel's action. In such a view, obedience is not a crucial dimension of faith. In the text of ch. 7 Jeremiah frontally attacks such a claim as

---

1. The critical matters related to the historicality of this text are very complicated. See Brevard S. Childs, *Isaiah and the Assyrian Crisis,* Studies in Biblical Theology, 2nd series 3 (Naperville: Allenson; London: SCM, 1967). Whatever precise conclusion is reached concerning historicity, it is clear that that ideology which Jeremiah resists is in some way a legacy of the Isaiah tradition.

"organized hypocrisy,"[2] and insists that God's way with Jerusalem is fundamentally concerned for obedience.

7:1-15 This section presents the core of the proclamation credited to the prophet. Jeremiah is commanded to have his say in the temple, though we cannot determine if his action is *ad hoc* or a part of the program for a special festival. The main theme of the proclamation is articulated in vv. 3-4. Judah is confronted with only two options. Judah may "amend," which will allow it to stay in the land, or Judah will blindly trust the temple and its ideology. The key word in Jeremiah's proclamation is "false" *(sh-q-r)*. The prophet is not rejecting liturgy or temple claims in principle, but those formulations which are false, that is, incongruent with the torah and with the LORD of the covenant. The implicit counterpart, later made explicit, is that if Judah does not amend its ways, it will not be kept in the land but will be sent into exile. Land is not an unconditional gift, but is premised on torah obedience. Land cannot be held simply by reliance on the legitimating ideology of the regime, but requires a quite explicit obedience.

Verse 4 alludes to the words of the Jerusalem liturgy that were boldly, endlessly, and uncritically repeated. Jeremiah dismisses those words of the liturgy as banal and ineffective, and mocks the unthinking reliance on the status quo that they reflect and embody. The accent is on *trust:* do not trust in, do not count on, do not stake your life on. In one deft move, the prophet has exposed the dysfunctional character of the Jerusalem temple. The temple and its royal liturgy are exposed as tools of social control, which in a time of crisis will not keep their grand promises. The temple is shown to be not an embodiment of transcendence, but simply an arena for social manipulation. The poet delegitimates the temple claims of absoluteness.

Verses 5-7 explicate the theme of v. 3 with an "if-then" argument indicating the conditionality of Judah's well-being. The introduction of an "if" of obedience aligns the text with the Mosaic tradition (cf. Exod. 19:5) and distances it from the unconditional promises claimed for David (2 Sam. 7:14-16). The first "if" in Jer. 7:5 is a repetition of the opening proclamation of v. 3. The second "if" makes torah obedience more explicit: "do justice, do not oppress sojourner, widow, orphan, do not shed innocent blood, do not go after other

---

2. John Skinner, *Prophecy and Religion* (1922; repr. Cambridge and New York: Cambridge University Press, 1955), 175.

gods."[3] This is a summary of the main requirements of the torah. In v. 7 the "then" clause of consequence is a permit to stay in the land. These verses, then, explicate in detail the same perception of reality announced in v. 3. Retention of the land is not by inherent right, not by might, not by liturgy, but only by the practice of justice and obedience. The call to torah obedience is raised as a bold challenge to the claims of the state.

Verses 8-11 present the harsh realism of the prophetic alternative. In the preceding verses the speech of the prophet sounds as though "amending" is still possible. Now with the opening term "behold," however, the prophet announces a conclusion and a verdict that suggest the time for amending is past and the decision about land loss is already made. Thus, while vv. 1-7 seem to allow time for a change, vv. 8-11 seem to suggest that the time is past. The reality of exile hangs over the entire tradition of Jeremiah. That exile is presumed here is not unambiguously clear, but the rhetoric tilts in that direction.

These verses characterize two stages of Judah's disobedience. First, v. 9 is a catalog of Judah's massive disobedience of torah in the conduct of its public life. The catalog of disobedience is a direct reference to the Ten Commandments, one of two such catalogs found in the prophets (see the other in Hos. 4:2). Judah regularly violates the main claims of its covenant with Yahweh. Second, those who violate the torah then go into the temple to conduct liturgy as though they are obedient to the LORD of the liturgy. They have no sense of shame at the distance between their liturgy and their ethics. The piercing, biting question of Jer. 7:11 does not suggest that temple disobedience is the problem. Rather, the temple has become a place of refuge, hiding, and safety for those who violate torah through their life in the world. The torah violators attempt to hide in the sanctity of the ritual. The temple becomes a means of cover-up for the destructive way life is lived in the real world. This escapist use of liturgy is self-deceptive, for it will not protect Judah from the realities of the covenant. Since the text addresses the power establishment, it is fair to conclude that the crimes targeted are not simply individual acts of exploitation but are acts of the entire system, which proceeds at the high cost of human well-being.

In vv. 12-15 the argument reaches its stunning and devastating conclusion. The prophet draws a shocking parallel between Shiloh

---

3. Note that the word order is inverted in Hebrew for purposes of emphasis.

and Jerusalem. Everyone listening knew of Shiloh—that it was a northern shrine and that long ago it had vanished from history, destroyed because of disobedience. It was also a part of the rationale and self-understanding of the southern royal community that northern Shiloh and southern Jerusalem are precise opposites.[4] Whereas Shiloh is rejected by Yahweh and therefore destroyed, Jerusalem is chosen and valued by God, and therefore safe. The contrast between Shiloh and Jerusalem shows the power of self-serving, vested interest in shaping the truth claims of the royal ideology. The managers of the Jerusalem establishment could not believe Jerusalem might be treated by God as Shiloh was.

Jeremiah vigorously denies this self-serving, ideological contrast and argues that Jerusalem is just like Shiloh. It is just like Shiloh in that it must obey to survive. It is just like Shiloh in its profound disobedience. And therefore, it is just like Shiloh in that it must be destroyed. The Jerusalem establishment's main claims of legitimacy are harshly and summarily dismissed. One can hardly imagine a heavier, more sobering message. Jerusalem has no preferential option from God and must answer to the demands of the torah. In the face of Jerusalem's failure to meet these demands, the verdict can only be destruction and death. The Jerusalem temple is under death sentence, and a whole world of religious and political self-interest with it. Jerusalem enjoys no "safe-conduct" in the midst of its policies, faith, and decision-making.

The parallel drawn between Jerusalem and Shiloh invites our imaginative parallels. The people of Jerusalem could not imagine their own precious system to be in jeopardy like Shiloh. Nor can we imagine that our own system—industrial, military, economic, political—might be in the same jeopardy as Shiloh and Jerusalem. Drawing analogies in contemporary life is hazardous. But imaginative preaching invites us to dare such analogies as did Jeremiah. His analogy in his time was as risky as any we might propose.

Jerusalem will be an empty crater, just like Shiloh (cf. 51:34). The royal establishment of the Davidic dynasty has no special claim upon

---

4. That self-serving Jerusalem ideology is precisely articulated in Ps. 78:56-72. See Anthony F. Campbell, "Psalm 78: A Contribution to the Theology of Tenth Century Israel," *Catholic Biblical Quarterly* 41 (1979): 51-79; and Richard J. Clifford, "In Zion and David a New Beginning: An Interpretation of Psalm 78," in *Traditions in Transformation,* ed. Baruch Halpern and Jon D. Levenson (Winona Lake, Ind.: Eisenbrauns, 1981), 121-141.

God. Everything depends on torah justice, which has been massively distorted and denied. Even Jerusalem must meet the same requirements as Shiloh. Yahweh will "cast out" even favored Jerusalem. Exile is coming. At least in these verses this prospect will not be averted. Practitioners of injustice will lose land and be displaced. It is a harsh, unqualified verdict.

We should note not only the radical character but also the discerning quality of this insight. Long before Karl Marx, the prophetic tradition has seen that religion may serve to legitimate the dominant class. Jeremiah is able to see and express quite clearly that such religion has an important positive social function. That positive social function, however, is subject to the critique of God's sovereign will. Thus religion that flies in the face of the character of God (who is allied with widows and orphans) cannot sustain a religious establishment.

7:16-20   Here we are given access to a private oracle received by Jeremiah concerning his vocation. The address "as for you" makes a distinction between the person of the prophet and the community under judgment, the same distinction we have found in 1:15-19.[5] The special instruction to Jeremiah, articulated with three negatives in 7:16, is that he is no longer to make intercession on behalf of Jerusalem, because Yahweh is past listening (cf. 15:1-3 for the same motif). God's patience is exhausted, and now there is no turning back. A lawsuit speech follows.

The indictment (7:18-19) characterizes the embrace of other gods, which is intolerable to Yahweh. The mocking description shows that worship of the "queen of heaven" has become a cottage industry that engages the entire domestic economy. The sentence (v. 20) is the release of the wrath of Yahweh, powerfully expressed with the fourfold "upon" (*'al*) (cf. 1:15-16). Judah's infidelity is so severe that Jeremiah's intercession must stop. The provocation is decisive. There is no religious act now available that could revoke this decision. Religion cannot override the cost of covenant nullification.[6]

---

5. On the person of the prophet in relation to the community, see Timothy Polk, *The Prophetic Persona*, JSOT Supplement 32 (Sheffield: University of Sheffield Press, 1984).

6. The nullification of the promise of which Jeremiah speaks has its contemporary parallel in the notion that a nuclear holocaust would nullify all cultural continuities and all religious underpinnings for cultural continuity. See Robert J. Lifton, *The Broken Connection* (New York: Simon & Schuster, 1980). The intent of Jeremiah is to articulate a cultural break

7:21-28 These verses expand on the contrast already made in vv. 3-4 between covenantal obedience and manipulation in liturgy. The assault on the ideological claims and practices of the Jerusalem establishment is unqualified and relentless. On the one hand, it is asserted that the God of Israel has never been interested in sacrificial liturgy (vv. 21-22). Those practices are fundamentally alien to the character of the God of Moses. Such acts are not intrinsically wrong, but they are invariably allied with the dominant values of control and oppression. The practice of such sacrifice tends to serve and legitimate vested social interest, and thus takes aim against covenantal obedience.

On the other hand, what is commanded and required is listening (*shema'*, v. 23.) That is all. Verses 21-28 appear to be much influenced by the Deuteronomist, for whom listening is the primal act of covenantal responsiveness (cf. Deut. 6:4). Listening is readiness to be addressed and commanded, to have life ordered by Yahweh. Listening is to cede control rather than to retain control through religious manipulation and ritual acts.

In what follows, the verdict, "they did not listen," appears four times (Jer. 7:24,26,27,28). The alternative to listening is autonomy (cf. 18:12). Israel organized its life for self-serving and self-sufficiency, thereby denying its character as a people bound in covenant with this One who is sovereign. According to the claims of this Deuteronomic tradition (which is to some extent a contrived scheme), there has been a steady, identifiable line of prophets.[7] Judah has had sustained opportunities to become a community of obedient listening (2 Kgs. 17:13). The refusal to listen and respond has been massive and pervasive, however, and continues to the present moment. Thinking it could determine its own best interest, Judah refused to receive corrective discipline or nurture (cf. Jer. 6:8, where the same word "correction" [*musar*] is used).

7:29-34 The focus in this section is on Judah's evil and Yahweh's punishment. The language used to describe evil moves from the torah categories of vv. 5-7 into the more extreme language of defilement. It is argued that the whole land has been defiled (v. 30). God

---

that in its emotive power is as strong as that articulated in quite different terms by Lifton.

7. On the Deuteronomic construct of prophetic continuity, see Robert R. Wilson, *Prophecy and Society in Ancient Israel* (Philadelphia: Fortress, 1980), 156-226. Jeremiah seems to be the principal example of the ways in which the Deuteronomic tradition has recast prophetic traditions.

cannot govern and life is not possible in a land that is ritually unclean and unusable. Living in such a land may make people exiles even if they never leave the territory. The rhetoric about punishment also takes extreme form. It does not speak simply of destruction and exile, but offers imaginative scenes of massive, ungrieved death. In these verses language for both indictment and sentence is escalated, perhaps to establish more fully the guilt of Judah and the legitimacy of Yahweh's claim.

Verse 29 invites lament because Judah is rejected. The covenant is terminated, and Yahweh withdraws protective care from the city. Verses 30-31 characterize the pagan religious action of disobedience. Verses 32-34 describe the punishment that comes with such religious promiscuity. Verses 32-33 concern death, which is so massive and comprehensive that there are no adequate social forms to cope with the disarray. As a result, the dead go unhonored and unburied, and they are left exposed in the most ignoble manner, surely contributing to the pollution. Verse 34 describes the end of the conventional celebrations of life. Society draws so close to total death that any such celebration is impossible and unthinkable. Life becomes barbaric, and all structures of plausibility are discredited. The poet searches for the most extreme language to invite his listeners to embrace the chaos at hand.

8:1-3 This passage carries the image of judgment and death to one more extreme dimension. Not only will there be death, but even the dead who previously have been honored and laid in their tombs will be dislodged. Not only will forms of civility in the present and future be dysfunctional, but past acts of civility will be nullified. Present wretchedness will nullify past decency. Nothing is sacred or honored or beyond the reach of the wrath of Yahweh now unleashed. The punishment here fits the sin: Judah has gone after the gods of the heavens; now the bones of the disobedient dead will be spread before those gods.[8] At the end, life is worse than death (v. 3).

The rhetoric of the text is not "realistic" in the sense that it describes what is known. Rather, it is an imaginative anticipation of what is as yet unknown and unexperienced, for which there is no precedent. But this future is boldly envisioned by the prophet. The judgment to come is so unprecedented that only such ominous images

---

8. On the "fit" between sin and punishment, see Patrick D. Miller, Jr., *Sin and Judgment in the Prophets,* SBL Monograph 27 (Chico, Calif.: Scholars Press, 1982).

are adequate to communicate it. Biblical eschatology always pushes to the limits of our imagination. Poetic characterizations of God's new age of blessing and poetic scenarios of God's judgment are always extreme cases of imagination, in the NT as in the OT. Such extreme imaginations are to be taken seriously. But when the poetic mode of imagination is forgotten and such anticipations are treated as flat predictions or descriptions, they are sure to be misunderstood and distorted. In such a reductionism, poetic efforts are robbed of their imaginative power. Any language that is used must match the unprecedented character of the impending judgment. The language of 8:1-3 does that. Practically, it may have been sufficient to impress upon Judah the impending historical realities of exile and displacement, but the prophet is not engaged in practical reasoning. Jeremiah seeks to penetrate and break open the imagination of the self-satisfied community so that it will see that the present circumstance is so extraordinary in its departure from torah that there can be no business as usual, not for Judah and surely not for Yahweh. Business as usual is dysfunctional because the indignant power of God is mobilized against Judah, and that mobilization is irreversible. This text seeks language to match that awesome, devastating theological reality. The text offers a "limit expression" to match an anticipated "limit experience."[9]

The theologically abrasive nerve of this text confounds conventional notions of the Bible. Popular propensity is to stress the ultimate continuity of God's commitment to the religious community. When all else fails, God will still be faithful. But in this remarkable statement the text opts for a final discontinuity. We cannot of course claim that this notion is pervasive in the Bible. It is important to recognize, however, that the Bible dares this unthinkable notion, and that it was asserted to real men and women in real historical circumstances. The prospect of theological discontinuity is an important dimension of biblical faith. This text bears witness to one aspect of God's inscrutable way with God's people. This text asserts something about the human prospect that we would prefer be left unsaid.[10] The text of 7:1–8:3 ends without relief.

---

9. On "limit expression" to match "limit experience," see Paul Ricoeur, "Biblical Hermeneutics," *Semeia* 4 (1975): 122-128.

10. The contemporary analysis of Robert L. Heilbroner, *An Inquiry into the Human Prospect* (New York: Norton, 1974), dismal as it is, is in keeping with the Jeremian analysis of the human prospect seen through the prism of Jerusalem's future.

NO BALM IN GILEAD

Jeremiah 8:4–10:25

This collection of poetic units (with a few prose elements) contains some of the most poignant imagery in Jeremiah. This material is commonly regarded as deriving from the earlier period of the prophet, largely from the prophet himself. Many of the same images and phrases reappear that are present in chs. 2–6. The main thrust of the poetry is to "redescribe" the people and the city as a community on its way to death because of its refusal to be faithful to Yahweh. The two formal elements of the lawsuit speech, indictment and sentence, are at the center of this poetry. That is, the poetry demonstrates that Judah, and not Yahweh, is guilty of abandoning covenant. As a result, judgment will come, either in the form of invasion, destruction and death, or exile.[1] What is most amazing in this section is the rich, imaginative variety with which the poetry can work and rework these few central themes. Engagement with the poetry requires not simply that we get "the main point," as that is relatively obvious. What matters is that we attend to the nuance of language and the suggestive, imaginative quality of the literature. A countertheme to the lawsuit of guilt and judgment is the expression of grief that is felt by the poet and, we dare believe, by Yahweh. Some of the most eloquent and pathos-filled poetry in 8:4–10:25 attends to this motif.

JUDAH TURNS FROM YAHWEH (8:4-17)

This poetic segment consists in an extended characterization of the failure of Judah (vv. 4-13) and a statement of impending judgment (vv. 14-17).

---

1. On the various ways in which the tradition of Jeremiah nuances the coming judgment, see the discussion of Christopher R. Seitz, "The Crisis of Interpretation over the Meaning and Purpose of the Exile," *Vetus Testamentum* 35 (1985): 78-97. This study is a part of his exhaustive dissertation from Yale.

8:4-7　In this passage the poem takes up the theme we have seen in chs. 3–4, the act of *turning away* and the prospect of *turning back*. It is taken for granted that Judah has turned away in disloyalty. That Judah refuses to turn back to a right relation is the astonishing thing that bewilders the poet. The primary poetic device is the word "turn" *(shub)*, which is used six times in vv. 4-6.

> If one *turns away,* does he not *return* . . .
> Why has this people *turned away*
> in perpetual *backsliding* . . .
> They refuse to *return* . . .
> Every one *turns* to his own course . . .

Judah's life consists in turning away from Yahweh, who is the only one who can give life. Jeremiah's analysis leads to a thin hope that Judah may turn back to life.

The summons of Yahweh, issued in pathos and in sternness, is that Judah should return to covenant loyalty. The inhabitants of Judah can only be genuine Israelites when they are turned to Yahweh. But Judah violated this identity received from Yahweh and has done so jealously. Turning away is not only disobedient, but unnatural, violating the true character of this people. The repeated use of *shub* is supported by the use of *niham,* "repent," in v. 6, which carries the same meaning. The main assertion of the poems of the early period of the Jeremiah tradition is that Judah is out of covenant relation and must intentionally return to the discipline of that relation.

The metaphor of fickleness as unnatural act is explored in vv. 6b-7 by comparison with other creatures of God (cf. Isa. 1:2-3). Every one of God's creatures has an ordered way to live. It is proper that a horse should boldly head into battle. It is proper that storks and other birds know when to migrate, when to come and go. They have an uncanny sense of knowing what behavior is proper, and when. The poet turns to creation imagery in order to comment on the right ordering of life.

This appeal to creation reveals that every creature is wiser than fickle Israel. Just as every creature knows how to live, Israel is to know Yahweh's justice, to know Yahweh's will and purpose for the proper ordering of communal life and the proper handling of public issues and neighbor relations. But unlike every other creature, Israel is stupid and does not undertake the behavior that properly belongs to its covenantal character. Israel's stupidity is supportive of the *shub* motif that identifies proper behavior as return to Yahweh and

Yahweh's justice.[2] Israel violates its own character as Yahweh's covenant mate.

In these verses the poet juxtaposes covenant language (Jer. 8:4-6a) and creation language (vv. 6b-7). The former concerns fickleness and inability to return. The latter is about the violation of one's true character. The juxtaposition is a powerful one, because it asserts that Israel's true character as a creature consists in being faithfully obedient to Yahweh. In refusing this obedience, Israel violates covenant vows and violates God's created order as well. In this act of violation, Israel has ceased to be the creature God has intended.

The poem becomes more specific about Israel's violation in vv. 8-13. These verses are framed as two lawsuit speeches, each of which states an indictment and a sentence.

8:8-10 The first lawsuit (vv. 8-10) is mostly indictment, but vv. 9a and 10a are a sentence. The indictment is directed toward the leadership, which has misled the community by its own fickle practice. (On the indictment of leaders, see Ezek. 13.) The "wise," who are to handle the torah, and the scribes, who are to understand how life with God is ordered, are in fact false. They are the "experts," but they have reneged on their proper role. The falseness of Judah concerns a fundamental betrayal and distortion, indeed, a systemic distortion of what matters for Israel. Israel has "rejected" the purpose of Yahweh (Jer. 8:9a), which means they have acted autonomously. In v. 10b prophets and priests, along with scribes and lawyers, are condemned. The entire public leadership is guilty of acting only in self-interest. The covenantal foundations of communal life have been completely jettisoned by the entire leadership apparatus.

The result of such falseness is sure and unavoidable, because covenant violations lead to judgment. Since Israel's only ground of life is covenant, when that is ignored trouble is sure to come. Verse 9a is general and says that Jerusalem is "captured." Verse 10a is more explicit. It anticipates invading forces, an occupying army. What is to be lost are wives and fields, property and relation, the two objects that are not to be coveted (Exod. 20:17). In the prose of Jeremiah the threat of invasion is explicitly identified as Babylon. But the poet is not so specific, because his aim is theological and artistic, not descriptive. The poet asserts that when covenant violations eventuate

---

2. On the intent of the verb *shub*, see the thorough exploration of the theme in John M. Bracke, "*šûb šebût*: A Reappraisal," *Zeitschrift für die alt-testamentliche Wissenschaft* 97 (1985): 233-244, and the literature he cites.

in broken relations, anticovenant forces are unleashed that will undo all of life. What amazes one is the bold capacity of the poet to make connections between evident religious perversion and happenings in the historical process that are interpreted as punishment. Only such a poet with an odd view of reality would dare to assign such cause-effect relation to these seemingly unrelated events.

8:11-13 In these verses the motifs of the lawsuit are reiterated again. The indictment is in three elements. The first (v. 11) is quite familiar. The leadership has lied. They have deceived the people by announcing a situation of well-being that in fact denies reality. The official ideology of the royal-temple establishment made claims of "peace and prosperity" that failed to acknowledge the profound theological sickness that is destroying the community. The lie is probably not a deliberate falsehood. Rather, it is a deep distortion that is so skewed and blind that it denies and prevents seeing how things really are. This people is so stupid that it accepts the cover-up offered by the leadership. It cannot see the gap between the claims of the establishment and the reality of its life (cf. 4:22).[3]

The second indictment (8:12a) is a loss of shame. The inability to blush means that there is no outside reference point to whom one must answer and by whom one is measured. Faithful people blush in the presence of the faithful God because the contrast between Yahweh's hope and their conduct is so stark. When as here, however, the faithful God has been effectively banished, the fickleness is no longer recognized as embarrassing.[4] Abraham J. Heschel has said that the "loss of embarrassment" is a decisive step toward loss of humanness.[5] Israel has taken that step through a presumption of autonomy, so that there is no one to whom to refer and therefore no norm that evokes blushing.

---

3. The incapability of Israel to notice, to see, or to hear is most dramatically expressed in Isa. 6:9-13. See Gerhard von Rad, *Old Testament Theology,* 2 (New York: Harper & Row; Edinburgh: Oliver & Boyd, 1965), 151-155.

4. The absence of an effective norm is reflected in 2 Sam. 11:25, "Do not let this be evil in your eyes," which is contrasted with v. 27, "the thing was evil in the eyes of Yahweh" (author's translation). David is shameless because he fails to refer his conduct to the uncompromising righteousness of Yahweh. The shape and deliberate contrast between evil "in your eyes" and "in the eyes of Yahweh" is lost in most English translations.

5. Abraham J. Heschel, *Who Is Man?* (Stanford: Stanford University Press, 1965), 112-114.

The third indictment is in v. 13. This judgment seems to have echoes of Isa. 5:1-7. Israel is characterized as a vineyard or a fig tree. Its task is to produce the fruits appropriate to its life and species, but there are no fruits, no produce. There is no ethical outcome of faith proper to Israel, no manifestations of covenant. There is a complete incongruity between the expectations of Yahweh and the failure of Israel, an incongruity so foundational as to require judgment and rejection.

On all three grounds, therefore, Israel is guilty of: (1) systemic denial of reality and pretense (Jer. 8:11); (2) loss of a reference for shame and therefore autonomy (v. 12a); and (3) failure to yield appropriate outcomes (v. 13). All three constitute failure to be genuinely Israel. The "therefore" of the sentence in v. 12b is inevitable: they shall fall and stumble. Notice how elusive the language is. It does not prescribe or predict. It is lacking in specify and concrete reference. It is poetry, not policy. The poetry is uncompromising, however, in its conviction that nullification surely follows the refusal to be who one is intended by God to be. This community will be nullified if it rejects its vocation as God's people. Judah in its disobedience has passed the point of having alternative choices. That nullification is now lamentably, inexorably underway.

8:14-17 These verses, which seem like an interlude in the flow of poetry, are an imaginative presentation of the destruction that is already underway. Only in v. 14b is there another reference to guilt. Otherwise, this poetic element is a characterization of the judgment now set in motion against Judah. The dominant metaphor is military. In the face of the invading army (quite unspecified), Israel is summoned to retreat and prepare for siege. The enemy is from the north, as Dan (v. 16) is the northernmost territory. (On the ominous character of the north as a source of threat, see 1:13-14.) That invasion, before which Israel is helpless, is articulated in a variety of gripping metaphors. Israel will perish. Israel's water, its basic support, is poisoned (cf. 2:13). There is only terror. The invading army is coming on great, terrifying, imperial horses. The army that comes will follow a scorched earth policy, devouring everything along the way (cf. 5:17). In this moment of poetry the experience of the confusion, threat, and upheaval that comes with the invasion is made available to the listeners. It is not necessary to await the arrival of the army. The experience of dismay can begin now with the poem.

The metaphor changes in 8:17 to a snake. The shift from horse to snake is a stunning one, from the massive rush of power to slow, creeping terror. The figure is employed to communicate that the danger facing Israel is sure and unavoidable (cf. Amos 5:19). The community will be poisoned to death if it does not first die of fear— all because Israel has refused its proper role in history. The price of covenant nullification is nullification of Judah as a viable, historical community. The poet creates a scenario that shows the utter undoing of this historical entity that the royal-temple ideology promotes as perpetually guaranteed. History is governed by this betrayed lover, this disappointed creator who has been casually disregarded by Israel. The price of such disregard is massive and unavoidable.

GRIEF BEYOND HEALING (8:18–9:3)

This poetic unit is one of the most powerful in the Jeremiah tradition. It is also one of the most pathos-filled. Its central images are sharply contrasted to the preceding ones in 8:4-17. Now it is not threat and terror, but dread, sickness, and sadness. The poet asserts that this people is "sick to death." The poetry also probably asserts Yahweh's "sickness to death" over the terminal illness of this beloved people. The formula, "says the LORD" in 9:3 is textually insecure.[6] The use of this formula, however, makes it likely that the pathos of God and of the poet here are indistinguishable. With the formula attributing the poem to Yahweh, the pathos cannot belong only to Jeremiah. This is poetry that penetrates God's heart. That heart is marked by God's deep grief.[7] God's anger is audible here, but it is largely subordinated to the hurt God experiences in the unnecessary death of God's people. God would not have it so, but the waywardness of Israel has taken every alternative response away from Yahweh.

8:18-21 This section may best be understood as a dialogue between the liturgic *pretense* of Israel and the corresponding *pathos* of God over this people that understands nothing. It is structured so that the beginning and end speak the pathos. Within that envelope are two quotes from the liturgy, and at the center is God's dismissive question of indignation. Thus, the structure of this unit is:

---

6. The phrase is lacking in the LXX. The change is not an incidental textual correction. It matters whose "voice" is sounded here, in terms of the weight and intent of the poetry.

7. See Terence E. Fretheim, *The Suffering of God* (Philadelphia: Fortress, 1984), 135, 160-162.

A   pathos (vv. 18-19a)
B   question of the people concerning presence (v. 19b)
C   God's question of indignation (v. 19c)
B′   question of the people concerning timing (v. 20)
A′   pathos (v. 21).

The pathos of God (or of the poet) in vv. 18-19a,21 is a heartsickness of a betrayed lover or a yearning parent.[8] One sees the trouble
of the lover or child, wants to head it off, but must stand helplessly
while the disease works to its dread conclusion of death. Yahweh
(and the poet) could see it all coming long before the leadership in
Jerusalem had an inkling, if indeed they ever suspected it. God's hurt
(v. 21) is derivative from Israel's hurt. Unlike Judah, God recognizes
and embraces Judah's hurt. God has no alternative. That is the kind
of God Yahweh is. But the people, where the hurt has its locus,
neither know nor care. Their ignorance and indifference make the
pain much more intense.

The pathos of the poem is derivative from the cynical indifference
of Israel that continues with business as usual in the face of sickness
to death. In v. 19b the people are quoted as presuming and insisting

---

8. On the helpless yearning and heartsickness of a parent over a child,
see Frederick Buechner, *Now and Then* (San Francisco and London:
Harper & Row, 1983), 54-55:

To love another, as you love a child, is to become vulnerable in a
whole new way. It is no longer only through what happens to yourself that the world can hurt you, but through what happens to the
one you love also and greatly more hurting. When it comes to your
own hurt, there are always things you can do. You can put up a brave
front, for one, and behind that front, if you are lucky, if you persist,
you can become a little brave inside yourself. You can become strong
in the broken places, as Hemingway said. You can become philo-
sophical, recognizing how much of your troubles you have brought
down on your own head and resolving to do better by yourself in
the future. . . . But when it comes to the hurt of a child you love,
you are all but helpless. The child makes terrible mistakes, and there
is very little you can do to ease his pain, especially when you are so
often a part of his pain, as the child is a part of yours. There is no
way to make him strong with such strengths as you may have found
through your own hurt, or wise enough through such wisdom, and
even if there were, it would be the wrong way because it would be
your way and not his. The child's pain becomes your pain, and as
the innocent bystander, maybe it is even a worse pain for you, and
in the long run even the bravest front is not much use.

that God must be present. After all, it is God's business to be present, and it is Zion's claim that God is present (cf. Exod. 17:7; Mic. 3:11). This people is so cynical as not to notice that the temple claims are dead and have failed (cf. Jer. 7). The temple is no longer God's habitat, and so the liturgy makes an empty promise and relies on a nullified claim. The fakery of such an appeal to the holy place of Zion as a place of God's presence is matched in 8:20 by an appeal to time. Now the quoted liturgy reminds God that the saving season is almost over. The community expects to be healed by a certain point on the calendar. God may be a bit behind schedule, so the community attempts to remind God about the proper order of events. But just as the promise of place is voided, so too the claim of time is irrevelant. God will not respond to any liturgic calendar or the state's "five year plan."

Both liturgic formulae of place and time assume that God will respond to the plans of the establishment. Those in Jerusalem who engage in acts of ideological self-deception imagine Yahweh to be only a patron and therefore available at particular times and places. Those conventions have been obliterated by the grief that makes all old practices null and void. Nothing will work now except radical repentance, but repentance is remote from Israel.

At the center of this poem in v. 19c stands the reason for the rejection of old traditional claims. God's pathos is evoked by affront. God hurts because God is offended. The ground of the sickness to death is idolatry, the attempt to organize life around controllable objects rather than in reference to holy subject. The text moves from the center of v. 19c out toward both its beginning and its end. Yahweh is affronted by the idolatry. Israel is driven to fraudulent liturgical assertions, which reflect idolatrous miscalculation. Israel wishes for God's presence in place and on time, but in fact Israel is terminally ill because of idolatry and should entertain no wish. Wishful thinking is inadequate religion. Because Yahweh discerns the pathology as Israel does not, Yahweh is pressed to deep grief. The structure of the poem suggests that the reality of idolatry precludes healing and deliverance. Israel's close commitment to fake loyalties immobilizes the very power of God that would save.

8:22–9:3   In these verses, God, the power that now cannot (or refuses to) save, is driven from rage to painful wistfulness. Perhaps elsewhere (not in Jerusalem), perhaps in Gilead, outside the normal range of royal administration, there is a cure. Perhaps there, there will be a doctor who can make a difference (v. 22). But the yearning question of v. 22 remains unanswered. The reader (along with the poet and God) is required to deduce from the lack of answer that there is no help in Gilead either. Indeed, no healing is possible. The sickness is too deep. The idolatry is too pervasive. Judah refuses the medicine that is available.

The poet (and God) are pressed by this awareness to a new wave of grief. In 9:1-2 the poet utilizes the Psalmic tradition (Ps. 55:6-8), which is surely familiar to his listeners. The familiarity of this tradition does not lessen its poignancy, however. The poet wishes first that his head and eyes were more available for weeping (Jer. 9:1). The hurt in the face of Judah's death requires and evokes more grief, more crying, and more tears than his body is capable of transmitting.

God is inadequate for the grieving now to be done, for "my people" are very close to death. In a second figure (v. 2a) the yearning is not for more adequate tear ducts, but for an escape from this unbearable people. The decisive verb is "leave" *('azab),* a word we have seen in ch. 2 dealing with Israel's abandonment of God. Now it is God (or the poet) who yearns to leave, because the fickleness is beyond bearing. This is not a God who loves eternally. There is only so much this God will tolerate. Now it is time to depart because the affronts and betrayals have become a burden too great for God.

Jeremiah 9:2b-3 catalogues the ground of grief and the basis for God's abandonment. The scandal of Israel's violation of covenant is based in idolatry, a falsely-placed loyalty, and is embodied in adultery, unjust gain, slander, evil. The telling phrase is "falsehood *(sheqer),* not truth *(emunah)* is mighty in the land" (author's translation). Every practice of fidelity—theological, moral, juridical, economic— has become a practice of fickleness and self-deception. This is rooted in the fact that "they do not know me," that is, they do not recognize Yahweh as covenant LORD. The pathos of the line, "they do not know me" echoes 8:7,12. Judah has forgotten everything necessary to survival, forgotten commitments, forgotten shame, forgotten accountability, forgotten God. When that core commitment is disregarded, there are not enough arms, strategies, policies, prayers, or sacrifices to survive. The God "not known" is the one drawn to grief, because the end is sure. Yahweh now has no rescue mission that can be undertaken.

The poignancy of the poem is matched by an absence of specificity. The poetry is left open and inconclusive. It does not allude to particular acts or kings or invading armies. No doubt the poet and his listeners have something particular in mind. But what lets the poetry function in every generation as a powerful disclosure is the concreteness of the language that is porous enough to let it touch new historical specificities. The first articulation of the poem can always be freshly presented with new concreteness. Heard in a new situation, this poem will have its powerful say toward new concreteness, almost without interpretation. Each new rendering in new circumstance permits the poem to be God's grief-stricken word in a quite fresh way.

NEIGHBORS BEWARE (9:4-11)

The historical existence of Judah is coming to an end. The specific mention of Jerusalem in v. 11 is the first concrete reference in this long poetic unit beginning in 8:4. But listeners who follow the poetry could not have missed the allusions all along the way. This historical institution Jerusalem is under final threat, because its relation with Yahweh has been monstrously violated. Contrary to the reading of reality promoted by the self-serving establishment, city, temple, and throne all in fact depend on covenantal fidelity. This alternative reading insists that relational metaphors tell us more about historical consequences than the formal posturing of the people ostensibly in charge (cf. Mark 10:42-44). Prophetic poetry has more to tell us about Jerusalem's future than carefully-crafted government news releases, because the ones who authorize such releases seem to know so little about the realities.

9:4-6 These verses open with an indictment that focuses on social relations. Interestingly, the poet centers on the loss of honest speech between neighbors. The dominant modes of communication are now slander and deception. The poet believes that no public community can function properly unless communication is conducted in good faith. Such a poetic discernment may give us pause in our time when communication has largely become deft management of fraudulent symbols and images—in economic and religious life, in advertising and in public office. In v. 5 the decisive words (already seen in v. 3) are "no truth . . . only lies" (*emet* and *sheqer*). The poet observes that the fabric of human community has collapsed because neighbor no longer counts except as an object of exploitation. The outcome of such calculating speech, which uses people, is treachery. The alternative to all such destructive deception is to "know Yahweh," but that has been refused. The analysis offered by the poem is subtle. It recognizes that the rejection of covenantal, theological references and underpinnings invites the erosion of all viable human relations. The freedom of the true God keeps human interaction open and faithful. Where there is a loss or diminishment of that God, the loss of serious human exchange follows quickly and surely.

9:7-9   This passage, introduced by "therefore," is the predictable sentence following the indictment of vv. 4-6. God cannot and will not be indifferent to such a violation of everything hoped for. The first judgment is refinement and testing, a motif we have encountered in 6:27-30. We should not be misled by the metaphor, however. The metaphor of refining may suggest that God will find and save the good elements of society; but the poem in its passion asserts that there are no good ones. The metaphor of sifting is pressed to its extreme, to announce that all are tested. All are found wanting. None are exempt. (See parallel imagery in Amos 9:9-10.)

The sentence is interrupted in Jer. 9:8 with a return to the indictment that reiterates the theme of vv. 4-6. Verse 8 articulates an incongruity and contradiction between speech and intent, between public appearance and actual motivation. The language is powerful: a deadly arrow, an ambush. The neighbor is under assault in ways that make community impossible. The sentence in v. 9 is a "visit," a harsh coming of judgment in which God's very life must be avenged. God's honor is at issue, and finally God will not be mocked—even by God's precious covenant partner. The basis of threat from Yahweh is finally not moral, but theological. God is God and will manifest that Godness against this people who mock. No social establishment, not even this holy one in Jerusalem, can finally banish God's awesome self, God's own life. The manipulative posturing of Judah does not paralyze God, for God need not and will not be trapped in these manipulative postures.

9:10-11   Beyond the lawsuit speech (indictment in vv. 4-6, sentence in vv. 7-9), vv. 10-11 summon to lamentation (cf. Amos 5:16-17). Such a poetic move may reflect the poet's deep pathos and/or the historic sense that the end is now very close to fruition. The poetry concerns both historical realism and poetic discernment. Grief comes because creation is undone (cf. Hos. 4:3; Jer. 4:23-26). Because of social falseness, cattle, birds, beasts are gone. The ecosystem has collapsed. This is indeed "the day after"—the day after reckoning, after social disintegration, after fickleness, after death. The lamentation focuses on the beloved city. This is the return of urban creation to chaos, the end of the system, end of ideology, end of security, end of meaning.

This poetry is flung audaciously in the face of every self-deceiving ideological claim. The words of the poet work against every sooth-ing patriotism, every self-confident creed, every ideological ploy. It is only a poem, but it is received as a truth-telling by the communi-ty around the prophet. The poet does not linger over the juridical elements. He is a pastor. His community can begin grieving because the die of historical dismantling has been cast. None in Jerusalem can avoid the loss by their policy or by their buoyancy. History under God's governance is not so easily or painlessly reduced.

THE LAND LAID WASTE (9:12-16)

The prose of vv. 12-16 lacks the passion of the preceding unit and may reflect the more measured articulation of the Deuteronomist. The unit is in three parts. First is a question (v. 12) that reflects as-tonishment at the poetry. The announced judgment violates com-mon sense. It simply does not seem plausible that the entire world will end. The announced judgment also violates the most cherished tenets of the royal-temple ideology. This verse, in a threefold ques-tion that may function as a rhetorical ploy, asks, how can anyone make sense of what is happening?

Second, the answer given in vv. 13-16 seems to say: it is not all that difficult, complicated, or obscure to understand. There are very good grounds for all of the destruction to come, and those grounds are derived from the old tradition. To understand this astonishing threat, one need only ponder the main claims of the covenant tradi-tion that expose the false presuppositions of Jerusalem. But of course, Jerusalem is incapable of pondering the old tradition.

The reason for the indictment is given in three negatives and two positives. The negatives are: forsake torah (again, the verb 'azab'), not listen, not walk (v. 13). That is, this people has departed from the quite explicit demands of covenant. In Deut. 6:4 Israel's main summons is to listen. In Deut. 13:4 Israel is to "walk after . . . listen . . . cleave," which forms a nice contrast to our three verbs. The prob-lem for our poet is that on all three counts, Israel is unresponsive.

The two positives (Jer. 9:14) assert that not listening leads on the one hand to autonomy (stubborn heart) and on the other hand to idolatry (serving Baals). The two are equated: self-reference and idolatry are two forms of an alternative to covenant with Yahweh, two forms of escaping obedience to the torah, two choices that can-not bring life.

The third element (vv. 15-16) is the judgment introduced by

"therefore." The sentence is massive and unambiguous with a fivefold statement:

I will feed,
I will give drink,
I will scatter,
I will send,
I will consume.

The sovereignty of God over the historical process extends even to Jerusalem. No ideology of throne or temple protects Judah from this relentless God. The sentence reflects an ambiguity about punishment that recurs in the tradition of Jeremiah. The threat is on the one hand by sword and on the other hand by exile (scattering), which permits a new possibility.[9] The tradition at different times says both. In this passage both possibilities are forceful enough to announce an end. The poet's intent is to offer rhetoric through which the scenario of termination is experienced as a real historical happening, even though much of the poetic rendition precedes reality. It is an act of rhetorical interpretation, but not for that reason any less serious. It is poetry that claims to disclose God's full intent, and the reason for it.

ZION IN MOURNING (9:17-22)

In these verses the invitation to public lamentation sounded in v. 10 is now treated more extensively. The poetry of grief means to enact in the imagination of Judah the end that royal ideology denies. Public grief is an art form that requires expertise, and this unit therefore summons the women who are specialists in grief. In v. 21 the coming of death is treated like an intruding agent in the night who sneaks in the window (like a thief; cf. 1 Thess. 5:2), enters the safest places—like showing up in the queen's bedroom in spite of all security measures—and works its will even among the young who are the sign of life. The image affirms that the coming of death cannot be fended off. It will penetrate behind every device of protection. In this city, on these streets, in these squares, the power of death is deliberate, sure, and irresistible.

In the end (v. 22) there will be a pile of corpses, perhaps from

---

9. On the juxtaposition of death and exile as a live theological issue in the interpretive community, see Christopher R. Seitz, "Theology in Conflict: Reactions to the Exile in the Book of Jeremiah" (Ph.D. dissertation, Yale University, 1986).

slaughter, perhaps from plague (cf. Jer. 7:32-33). The poet offers as many metaphors as he can to evoke the inescapable, dreaded reality. The final metaphor is the reaper who cuts down with none to gather back up (cf. Amos 2:13-14). The bodies shall be strewn in the land. The inhabitants of Jerusalem shall be scattered around the Fertile Crescent. The center has not held, and things do indeed fall apart for Judah.[10] The pretense of the city is now fully exposed. Death presides in this city that has so craved life but that has carelessly squandered its chance for life and now must relinquish it.

TRUE GLORY (9:23-26)

In this prose section two very different sayings are placed back to back. The first (vv. 23-24) is a magisterial epitome of the claims of Israel's covenantal and prophetic faith. It articulates a sharp contrast between two very different ways of life.[11] The two ways of life are articulated in contrasting triads. The first triad is the way of wisdom, might, and riches. These modes of self-sufficiency are condemned. This triad figured large in sapiential instruction and seems to be embodied in King Solomon (on which see Matt. 6:29). The wisdom teachers reflected on the gains of wealth and power (see especially Eccles. 1–2) and concluded that they did not bring ultimate well-being. The meaning of "wisdom" in this triad is more difficult, but in this context it apparently means "technique," the means to control the outcome of life through technical data.[12] As such, wisdom ranks with might and riches as being unable to bring well-being.

The contrasting triad of "steadfast love, justice, and righteousness" (v. 24) reflects a wholly different orientation, congruent

---

10. The familiar lines of William B. Yeats, "The Second Coming," are peculiarly pertinent to Jeremiah.

Things fall apart: the center cannot hold;
Mere anarchy is loosed upon the world . . .
The best lack all connection, while the worst
Are full of passionate intensity.

11. See Walter Brueggemann, "The Epistemological Crisis of Israel's Two Histories (Jer. 9:22-23)," in *Israelite Wisdom*, ed. John G. Gammie (Missoula, Mont.: Scholars Press, 1978), 85-105.

12. On wisdom as a form of administrative power, see George E. Mendenhall, "The Shady Side of Wisdom: The Date and Purpose of Genesis 3," in *A Light Unto My Path*, ed. Howard N. Bream, Ralph D. Heim, and Carey A. Moore (Philadelphia: Temple University Press, 1974), 319-334.

with the character of God who delights in these qualities and insists upon them. Yahweh champions and embodies fidelity, equity, and humanness in the community. Thus, Yahweh is contrasted with other gods who seek satiation (might, riches). If God is committed to covenantal life as marked by steadfast love, justice, and righteousness, it follows that the community is to be ordered differently in light of that which delights Yahweh. The saying posits a close cause-effect linkage between the delights of God and social policy in Israel that reflects covenant faith.

This rather simple statement of contrasts identifies the social values that lead to death and the social relations that lead to life. Clearly Jeremiah's contemporaries had made the wrong choice and had chosen death. In 1 Cor. 1:18-31 Paul takes up the language of Jeremiah. In critiquing the practice of the Corinthian church, Paul contrasts the wisdom and power of the world and the weakness and foolishness of the Cross. As with Jeremiah and Paul, the issues in our own time have not changed. The same demanding choice between human fidelity and equity on the one hand and the self-serving ways of worldly security on the other hand is present among us.

In the verses that follow (Jer. 9:25-26), a verdict is given on Israel's choices. Verses 23-24 presented the choices Israel was called to make. Verses 25-26 review the choice that was made and the destiny received. The opening formula of v. 25 looks to a future that may be distant, but nonetheless very certain. The sure destiny of harsh "visitation" is on both the circumcised and the uncircumcised. Indeed, those who ostensibly practice the form of circumcision are in fact the uncircumcised. (See a parallel use of the theme in Rom. 2:25-29.) This bold assertion argues that the ritual practice of circumcision is in fact a fraud that has no reality. The result is that the chosen people are as ritually unacceptable and disqualified as any other *goy*. It is not only a judgment on both Israel and the *goyim*, but an argument that there is no distinction. The people who presumed a favored position in fact have no distinguishing characteristics to which any attention is paid. Chosen status is harshly dismissed. Judgment is the same on all. This assertion of impartial judgment is the inversion of impartial grace, reflected in Deut. 10:17 and Acts 10:34-35.

The specific reference to the other nations (Jer. 9:26) seems to be quite incidental. The point of the list of nations is simply to assert that Judah stands among the uncircumcised, and so is on equal basis with the other nations. Attention is thus focused in v. 26 on Israel, "uncircumcised in heart." (On this formula, see Deut. 10:16; 30:6;

Jer. 4:4.)[13] The heart is the organ of response and covenant-making. When the heart is uncircumcised, it lacks sensitivity and ability to function. When Israel's heart is not responsive to Yahweh (as it has not been in the experience of this poet), Israel can make no covenantal claim on Yahweh.

Unlike the other uses of the circumcision metaphor, this is not an imperative urging circumcision and, with circumcision, repentance. Instead the formula of circumcision is a final judgment given without any new chance being voiced. Yahweh's harsh visitation is coming. When it comes, this people is no more chosen than any other. Surface rituals will not save. All that would save is the covenant practice of steadfast love, justice, and righteousness. But according to Jeremiah, Israel rejected these practices long ago. The argument on circumcision here, though negatively stated, is an anticipation of Paul (Gal. 5:1-6), who sees that ritual cannot save. Only a reoriented heart can save, but that is now impossible for Judah.

NONE LIKE THE LORD (10:1-16)

In Jeremiah's time as in our own, the critical faith issue is not atheism, but idolatry.[14] In Jeremiah's time the temptation was the attraction of the gods of Babylon. In our day the comparable temptation may be the gods of militarism, of nationalism, of naturalism, of consumerism, of technology. In both cases the temptation is to vest one's life hope in the things we ourselves generate, instead of receiving life as a gift from this One who stands beyond us and for us. Characteristically the Bible does not deny the existence of other gods. The Bible makes an assumption that the world is polytheistic. The other gods exist. They have seductive power, but what they lack is power for life. They cannot do anything, and in that decisive test

---

13. It is worth noting that in Deut. 10:16-17 the command to circumcise the foreskin of the heart is followed immediately with the assertion that God is impartial and takes no bribe. That is, circumcision is a mark of covenant obedience, but it gives Israel no preferential status. The distortion of circumcision, as argued by Paul, arises when the command to obey is distorted to indicate a preferential status. That distortion is rejected by Jeremiah as by Paul.

14. On the centrality of idolatry rather than atheism in contemporary discussion, see Pablo Richard et al., *The Idols of Death and the God of Life* (Maryknoll, N.Y.: Orbis, 1983), 1 and *passim.*

they are utterly unlike Yahweh, who has the power to give life and therefore also the power to judge life.

The text of Jer. 10:1-16 is organized as a litany of contrasts between the true God and false gods.[15] The false gods, and their foolish subjects who have manufactured them, are characterized in vv. 1-5,8-9,11,14-15. These gods are characterized by a series of negatives:

> cannot move (v. 4),
> cannot speak,
> cannot walk,
> cannot do evil,
> cannot do good (v. 5),
> did not make (v. 11).

Three times they are described by the Hebrew word *hebel* (vv. 3,8,15; cf. 2:5), which means "vapor, nothingness, vanity." Jeremiah 10:14 says that these other gods have no spirit (i.e., no vitality) and are in fact "false." They cannot keep their promises. The contrast with Yahweh leads to the conclusion that they are unworthy of trust or loyalty, commitment or obedience.

We should not imagine that such would-be gods are merely religious projections. A critique of the idols must be more realistic and critical than that. First, the idols are linked to the way of the nations (v. 2) and the customs of the peoples (v. 3). They reflect the practices of noncovenanting peoples. Second, not only are the idols stupid and foolish (v. 8), but those who make and serve them are equally foolish. Third, the weight of the description falls on what the idols are made of—silver and gold, violet and purple. The false religion of the idols is therefore directly tied to the false economics around which Judah structures its life.[16] The idols are not only religious objects. They are commodities with economic value that lead to a false and destructive organization of community life. A misdirected religious loyalty is attached to a misorganized community life. Indeed, we may imagine that the poet wishes to comment on both at the same time, for religion and economics are intimately connected. The poet surely is not preoccupied simply with an ab-

---

15. See Jože Krašovec, *Antithetic Structure in Biblical Hebrew Poetry, Supplements to Vetus Testamentum* 35 (1984): 76-85.

16. See Walter Brueggemann, "Old Testament Theology as a Particular Conversation: Adjudication of Israel's Socio-Theological Alternatives," *Theology Digest* 32 (1985): 303-325.

stract religious habit, but with the concrete practices that shape communal life.

Yahweh, the God of Israel, is contrasted to the idols in vv. 6-7,10,12-13,16. There is none like Yahweh (vv. 6,7,16). Indeed, these verses demonstrate that there is no serious point of comparison. This one is a God with power to act. The wrath of Yahweh terrifies (v. 10). This God is to be feared (v. 7), as the other gods need not be feared. The decisive and powerful actions of Yahweh are seen in contrast to the other gods who do no actions. Unlike the idols, this God is capable of doing something that matters.

The verbs used to speak of Yahweh are indicative of the power of this God:

He made,
he established,
he stretched out (v. 12),
he utters,
he sends up (makes rise),
he makes,
he brings out (v. 13),
he formed (v. 16).

The language is of creation, which is done by Yahweh's powerful speech and by Yahweh's forming activity. The modes of creation of both Gen. 1 and Gen. 2 are captured in these verbs. In Gen. 1 God creates by powerful speech. In Gen. 2 Yahweh makes by acting, as a potter. Both modes are utilized in our text.

The appellations of Yahweh are stunning: "true God," "living God," "everlasting King," "portion of Jacob," "LORD of hosts." Yahweh is the true and reliable God (Jer. 10:10), contrasted with the idols of falseness (v. 14). This God does what has been promised and keeps commitments to the world God has made. This God is a living God.[17] This God has the power for life, the capacity to work a real newness, to cause life where there is only death and chaos. The everlasting King (v. 10) gives the assurance of keeping the world order against every threat of chaos. This king is able to constrain the waters, to drive back the flood (v. 13). The name "portion of Jacob" links Yahweh to the election tradition of Israel in Genesis, and "LORD of hosts" is an old martial name celebrating power. The col-

---

17. See Hans-Joachim Kraus, "The Living God: A Chapter of Biblical Theology," in *Theology of the Liberating Word,* ed. Frederick Herzog (Nashville: Abingdon, 1971), 76-107.

lage of terms and phrases credits this God with power both in creation and in history.[18]

This poem is content to state the contrast between Yahweh and the idols and is not compelled to draw any implications. The contrast is powerful enough. Israel has the option to be in relationship with and loyal to the God who can give new life. This God must be trusted and served and is never at the disposal of Israel. The alternative is to be allied with gods who have no power for life and cannot be trusted. The structure of the text requires a decision (cf. Matt. 6:24). It is a decision Israel does not want to make, and one that Israel characteristically makes wrongly. The total tradition of Jeremiah affirms that Judah is in the jeopardy which Jeremiah announces, precisely because it has abandoned Yahweh and embraced other gods who cannot give life.

The faith question raised by the sharp contrasts of Jer. 10:1-16 concerns the character of God and the nature of faith. False faith is linked to the idolatry of false gods and to the ideology of false imperial claims. Israel's source of life falls outside such practices. The text requires a choice, which is indeed life and death (Deut. 30:15-20). Those who practice idolatry are consigned to powerlessness. The alternative of the power of the real God is offered here, but Judah seems never to understand or embrace this singular life-giving alternative.

In some ways this text seems quite remote from us because we understand ourselves to be removed from the ancient temptation to idolatry and polytheism. We do not credit the presence of other gods in our religious conversations. If we do a careful analysis of the modern situation, however, important parallels emerge. That analysis may be aided by the thought of Karl Marx, who sees that idols are made out of the most precious commodities, silver and gold.[19] That is, we come to worship the things we have made, the creation and not the creator (Rom. 1:25). The analysis of Paul (and Marx) is paralleled by that of Sigmund Freud, who critiqued religion as an illusion that projected a yearning and social value on the things we have

---

18. A similar cluster of terms and phrases occurs in like usage in John 1:19-51 concerning Jesus.

19. Marx has helped us see that it is not commodities in general that are the problem, but precious commodities—gold and silver—which are assigned transcendent value and so function as fetishes. On such fetishism in American consumerism, see John F. Kavanaugh, *Following Christ in a Consumer Society: The Spirituality of Cultural Resistance* (Maryknoll, N.Y.: Orbis, 1981).

produced. Both Marx and Freud offer a critique of religion that is faithful to the tradition of Jeremiah. They assert that it is a lie when we try to derive the source of devotion, loyalty, and obedience from ourselves and the things we have made, whether that dimension of self is economic, political, psychological, or religious. The root of idolatry is to try to find ultimacy within the world of our own control and production.

The positive assertion of the text concerning Yahweh moves beyond the criticism of Marx and Freud to say what is true. With the positive assertions of the truth about Yahweh, biblical faith parts company with the critique of Marx and Freud, for it asserts that the holy, incomparable God of judgment and deliverance is not a projection out of our economics or philosophy.[20] This God—true and living—is a free agent who moves toward and against established reality according to his own irreducible purposes. It is this reality of genuine, holy freedom that is the ground of the prophetic judgment against Jerusalem, for God is not dependent on what is in the world. This same reality of genuine, holy freedom is also the ground of hope after judgment for Jerusalem, for God can do a newness not derived from what is old and now nullified.

The "smashing of idols" and the assertion of the true God are the proper work of prophetic poetry.[21] In our own time, we seem to be deeply—if not hopelessly—enmeshed in our self-created systems of security, well-being, and prosperity. But the enmeshment destroys us, for it talks us out of neighbor love, out of genuine freedom, and destines us to the anxiety of competence and finally to despair. That the source of life lies outside us and moves freely delivers us from being self-generated and self-sufficient. The modern form of idolatry is finally autonomy, the sense that we live life on our own terms. But such autonomy is a lie. The truth concerns this other One. It was so for Jeremiah and his contemporaries. It is so now, for us.

---

20. On a theological understanding of faith that is not simply projection, see Hans Küng, *Does God Exist?* (Garden City, N.Y.: Doubleday, 1980).

21. See Walter Brueggemann, "'Vine and Fig Tree': A Case Study in Imagination and Criticism," *Catholic Biblical Quarterly* 43 (1981): 188-204. More programmatically, see Paul Ricoeur on demystification and assertion, respectively, in his two essays, "The Critique of Religion," in *The Philosophy of Paul Ricoeur,* ed. C. E. Reagen and David Stewart (Boston: Beacon, 1978), 213-222; and "The Language of Faith," *ibid.,* 223-238.

PACK YOUR BAGS (10:17-25)

This unit has the poet moving back and forth between public calamity and personal, grieved reflection. In vv. 17-18 the poetry concerns the public calamity of exile. The people are to be thrown off
the land. For that reason, they are summoned in v. 17 to pack up and
be ready to go. (The image of being packed for exile is echoed in
Ezek. 12:1-16.) That same motif is resumed in Jer. 10:22. The
"threat from the north," anticipated in 1:13-14, now draws close.
This unnamed threat has the effect of reducing Judah to an unin-
habited thicket. The dismantling of Judah is an historical loss of
created order and a return to social chaos (cf. 4:22-26). The twin
motifs of exile and devastation are thus sounded in these verses.
Some will be carried away. Some will be killed. Both groups are
under harsh judgment.

Such a scenario about which the poet is so sure drives him to personal, grieved reflection. Jeremiah 10:19-20 is a statement of the
poet's anguish over the scenario of devastation that he envisions. The
loss is an experience of death: death of home, death of children. The
first person pronouns are numerous. These two verses may contain
a word play on *hal* ("affliction") and *ohel* ("tent"). The posture of intense personal devastation may reflect the poet's actual condition,
but it is also a rhetorical strategy. He wants the listening community to enter in prospect into the public disaster. He wants to lead the
community into grief by an act of imagination that anticipates the
actual event.

Only in v. 21 is any reason given for the coming of the announced devastation. The shepherds (i.e., the kings) have turned against
the wisdom of obedience. Such failed leadership leads to a scattering, to exile. In Ezek. 34 a new shepherd is promised who will gather
in homecoming, but here there is only scattering (see also Jer. 3:15).
In a variety of images the poet articulates and grieves the scattering
of Judah, the outcome of failed covenant.

Finally, vv. 23-25 are a reflective prayer that sounds much like the
prayers of complaint which come later in the book of Jeremiah. The
premise of the prayer is stated in v. 23 in language that sounds
sapiential (cf. Prov. 16:9–19:21). It is conceded that the human
agent does not understand or decide. The inscrutable historical
process is governed only by God, who need not justify or explain
such action. The devastation to come upon Judah is inexplicable to
Jeremiah, and the purpose of it is inscrutable.

The prayer of Jer. 10:24 is an act of repentance. In v. 25 the poet prays for God to act against the nations for their cruel treatment of God's people. It could be that the prayer of vv. 23-25a is only a personal one by the prophet, but its substance serves a public intent. Much later in the tradition (Jer. 25, 46–51) this very judgment against the nations is implemented, but not before Judah and Jerusalem are defeated. The reversal of the situation of Judah and the nations is sounded with the use of the verb "devour" in 30:16: "all who devour you shall be devoured." That is, this prayer of the poet is indeed answered, but not in time to avert the devastation. This prayer of 10:24-25 is offered against the devastation, but it is answered only after the fact. This grieving reflection leads to hope, but it is hope in a context of assault from God. In the immediacy of the situation, the wrath of Yahweh overrides a hope for deliverance.

THE COVENANT BROKEN

Jeremiah 11:1-17

This prose passage contains a formal, highly stylized statement of covenant theology. As a result, it is commonly regarded as Deuteronomic. Much critical attention has been given to the precise identification of the covenant that the unit proclaims, and there is much speculation about the historical process behind this text. Because the tradition of Jeremiah is profoundly linked to the book of Deuteronomy, many scholars hold that this text shows the inclination of the prophet in his early period to be a supporter and advocate of Josiah's covenantal reform (cf. 2 Kgs. 22–23).[1] However, such a view is tenuous and is excessively focused on historical issues. We may do better to follow the contours of the text itself without settling questions that lie outside the evidence of the text.

11:1-5 These verses are an initial summons to the prophet to articulate the covenant and its demands. There is no hint of what covenant, but the following verses make clear that it is the covenant of Sinai with its torah demands. Here, as everywhere in the tradition of Jeremiah, the torah demands of the Sinai covenant are held in confrontational tension with the confident guarantees of the royal covenant so cherished by the power elite in Jerusalem. The seriousness of this Sinai covenant and its required obedience is evident in the negative of v. 3. The one who violates such covenant is "cursed." This is a radical either/or from which Judah cannot escape.

These verses present three overriding themes of the tradition.

---

1. On the possible relation of this text (and Jeremiah generally) to the reform of Deuteronomy, see the classic essays of H. H. Rowley, "The Prophet Jeremiah and the Book of Deuteronomy," *Studies in Old Testament Prophecy* (Edinburgh: Clark; New York: Scribner's, 1950), 157-174; and John Bright, "The Date of the Prose Sermons of Jeremiah," *Journal of Biblical Literature* 70 (1951): 15-35. Since these articles, the change in methods of interpretation has shifted the issue and made it much more complex and elusive.

First, Judah and Jerusalem are required to listen (cf. Exod. 19:5-9; Deut. 6:4; 15:5). To "listen" means to be addressed, to know that life comes as a gift from another (cf. Jer. 7:21-28). This listening is not simply an auditory response, but requires obedient action. Second, the act of obedient listening permits the covenant formula of 11:4. This formula of mutuality and solidarity indicates that, through speaking and listening, through command and obedience, this God and this people now belong peculiarly to each other.[2] It is probable that the covenant formula as such is not much older than the book of Jeremiah (and perhaps the covenant of Deuteronomy).[3] But even if the formula is not ancient, it expresses a conviction that is foundational to Israel's faith. It is the mystery of Israel's life with Yahweh that Israel and Yahweh are on the way in history together and must take each other with ultimate seriousness.

The third theme of the tradition occurs in the stylized formula of v. 5. This Mosaic-Sinaitic claim is linked to the promise of land made to the ancestors in the book of Genesis. By the linkage of promise and command, this text proclaims the covenantal condition of Judah keeping the land. That proclamation is set in the midst of an invading army and the immediate prospect of exile and land loss.

All three elements indicate that Jeremiah is here commissioned by Yahweh to express and summon Israel to the most demanding and elemental claims of covenant faith. The prophet is to insist that his contemporary community should shape its life according to the costly demands of solidarity with Yahweh.

11:6-8 These verses provide historical retrospect. Jeremiah is once

---

2. On the peculiar power of speech to bind in covenant, see Robert Alter, *The Art of Biblical Poetry* (New York: Basic Books, 1985), 212, who comments on "the quintessential biblical notion of the nexus of speech that binds man and God. . . . God speaks the world and man into being, and man answers by speaking songs unto the Lord."

3. Lothar Perlitt, *Bundestheologie im Alten Testament,* Wissenschaftliche Monographien zum Alten und Neuen Testament 36 (Neukirchen-Vluyn: Neukirchener, 1969), has most strongly argued that the notion of covenant originated in the circles of Deuteronomy (and Jeremiah) in the 7th century. However, such a judgment seems to be an overstatement and inherently implausible. Cf. the careful and judicious statement of Dennis J. McCarthy, *Treaty and Covenant,* rev. ed., Analecta Biblica 21A (Rome: Biblical Institute Press, 1978), 13-24 and *passim;* and most recently Ernest W. Nicholson, *God and His People* (Oxford and New York: Oxford University Press, 1986).

again commissioned. His mandate is in the context of a historical memory. The old community was summoned to listen, but it did not. It had a very long history of not listening. Because the community did not listen, the covenant curses are implemented (cf. Deut. 28). Yahweh reminds Jeremiah that the old generation of Sinai and wilderness was judged for its disobedience (cf. Num. 14). The ancient memory of the Sinai covenant is structured as indictment ("did not listen") and sentence ("I brought covenant words on them"). The retrospect to Sinai serves to create a context for the immediacy of Jeremiah's present proclamation of broken covenant.

11:9-13 The historical retrospect on disobedient Israel is made contemporary in vv. 9-13. In v. 9 Yahweh speaks to Jeremiah for a third time. The charge that Yahweh brings against Judah is revolt, conspiracy (v. 9), a total rejection of Yahweh and of the covenant. The substance of the "revolt" against Yahweh is given in v. 10 in highly stereotyped language of the tradition. They refused to listen, they served other gods, they broke covenant. Notice the charge is completely lacking in temporal and circumstantial specificity. The sentence in v. 11 is equally lacking in concreteness. It is "evil" that matches the affront. Israel "did not listen." Now, as judgment, Yahweh "will not listen" (v. 11).[4] If Yahweh does not listen, this recalcitrant people will try alternative gods and sooner or later will discover that those other gods cannot save (cf. Deut. 32:38).

11:14-17 In these verses the judgment on this disobedient people is stated in a peculiarly theological way. The prophet may not intercede. Yahweh will not listen. This rebellious people has forfeited its right to approach God, and no ritual activity will compensate. Access to the throne of life is now denied. The living tree of much fruit is now only a dead tree set for burning (cf. Matt. 3:10). The end must surely come.

The entire unit of Jer. 11:1-17 is a meditation on Deut. 6:4.[5] This people must listen. When Israel does not listen, it rejects the One

---

4. The match between Israel's failure to listen and Yahweh's decision not to listen is precise and intentional. On this type of correspondence, see Patrick D. Miller, Jr., *Sin and Judgment in the Prophets,* SBL Monograph (Chico, Calif.: Scholars Press, 1982).

5. On the cruciality of Deut. 6:4 for Israel's faith and especially for Jeremiah, see S. Dean McBride, Jr., "The Yoke of the Kingdom," *Interpretation* 27 (1973): 273-306.

who summons, it violates its identity, and it must be destroyed. The sequence of the chapter offers an outline of the old covenant formulary.[6] That sequence is now utilized to offer an entirely fresh reading of Israel's life with Yahweh:

- (a) covenant foundation (Jer. 11:1-5),
- (b) covenant violation (ancient) (vv. 6-8),
- (c) covenant violation (contemporary) (vv. 9-13),
- (d) harsh judgment, end of covenant relationship (vv. 14-17).

We may take this covenant preaching on its own terms, without settling all the critical questions of reference and editorial work. The text takes up the old conventional language of covenant and applies it to Jeremiah's contemporaries (and subsequent generations) without being exact about the connections. The religious assertion is that Israel has found other gods to serve. The religious foundation of life has collapsed, but the punishment is public and political. Covenant violation leads to historical destruction. For this community defined in covenantal ways, disobedience to covenant can only lead to death (cf. Deut. 30:15-20). The conclusion is so sure that prophetic intercession is precluded. The covenant relation is decisive both for Israel's life with God and for Israel's life among the nations. That decisive relation is now about to be nullified. When it goes, everything goes. Israel is bereft of its partner and so is dangerously exposed to the nations. Only the covenant relation guarantees Israel among the nations. Without it, Israel is in acute jeopardy.

---

6. See Klaus Baltzer, *The Covenant Formulary* (Philadelphia: Fortress, 1971).

A HARD MESSAGE TO STUBBORN JERUSALEM

Jeremiah 11:18–20:18

These chapters of Jeremiah contain rich and diffuse materials. Beyond the identification of recurring themes and motifs, it is exceedingly difficult, if not impossible, to detect any sustained order or intentionality to the editorial process. One can detect here and there suggestions about the juxtaposition of certain elements, but that falls short of any general shaping of the materials. While there are some few elements of hope and an occasional didactic reflection, two central themes dominate this material. On the one hand, there is a steady insistence that Jerusalem will be destroyed, and the poet can find many ways in which to speak this word. On the other hand, interspersed with this theme is the countertheme of grief and anger on the part of the prophet for having to speak this hard message to a community that resists. Given that very general overview, it is necessary simply to take up the texts one at a time. As elsewhere in the book of Jeremiah, this material reflects both rich and imaginative poetry and disciplined prose assertion. There is a commonality in the general direction of all of the material.

A LAMB LED TO SLAUGHTER (11:18-23)

These verses comprise the first of a series of passages (11:18–12:6; 15:10-21; 17:14-18; 18:18-23; 20:7-18) called the Lamentations or Complaints of Jeremiah.[1] They seem to be the most direct, candid, and intimate prayers that we know about in the OT. Thus it is suggested that Jeremiah, in addition to his bold words to Judah as a prophet, also carried on an intense and often stormy conversation

---

1. On the complaints, see Gerhard von Rad, "The Confessions of Jeremiah," in *A Prophet to the Nations,* ed. Leo G. Perdue and Brian W. Kovacs (Winona Lake: Eisenbrauns, 1984), 269-284; and N. Ittmann, *Die Konfessionen Jeremias,* Wissenschaftliche Monographien zum Alten und Neuen Testament 54 (Neukirchen-Vluyn: Neukirchener, 1981). The latter recent work contains a complete bibliography.

with Yahweh. These passages are models for the depth of honesty that is appropriate in prayer. The hazard of such honest prayer, as we shall see, is that Yahweh can be equally honest and therefore abrasive in response to prayer.

Though the prayers are indeed direct, intense, intimate, and personal, it is clear that they follow a conventional form of prayer speech that is evident in the laments of the book of Psalms. This suggests that Jeremiah was so thoroughly saturated with the Psalter and its liturgic uses that he readily and naturally employed the speech conventions of this community. Or it may suggest, alternatively, that these prayers are an intentional imitation of such liturgic usage. My own judgment is that while the forms are important, they are used here in a way that evidences the power, courage, and imagination of an identifiable person.[2] Critical judgments that overlook the work of a creative personality in the poem fail, I suggest, to discern fully the offer of the poetry.

One may also ask whose "voice" is sounded here. Traditional interpretation holds that these are indeed the prayers of this one person, presumably Jeremiah. A recent suggestion holds that they are rather the speech of this person, Jeremiah, who acts as a mediator and who is in fact presenting the prayers of the community.[3] This notion, however, meets great obstacles because of the particular substance of the prayers, which concern personal pain, grief, and rage.[4]

Rather than choosing between these opposing views, we may opt for a mediating position. These prayers were in the first instance the specific prayers of a person rooted in the language and faith of the Psalms. But as the prayers of Jeremiah were taken up as communal literature, they were seen to have a larger pertinence to the entire community. That is, they were not canonized and regarded as "Scripture" simply in order to preserve Jeremiah's personal prayers. Rather, they were taken up and valued because they were found to be a poignant vehicle for Israel's faith. The canonizing process generalizes these

---

2. On the power of the person of the prophet midst the conventionality of forms, see Timothy Polk, *The Prophetic Persona,* JSOT Supplement 32 (Sheffield: University of Sheffield, 1984).

3. Henning Graf Reventlow, *Liturgie und prophetisches Ich bei Jeremia* (Gütersloh: Gerd Mohn, 1963).

4. John Bright, "Jeremiah's Complaints: Liturgy, or Expressions of Personal Distress?" in *Proclamation; Presence,* ed. John I. Durham and J. Roy Porter (London: SCM; Richmond: John Knox, 1970), 189-214, has provided the most acute critique of Reventlow's hypothesis.

prayers and transforms personal prayer into an expression of community issues. The prayers turn out to have power and compelling authority beyond the intent of the original speaker, but not in a way that cancels out the terrible pain and faith that is evidenced in them.

This unit contains three elements that follow the covential structure of the lament prayer: complaint (vv. 18-19), petition (v. 20), divine response (vv. 21-23).

11:18-19 *The complaint* serves to express the trouble the speaker is in, to describe it fully and intensely enough to evoke God's response.[5] The complaint is an accusation against an unidentified "they" (v. 19), who in v. 21 are identified as "the men of Anathoth," people from Jeremiah's home village (cf. 32:7,9). Reminiscent of the language of the psalter (Ps. 44:11,22), the complaint is of an innocent lamb about to be slaughtered. That language is given specificity in Jer. 11:19b by a quotation placed in the mouth of Jeremiah's adversaries. According to this alleged quotation, the prophet's adversaries are devising a scheme to eliminate him. The quotation includes a cluster of powerful words: "destroy, cut off, not remember." We have seen that the prophet opposed the royal-temple ideology in his repeated assertions that God had now determined the termination of Judah's life as organized around that ideology. We can imagine that Jeremiah had powerful enemies who wanted to silence such a treasonable voice.

11:20 *The petition* builds upon the complaint and makes a powerful request of God. Jeremiah did not deliver this unbearable message of judgment out of his own imagination (cf. 23:21-22). It is, rather, the verdict of the One who sends him. This prayer thus reflects the assumption that Yahweh will protect the messenger who delivers the message of the LORD, unwelcome as it may be. The appeal is addressed to "Yahweh of hosts," and is therefore an appeal to God's regal power. In the opening of the petition Yahweh is reminded that he "judges righteously" (cf. Gen. 18:25), that is, that such a judge actively intervenes on behalf of the faithful to see that they are fairly treated. The petitioner clearly presents himself as the righteous one who is entitled to such positive intervention. Thus the petition is based on a fundamental conviction Israel has about God.

---

5. On this intentionality in biblical prayer, see Moshe Greenberg, *Biblical Prose Prayer* (Berkeley: University of California Press, 1983), esp. 11-14.

The actual petition is reduced to one phrase, "let me see thy vengeance." In Jer. 11:18 Jeremiah already "knew" of the trouble. Now he wants to "see" a fair resolution. Jeremiah is not in doubt as to where righteousness is located in this dispute. He is the righteous sufferer who is wronged by evil devices. The uneven and unresolved relation between the righteous ones and the wicked ones is presently all in favor of the wicked ones, who will prevail—unless Yahweh intervenes. When Yahweh intervenes, the balance will be shifted to the righteous one who is allied with Yahweh. The new possibilities depend completely on Yahweh's readiness to intervene.

The language of "evil/right" and the summons to Yahweh to "judge and test" is court language. The final noun of the petition, "cause," means a legal case. The petition addressed to Yahweh seeks positively for acquittal and negatively for a countersuit against the offender. When the juridical language is recognized, the plea for "vengeance" is not a request for blind capricious retaliation, but for the implementation of a just legal claim and the implementation of Yahweh's justice on which the speaker has every right to count.[6] This is the court petition of one unjustly treated, addressed to a reliable judge against the unjust perpetrators.

11:21-23 *The divine response* indicates that the court of Yahweh has heard and accepted the claim of the speaker as a righteous one. The response of Yahweh is a court verdict. The guilt of those who scheme against Jeremiah is established in v. 21. The men of Anathoth are guilty of trying to silence a prophet. That offense is scandalous in Israel, for prophets are constitutive of communal life (cf. Amos 2:12; 7:16; Jer. 26:18-19). The silencing of prophets diminishes the identity of Israel.

The sentence against the ones Jeremiah accuses comes in 11:22-23. It is introduced by a characteristic "therefore." Yahweh will visit upon the men of Anathoth with death by sword and famine until none are left. They had done "evil" (v. 18). Now they will receive evil. We have no evidence of the implementation of this decree, but its rhetorical effect is the vindication of Jeremiah. The decree shows that Jeremiah's word is indeed from Yahweh, and that the prophet enjoys the formal support of the One who sent him.

Beyond the vindication of the person of the prophet, this prayer

---

6. On vengeance as a legitimate concern in a legal frame of reference, see George E. Mendenhall, *The Tenth Generation* (Baltimore: Johns Hopkins University Press, 1973), 69-104.

and its answer present a philosophy of history characteristic of prophetic faith. The men of Anathoth rejected a view of the historical process that asserted the end of the known world of royal-temple power. The divine response verifies such an establishment-ending word, however. It asserts that this prophetic word is authentic and enjoys the authorization and protection of the righteous Judge. What is guarded and endorsed here is not simply the person of the prophet, but the prophetic word that is indeed attested as the very word of Yahweh.

The prayer and response thus are to be heard in two ways. First, in its initial articulation, it is vindication for the person and message of the prophet. Second, canonically the text moves beyond the person of the prophet to endorse a view of historical processes under God's troublesome governance. It bears witness to Yahweh's judgment and Yahweh's sovereignty, which will not be outflanked. That righteous will is not frustrated or averted by violent resistance. History has moral shape *(tsedaqah),* and those who mock that shape are subject to death.[7] The covenant curses of sword and famine follow where the overriding will of Yahweh is mocked. The "conspiracy of the Jerusalem establishment" (cf. v. 9) cannot withstand this sovereign intent articulated by the poet. The prophet as bearer of this sovereign intent may suffer, but in this poem the outcome of God's sovereign will is not coterminous with the fate of the prophet.

PLIGHT OF THE RIGHTEOUS (12:1-6)

By common scholarly reckoning, this is the second "confession" of Jeremiah. It has important linkages to the first one in 11:18-23. The passage divides into two parts, complaint and answer.

12:1-4 *The complaint* raises the most fundamental question of faith, the reliability of Yahweh to stand by and look after faithful covenant partners.[8] Verse 1 states a premise: Yahweh is righteous.

---

7. The power of *tsedaqah* as a force governing history has been well exposited by Klaus Koch, *The Prophets,* vol. 1: *The Assyrian Period* (Philadelphia: Fortress; London: SCM, 1983), 56-76.

8. This text poses the problem of theodicy more frontally than any other OT text. See the essays on the theme in *Theodicy in the Old Testament,* ed. James L. Crenshaw, Issues in Religion and Theology 4 (Philadelphia: Fortress; London: SPCK, 1983). On the social dimension of the problem, not sufficiently emphasized in the Crenshaw collection,

The whole Bible is based on that premise. It means that the God who makes promises will keep them and will intervene in powerful ways when the promise runs amok. The same premise is operative in 11:20 (cf. Ps. 73:1). Because this God gives trustworthy decisions, Yahweh is the one to whom the speaker (and all Israel) turns in times of vexation. On the basis of the bedrock assumption, the second part of Jer. 12:1 states the question of theodicy, which rings in the ears of Israel even to the present day: why do wicked people prosper? That wicked people do indeed prosper is beyond debate. The unspoken counterpart is: "righteous people like me do not prosper." The question is an immediate, intense, and personal one and cannot be distanced as a speculative issue. The question (sounded in parallel fashion in Job 21:7) makes clear that the prayer does not seek an explanation. This is not an occasion for a theological seminar. Rather, Jer. 12:2 makes clear that this is an accusation of God, which anticipates action. It is God who causes the unjust to prosper, and that is against our expectation of God, if indeed God presides over a morally coherent creation.

Verse 3 expresses the righteousness of the speaker, which corresponds to the righteousness of Yahweh in v. 1. This complaint is a serious suit filed by a righteous petitioner to a righteous judge. The two of them, so the poem claims, should agree about the accused wicked, who surely must be judged. Jeremiah knows he is under scrutiny from Yahweh (cf. 11:20), but he also knows confidently that he is innocent. On that basis he proposes a sentence against the wicked, which would be an important righting of a wrong. Echoing 11:19, the wicked should be set for slaughter. What his adversaries have proposed against him, he now wishes for them. Jeremiah 12:4 is in the form of a complaint, designed to support the charge of guilt already asserted. The argument is that there is a severe drought ("the land mourns"). The drought is caused by the wickedness of the wicked (Hos. 4:1-3), and that drought will undo creation.

The opponents of the prayer and the targets of the petition are not named. We may assume a carryover of the "men of Anathoth" from the preceding unit. Or more generally, it is those who resist the harsh prophetic poetry now being announced. In any case, we are dealing not with a theoretical matter but with an intense and urgent issue about a real conflict over social reality. We are not, moreover, dealing simply with private wounds. Rather, we are dealing with an

---

see Walter Brueggemann, "Theodicy in a Social Dimension," *Journal for the Study of the Old Testament* 33 (1985): 3-25.

urgent question about the moral shape of reality and whether the reading of reality offered by the prophet can be sustained. If it can be sustained, it will only be by Yahweh's attentiveness. This poem is admittedly about the person of the poet. But more than that, it is a matter of the power of truth in a society where falsehood prevails. The quotation with which v. 4 ends means that the legitimacy of the prophetic announcement is in jeopardy.

12:5-6 *The answer* is a surprise to Jeremiah and to us. One would have expected a supportive answer, as in 1:8 and 19. But not here. Here there is only a hard-nosed response which reprimands and warns that more severe demands are still to come. The present threat is modest compared to what will come, like the comparison of human footraces to horses, like the easy terrain to the demands of an uncharted jungle. The safe or domesticated land is contrasted with the Jordan valley, which was hot, well watered, and so inhabited by wild beasts. The awareness of this geography intensifies the power of the contrast. The danger to come for the prophet is like the danger of living in the threat of the ominous jungle of the Jordan. Worse is yet to come. The danger of prophetic truth will grow more severe as the judgment draws closer. The petitioner gets no assurance and no relief. If the petition reflects uncertainty about whether God is indeed righteous and reliable, the answer is that the speaker will have to live with that uncertainty. There will be no relief from the uncertainty. God's righteousness is not articulated here. The issue of God's reliable righteousness is held in abeyance. In the meantime, severe obedience is required.

Beyond the reprimand, the second element of the response is a warning (12:6). The voice of Yahweh here acknowledges that the conspiracy of resistance (11:9,19) to the prophetic vision of reality is so pervasive that the poet should trust nobody. They are all untrustworthy. The warning is unequivocal: do not trust them. Perhaps the warning means that Jeremiah is cast as an isolated voice and must get used to his isolation. Or the warning may mean "trust me, Yahweh, and only me." Trust me instead of them. The isolation of the petitioner with this response is not unlike a citizen who learns of conspiracy in government but can find no place to report it, because everyone to whom report might be made is implicated in the conspiracy. Such a grasp of the realities of public life drives one into isolation and/or into life with God.

Notice, however, that the response of God in 12:5-6 completely evades the issue of v. 1 and the desperate petition. No response is made to the issue of theodicy. Yahweh's response is not unlike the whirlwind speech of Job 38–41, which simply overrides the theodic question. Those who raise this question are given no comfort. It is as though fidelity to Yahweh must be its own reward. The one who is faithful cannot expect that others will see and be changed. To serve such a God is not merely an act of dedicated loyalty and intentional decision-making. It is, rather, an inescapable destiny once one has grasped a certain reading of reality. The prophet is compelled to speak without any assured award.

The response only summons Jeremiah to more radical obedience. But the obedience itself is the only matter at issue. There is no hint that obedience leads to any benefit. Characteristically, Yahweh changes the subject and will not respond to the question of benefit. We are left with a God confessed to be righteous, who refuses to deal with the problem of wickedness. That is how the obedient regularly find the sovereign rule of God. The poet is left with his reading of reality, with a sense of incongruity, yet with a passion for a reading that awaits God's sanction.

THE PATHOS OF GOD (12:7-13)

Now a very different voice speaks. It is the voice of Yahweh. Yahweh's voice in the preceding poem (12:5-6) was harsh and uncompromising. That same voice now announces the devastation of the land of Judah. The words are not, as we might expect, however, judgment or indignation. They are words of exhausted grief by this One who so treasures the land and now finds it so abused that it must be abandoned. The poem is enveloped by powerful words that tell the whole story of land and people. It begins in v. 7 with a triad, "I have forsaken . . . I have abandoned . . . I have given over." That thought ends in v. 8 with the broken, harsh verdict, "I hate her." The first verb, "forsake," has been often used in Jeremiah to remark on Judah's abandonment of Yahweh. Now it is Yahweh who abandons. Yahweh can stand the affront, the pain, and the grief no longer. The poem ends in v. 12 with the outcome: "no peace." Verse 13 explicates this outcome, but the dramatic climax is at v. 12. Yahweh has abandoned Judah. The result is absence of well-being. Everything depends on the embrace of Yahweh. When that fails, all else is failed. The poem permits Judah to reexperience that central failure which, prior to the poem, had not been noticed. Yahweh has withdrawn fidelity. When Yahweh withdraws, Judah is helpless and hopeless.

Verses 7-8 begin with a threefold use of "inheritance" *(nahalah)*.

From the beginning Israel (land and people) had been Yahweh's special, intimate treasure (Deut. 32:9). The use of "inheritance" stakes out a claim. The land can be possessed by none other, for it belongs inalienably to Yahweh. Nor can the people imagine that the land is autonomous, for Yahweh has old and deep claims on this community. But all of that is over. Yahweh's beloved land is "handed over." Yahweh's intimate partner, beloved wife, precious son, is now written off. (The "handing over" is perhaps parallel to the surrender of Jesus to the authorities in Matt. 27:2; Mark 13:1,10,15.) The triple use of "inheritance" is reinforced in Jer. 12:10, with "my vineyard" (cf. Isa. 5:1-7) and the double use of "portion."

The metaphors in Jer. 12:8-9 suggest that this beloved people has been actively antagonistic to Yahweh. The images portray the strange wildness of a recalcitrant creation. The land is like a lion, hostile to Yahweh. The heritage is like a bird of prey, ready to spring and hunt and devour. The kings are destructive, ready to abuse. The images bespeak a situation of brokenness, antagonism, hostility, alienation in the land and the people. The poetry is wondrously abrasive in presenting the disjunction between the peaceably ordered kingdom of Yahweh's vineyard and inheritance, and this community now gone berserk in its destructive, rapacious way.

This contrasting play of images of beloved people/aborted community leads to the outcome in vv. 11-12. The language now is of terror, violence, destruction. Abuse of the land has turned heritage to desolation, precious portion to wilderness. Verses 10-11 have a fourfold use of "desolate." Israel's waywardness with the land has destroyed the life-giving potential of the land and the life-celebrating quality of the community. (This portrayal is reminiscent of 2:6-8, in which the good land is made desolate land.) The land has not been well treated. The people have not been well served. The result is that the land is unable to be the land Yahweh intended and hoped for. The community is unable to be the people Yahweh proposed.

It is no wonder that Yahweh grieves. Yahweh's pathos results from the fact that nobody notices and nobody cares. As a result of abuse by exploitive royal power, destroyers have come. They have not come because Yahweh is fickle or careless, but because Israel has distorted. And now comes the destroyer, the sword, and "no one lays it to heart" (v. 11). Verse 12b makes it clear that the invaders are not an accident nor are they unwelcome to Yahweh. The invaders are not an intrusion in God's rule, but in part an instrument of God's rule. Yahweh cries because the invaders are Yahweh's own instrument of anger and judgment. Yahweh has declared war on this beloved, recalcitrant inheritance. In v. 9 the poem summons wild beasts to "devour." Now in v. 12 it is Yahweh's sword that "devours."[9] Both uses of the verb presumably refer to an invading army, but the army is summoned by Yahweh, who is the One who wields the sword. The end result is that the land and the people are now utterly unproductive. The trade-off of thorns for wheat (v. 13) indicates that everything has come to a sorry, failed end. The language may refer back to the Creation narrative in which the land of blessing can only produce thorns (Gen. 3:18).[10]

The situation of the poem is concerned with (1) the indictment that the land has failed Yahweh (Jer. 12:8-11), (2) the judgment in the form of invasion, and (3) the outcome of nonproductivity. The initial statement of v. 7 produces the clue to all else. Yahweh's withdrawal causes fertility to end and exposes the land and the people to chaos. The last phrase of v. 13 is not unlike 4:26, which also speaks of the land reverting to chaos.

This poem is not descriptive. The poet's contemporaries could not yet see the failure of productivity. It is, rather, evocative and anticipatory. The poem seeks to look again at what is about to happen. It enacts a scenario for the land and the people that unimaginative observers would reject as remote from reality. They would have thought it remote because they were enveloped in an ideology that did not know that Yahweh could be driven to grief and finally to withdrawal. Thus the poem is a disclosure of the turmoil that goes on in the heart of God, which is then implemented in the life of Judah.[11] The poem enacts this strange future at two levels—theological imagination and political realism. The poem moves back and forth between them, even as the tradition wants the community to do. Theological imagination by itself seems lacking in specificity. But

---

9. That Yahweh wields a "sword" is a notion very deep in the tradition of covenant. Already in Exod. 22:24 Yahweh wields a sword on behalf of the marginal. Now that same sword which guards Yahweh's purposes is turned against Yahweh's people and city.

10. An inversion back to a functioning, joyous creation, from thorns to cypress, from briars to myrtle, is envisioned in Isa. 55:12-13. That vision is still beyond the horizon of judgment in Jeremiah, however.

11. This turmoil in the heart of God is crucial to the entire poetic tradition of Jeremiah. What eventuates in public history is derived from God's pain. This motif has been dramatically articulated by Abraham J. Heschel, *The Prophets* (New York and London: Harper & Row, 1962), 108-130, 221-278; and Kazō Kitamori, *Theology of the Pain of God* (Richmond: John Knox; London: SCM, 1965).

political realism by itself is inadequate for the pain that lies at the heart of the historical process. The failure of the community and the withdrawal of Yahweh come together. As 12:1 asserts Yahweh's righteousness, this unit defends God's action, which leaves Judah bereft. In this text the outcome is unambiguous, even though most in Jerusalem did not want to notice (cf. Lam. 1:12).

JUDAH'S NEIGHBORS PLUCKED UP (12:14-17)

This unusual prose oracle reflects a quite late situation in the tradition of Jeremiah. Apparently it is placed where it is because of the initial use of "heritage" *(nahalah)*, thus linking this unit to the preceding passage, which begins in v. 7 with the same word and ends in v. 13 with the like-sounding word *nahal* ("weary"). This passage is a play on the word "pluck up" *(natash)*, which has been identified as a governing word for the Jeremiah tradition in 1:10. In this passage the term is used in a variety of ways concerning both Judah and the nations.

The initial address (12:14) against evil "sojourners" (RSV "neighbors") refers to the other nations that have invaded and occupied Judah. The tone of the beginning is one of indignation, for the nations violated (smote) the heritage that had been designed only for chosen Israel. Yahweh is affronted at such a violation. The primary assertion of this oracle is the lead sentence of v. 14: "I will pluck up the nations from the land." With magisterial sweep, the prophet asserts Yahweh's sovereignty over the nations and announces that God will now displace the nations from the land of Israel. This odd assertion is consonant with the oracles against the nations articulated by various prophets.[12] For Jeremiah, God is in the business of plucking up, that is, displacing peoples who are disobedient. The Jeremiah tradition is mainly preoccupied with plucking up Judah, but here the shoe is on the other foot. No nation is named, but one thinks of Babylon in this context. Babylon has been Yahweh's agent in plucking up Judah and sending Judah into exile. But now the process is inverted and this nation is in turn to be plucked up and driven out. This inversion bespeaks the end of exilic occupation (cf. Jer. 50–51; Isa. 46–47). Such a verdict is best understood after the destruction of 587 B.C.E., after Babylon has done

---

12. On these oracles, the most complete discussion in English is that of Norman K. Gottwald, *All the Kingdoms of the Earth* (New York and London: Harper & Row, 1964).

Yahweh's harsh work of destruction. If one links this statement to the historical facts, then this unit may allude to the conquest of Babylon by Cyrus and the Persians. The great theme is that finally all the states and empires must answer to the rule of Yahweh.

In Jer. 12:14c-15 the oracle moves away from its focus on the judgment of the other nations. It is as though the use of the verb "plucking up" draws the tradition back to Judah. In these verses, the verb is used to trace Yahweh's dealing with Judah:

(a) In v. 14c Judah will be plucked up from among the nations. Judah will be taken from exile where it has been placed by God and brought home. This is a surprising use of the verb, which is characteristically negative in the Jeremiah tradition. Here it is positive, implying rescue and homecoming (cf. Amos 4:11).

(b) In Jer. 12:15 the same verb is used in its more characteristically negative way concerning Judah. This statement alludes to the deportation and Judah's departure into exile.

(c) Then, in v. 15b, the positive plucking up of v. 14c is reasserted so that the final action of God toward the nations is compassion, homecoming, and the end of exile for all nations. All of the nations are promised homecoming, each to its own land. This odd statement suggests that the action of a foreign nation in invading Judah, even if it is the will of Yahweh, is experienced by that nation as displacement. The outcome of the complex use of the metaphor "plucking up" is to announce that Yahweh will have compassion over the nations, even as over Judah.

Following this digression, vv. 16-17 continue the main theme of the oracle that began in v. 14a. These two verses take the characteristic language of Deuteronomic thought and apply it to the nations. The unit is presented as two symmetrical "if-then" statements, one positive and one negative. (For the same structure applied to Israel, see 1 Kgs. 9:4-7.) In this oracle the nations are treated exactly like Israel, subject to the same choices, possibilities, and threats.

The positive "if-then" statement of Jer. 12:16 asserts that the nations must learn the faithful ways of Israel, must submit to the torah, and learn to focus life upon Yahweh. If the nations do that, they will be established in the midst of Israel. The word "build" here is the counter word to "pluck up" in 1:10, so that a new season of well-being is promised to the nations. The negative counterpart of 12:17 is that if the nations do not listen *(shemaʿ)* and submit to the claims of the torah, they will be plucked up and destroyed. The nations will be nullified and eliminated from the historical process. The nations are treated as potential covenant partners for Yahweh and are offered the same terms of condition for covenant to which Israel is held accountable. Without compromising the demands of Yahweh, this is a remarkable articulation of a possible covenant beyond Judah's presumed special destiny.

Thus this prosaic oracle is a juxtaposition of two themes: (1) a provision of mercy for Judah, and (2) an extraordinary offer to the nations to be included in the scope of covenant well-being. The promises and threats made to the nations are the same as Israel has had since Sinai, which are classically expressed in Deuteronomy.

The historical placement of this text would seem to be late in the Exile. In substance (though not in style), the text offers hints that are not unlike the assertions of Second Isaiah, for there is talk of both homecoming for Judah and a displacement of nations, presumably Babylon. But what interests us is not the dating or location of the text. Rather, it is the remarkable theological claim of the text that is evoked by the word "pluck up" and its counterpart, "build." The exile and restoration of Judah are not unexpected. But the double "if-then" structure for the nations and the words "learn-obey" are remarkable. They suggest that the nations are invited in and judged by the standard covenantal norms. They are treated as is the chosen people Israel.[13]

The notion that the nations may be regarded along with Israel as peoples of Yahweh is a motif recurring in the Isaiah tradition. Isaiah 2:2-4 records a vision of the nations coming to Zion. But in that envisioned scenario, the preeminence of the Zion-David establishment is retained. Our passage has more in common with Isa. 19:23-25, which does not refer to either Zion or David. The Jeremiah oracle stands apart from Isa. 19:23-25, however, because it is explicitly torah-centered as Isa. 19:23-25 is not. The future of the nations is conditioned by the torah. The torah is made the explicit norm for the nations without reference to Israelite preeminence. The whole international process is envisioned as submission to Yahweh. The nations embrace the same obedience required of Israel and so are treasured by Yahweh. Otherwise, the nations, like disobedient Israel, will perish (Jer. 12:17).

Both an invitation to the nations to join the covenant and an offer

---

13. See the comments of Wilhelm Rudolph, *Jeremia,* 3rd ed., Handbuch zum Alten Testament 12 (Tübingen: J. C. B. Mohr [Paul Siebeck], 1968), 83. Rudolph notes the parallel between "my house" in v. 7 and "my neighbors" in v. 14. Moreover, the criteria are reminiscent of Amos 1–2, in which Israel is judged by the same norms as the other nations.

of compassion to the nations are unexpected in the tradition of Jeremiah. This unexpected oracle, however, offers important theological resources in a social climate that is too prone to link God with country. Even in Israel, with its passion for election as chosen people, it is here affirmed that God may choose elsewhere outside Israel. Here it is asserted that every kingdom with a readiness for obedience has an opportunity for Yahweh's special compassion. No more than that is offered even to Israel and Judah in this tradition.

THE LINEN WAISTCLOTH (13:1-11)

In as many different ways as possible, the tradition of Jeremiah asserts that Israel-Judah has violated its proper loyalty to Yahweh and so stands under severe judgment. Here that recurring assertion is presented through the action of a symbolic gesture. The narrative action here, as is characteristic of the genre of symbolic act, has two parts—the action and its interpretation.

The action of vv. 1-7 has three commands by Yahweh to Jeremiah, each of which the prophet obeys. First, Jeremiah is commanded to buy the linen cloth and wear it (v. 1). He does so in obedience (v. 2). Second, Jeremiah is commanded to take the loincloth and hide it in the rocks by the Euphrates River (v. 4). (Because the Euphrates River is a very long distance from Jerusalem, it is not clear that this is the river that is intended. The Hebrew term might refer to a town in Benjamin, Jeremiah's own home region. Or perhaps the entire narrative is a fantasy journey. The identification of the site has no crucial bearing on interpretation.) Jeremiah obeys the command (v. 5). Third, Jeremiah is commanded after a time to recover the buried loincloth (v. 6). He does so in obedience (v. 7). Thus far the structure of the narrative is perfectly symmetrical. And thus far we are given no clue to the meaning of the action. There is an oddity even in this symmetrical structure, however. Why does Jeremiah wear the loincloth before it is hidden and recovered? What is the significance of this initial act of command and obedience? As we shall see, the first action does serve a quite intentional purpose. The concluding statement of v. 7, introduced by "behold," breaks the symmetry of command and obedience. This assertion in v. 7c is something of a verdict that prepares us for the interpretation. The recovered loincloth is ruined and good for nothing. This conclusion prepares us for the interpretive comments that now follow.

The interpretation of the action of vv. 1-7 in vv. 8-11 is more complex than might at first appear. The interpretation can, I believe, be read in reverse order from the three commands of vv. 1-7. The link between act and interpretation depends upon the parallel asserted between loincloth and Judah-Jerusalem. Thus the action is a parable about Judah and Jerusalem. What has happened to the loincloth is taken up as a commentary about the life of Judah and Jerusalem.

First, in vv. 8-9 it is asserted that Judah-Jerusalem, like the loincloth, is now seen to be ruined. This first interpretive insight thus correlates with the third command and act of vv. 6-7. Second, in v. 10, in the second interpretive comment, Judah is as far from Yahweh as the loincloth is from Jerusalem. Judah is removed from Yahweh by refusing to listen, by acting in stubborn autonomy, by going after other gods. The language of indictment is characteristic of Deuteronomy and corresponding parts of Jeremiah. Third, in v. 11, in the third interpretive comment, we have a correlation to the first command and act of vv. 1-2. There Jeremiah is to wear the loincloth, so that it should cling to his body. In parallel fashion, Judah is to cling, to cleave *(dabaq)* to Yahweh, to be as intimately linked to Yahweh as clothes to a man (on clothes and person; see Ps. 109:18-19,29). The proper use of a loincloth is to be worn by a man. It is to be worn, not to be hidden and buried. Thus Israel's proper use is to cleave to Yahweh, not to be autonomous, stubborn, or committed to other gods. An improperly used loincloth becomes rotten and useless. An improperly postured Israel becomes rotten and worthless.

Thus, Jer. 13:1-11 forms a rough chiasmus.

1st command: buy and wear (vv. 1-2)	3rd interpretation: cling to Yahweh (v. 11).
2nd command: remove and hide (vv. 3-5)	2nd interpretation: Israel refuses Yahweh (v. 10).
3rd command: recover and find useless (vv. 6-7)	1st interpretation: Israel is worthless (v. 9).

The narrative of the symbolic act is climaxed in v. 7 with a verdict introduced by "behold." The interpretation is concluded in v. 11 with the verdict, "did not listen." An Israel that does not listen is as useless as a loincloth that does not cling to the man for whom it is purchased. The covenantal attentiveness of "hear" and "cling" is decisive for Israel's identity and value. When Israel hears and cleaves, Israel is a name, a praise, a glory—that is, designed to enhance Yahweh (v. 11). As the cloth makes a man, so this people is to enhance this God. But now Israel has no value to Yahweh, for Israel refuses the function and relationship to Yahweh for which it was "purchased" in the first place. (See the similar purchase metaphor in 1 Cor. 6:19b-20.)

The narrative is artfully constructed to make a shrewd identification of the proper historical function of Israel. The analogy of the loincloth is concerned with more than exile and rottenness. The first command and the third interpretive comment allude also to the proper use of the loincloth. It was taken for granted that the loincloth could be properly worn. That is its normal use. So also it was taken for granted that Israel could be properly oriented to Yahweh. That is Israel's normal purpose. But Israel refused and so is worthless. The parable is a comment on Israel's true identity and in fact replicates the entire history of Israel, both as intended for covenant and as having rejected covenant, and so being "good for nothing."

THE WINE JAR (13:12-14)

This unit of judgment is an oracle, not a symbolic act, even though it appeals to a visible object: jars full of wine. The initial statement, which gives no clue to its meaning (v. 12), appears to be a proverbial saying or even a riddle. The saying, "Every wine jar will be full," seems designed to evoke an inquiry. Indeed, it is followed promptly by an inquiry (v. 12b). This in turn is followed by the explanatory oracle in vv. 13-14, which is a statement of judgment.

In the move from proverb (v. 12b) to statement of judgment (vv. 13-14), however, the language has shifted.[14] "Full with wine" has become "full with drunkenness." The latter term is a metaphor for destruction. The language suggests bitterness, lack of control, shame. While we speak of the "cup of blessing" in the eucharist, this is the cup of reeling and death (cf. Jer. 25:15-29; Mark 10:38-39; 14:36).

No indictment or ground for judgment is given. The resolve of God is firm and massive nonetheless. The harsh conclusion is addressed to all the principal people of Jerusalem (kings, priests, prophets). This unit sounds one more time the familiar theme: Jerusalem is under death sentence not from Babylon, but from Yahweh. God speaks a threefold negative against God's own exercise of compassion (Jer. 13:14). Israel's old habitual ruthlessness against Israel's enemies (Deut. 7:16; 13:8; 19:13, 21) is now utilized as ruthlessness against Jerusalem. The formula of ruthlessness articulates God's final resolve to destroy his own beloved city.

The first action of Yahweh is "I will fill" (Jer. 13:13). There will

---

14. See the interpretive comments of William McKane, "Jeremiah 13:12-14: A Problematic Proverb," in *Israelite Wisdom,* ed. John G. Gammie (Missoula, Mont.: Scholars Press, 1978), 107-120.

be ample wine to evoke drunkenness. But the intent of Yahweh's action is not clarified until v. 14: "I will dash." The figure of full wine jars is used to assert that all inhabitants of the community will be filled with drunkenness (v. 13). But the metaphor remains enigmatic, until it is recognized that drunkenness may be taken as a protoapocalyptic figure for instability and judgment (cf. 25:15-29). The notion of drunkenness here is not related to immorality, but to a loss of equilibrium, of being dizzy and unbalanced.[15] The image is of persons so unstable, as in a crazy drunk, that they will bump against and hurt each other. They will be helpless, unable to act differently or responsibly. They will be at the mercy of their condition, out of control. Indeed, the only one who could save them from this uncontrolled act of self-destruction is Yahweh, who made them drunk in the first place.

Yahweh, who instigated the condition of instability, will not intervene:

I will not pity,
I will not spare,
I will not have compassion.

Self-induced destruction is permitted to work its own way without intervention from Yahweh. Israel's current drunkenness (instability resulting from lack of reference) will be permitted to run its full course. According to this metaphor, Yahweh does not actively intervene to destroy or punish. Yahweh only creates a condition of drunkenness, which leads to a hopeless conclusion. The last term, "I will not have compassion *from their destruction*" (author's translation), is heavy and decisive. It is the word we have seen as "spoil" in 13:7-9. The outcome is the same in the acted parable (vv. 1-11) and the oracular riddle (vv. 12-14). Worthless Israel is coming to a sorry end. The judgment and punishment come without any intervention by Yahweh. As a result, the deathliness of Jerusalem's own life will work to its destination of death. Their own drunken disorientation will be their destiny.

LAST CHANCE TO REPENT (13:15-19)

This poem is another reflection of the ominous fate that the prophet anticipates for the Judean community. Verses 15 and 17 juxtapose

---

15. McKane, *ibid.,* in parallel fashion shows that the subject of the unit moves from intoxication to "shattering."

two uses of *shemaʿ*, "listen/not listen." According to vv. 15-16 there is still time to listen. To listen would be to concede glory to Yahweh and, conversely, not to presume glory for one's own program and policy. The invitation of v. 16 (echoing Amos 5:18,20) suggests that if Yahweh is honored, judgment and death will not come. But if Judah does not turn, then the judgment of darkness, stumbling, twilight, gloom, deep darkness is sure to come. The language is not precise, for the poet prefers to use impressionistic speech that is all the more dread-filled.

The alternative of "not listening" (Jer. 13:17; cf. 7:24-27) will lead to death. "Not to listen" asserts a statement of autonomy and a rejection of Yahweh, an act of self-serving pride and self-sufficiency. Such a choice on the part of Judah drives the poet to grief, for "not listening" leads to exile *(shebah)*. The linkage of *"not listen"* . . . *"exile"* is structurally the main claim of the prophetic lawsuit (cf. Amos 7:16-17; 6:4-7). The indictment is Israel's refusal to be addressed in covenant. The result is expulsion from the land. The reality of exile is rooted in violation of the torah, which Yahweh will not countenance.

Jeremiah 13:18-19 expounds the negative judgment of v. 17. The double use of *shemaʿ* in vv. 15,17 makes it seem as if Judah still faced a choice (cf. Deut. 30:15-20). But the exposition of Jer. 13:18-19 suggests that the positive alternative is long since forfeited. In v. 17 the decisive choice is already made in the negative. This twofold address contains a specific message and a more general one, both of which have a mood of grief. In v. 18 the grief is addressed to the king, presumably Jehoiachin, who is exiled into Babylon with his mother (cf. 2 Kgs. 24:12).[16] The verse is an announcement that the royal claim is now nullified. The crown is removed and the king and queen mother are treated like common exiles, or even slaves. The language of dethronement is parallel to that of Isa. 47:1-3, only there it is addressed to Babylon. In this disclosure of an ending, we have symbolization of the end of the entire reality of dynasty and temple, the forfeiture of the dynastic promise, all because of not listening.

---

16. Christopher R. Seitz, "Theology in Conflict: Reactions to the Exile in the Book of Jeremiah" (Ph.D. dissertation, Yale University, 1986), 164-171, has drawn a remarkable conclusion that the confused status of the monarchy in the period of Jeremiah was much influenced by the role of several competing "queen mothers." That is, which members of the royal family controlled power and lasted in power seems related to the various mothers of princes, who are identified in the text.

The specific address in Jer. 13:18 is matched in v. 19 with a more general comment about the whole territory of Judah. The language is vivid and decisive: "closed . . . none to open." Judah has become occupied land. Then the poet lets fall the decisive word "exile" (*golah*). That reality is announced in v. 17, but now it is decisive. In v. 17 there had still been a wistful "if." That chance is now gone in v. 19.

Thus far in this chapter then we have three units—vv. 1-11, 12-14, and 15-19—all of which make the same point, but in astonishingly different ways. All of them announce an ending. All of them credit Judah with conduct that has evoked this outcome. By inference, all of them exonerate Yahweh. The judgment is more than warranted.

THE SHAME OF JERUSALEM (13:20-27)

This is an exceedingly difficult text, one that most commentators prefer to treat very briefly. The main thrust is clear, but the specifics of the text are problematic. It is not clear who the various persona in the poem are. The oracle is addressed to Jerusalem (cf. v. 27; most commentators follow the LXX and insert "Jerusalem" as a vocative in v. 20).

The main theme follows the skeletal structure of the lawsuit speech. Jerusalem is again reminded of its enormous evil: iniquity (v. 22), the doing of evil (v. 23), lies (v. 25), abomination, and harlotry (v. 27). All of this will cause royal Judah to lose its way and end in humiliation. If this poem is a continuation of vv. 18-19, then it may be an oracle again addressed to the king, who is now, in the drama of the poem, deposed. The threat from the north in v. 20 (cf. 1:13-15, here likely Babylon) caused the king-shepherd to lose the flock over which he rules.[17] As the Babylonian invasion caused the sheep to be without a shepherd (cf. the deportation of the king), so it also caused the shepherd to be without sheep (cf. Isa. 53:6). The "beautiful flock" of Jer. 13:20 suggests the kingdom entrusted to the crown. The same word, "beautiful," is used here for the flock as for

---

17. The metaphor of shepherd-sheep to speak of king and kingdom is pervasive in the OT and is used in the Jeremiah tradition (cf. 23:1,4; 25:34-36; 31:10). It lends itself nicely to the notion of exile, which is a scattering of the sheep. Clearly the shepherd has obligations to the sheep, on which see 23:1 and Ezek. 34. The general use of the metaphor connects the failure of the shepherd and the scattering of the sheep.

the crown in v. 18. Both flock and crown are beautiful and prized. Now both are lost. Indeed, everything is lost.

A tone of grief is appropriate for the poet's scenario. Verse 21 is especially difficult. William L. Holladay proposes to read the first line, "when your lambs are missing," with an allusion to the parable of 2 Sam. 12.[18] But it is difficult to know (even with such an emendation) what that means in this context. The corrected reading seems to suggest that the king has lost what is most precious. That loss will cause pain and hurt like a woman in labor (Jer. 13:21b). The judgment to come "from the north" (v. 20) will, in any case, mean loss of what is precious. The loss will be wrenching. But, says the poet, the king and the people need not ask long what is the cause of the loss and exile. It is Israel's disobedience.

Verse 23 is a well known verse. Along with Ezekiel, Jeremiah takes the dimmest view of Israel's chance of obedience. Jeremiah's assessment of a possibility of change is specifically a comment on wayward Israel and not a more general comment on "human nature." The conclusion the poet reaches is that Israel is as sure to do evil as an Ethiopian has black skin or a leopard has spots. That is, evil has become so habitual for Israel as to be definitional. Israel no longer has any option or choice to exercise.

The result of this massive and irreversible disobedience is presented in three different metaphors. First, the disobedient people is blown like chaff (v. 24). The metaphor echoes Ps. 1:4 and refers to being "scattered." Thus the metaphor is yet another way to speak of exile. Second, the language of land apportionment is used (Jer. 13:25; cf. Mic. 2:1-5; Ps. 16:5-6). Here the language concerns assignment of a specific piece of territory to be held as personal property. The image is used ironically here, for the portion given is now exiled land, that is, land that is ritually unclean and religiously worthless (notice a positive use of the same matter in Jer. 32:1-15). Third, in 13:26 we have again the image of a humiliated slave in exile.

This elusive poem is clear in its main intent. Very simply, disregard of Yahweh leads to exile and the loss of all precious sources of well-being. But that very simple message is presented with a rich variety of suggestive images that run from a woman in labor (v. 21) to a humiliated slave girl (v. 26). The abruptness of the figure of a woman being shamefully exposed is intended to shock by offering a scenario of the queen mother treated like a common prisoner of war

---

18. In a private communication. See also his commentary, *Jeremiah 1*, Hermeneia (Philadelphia: Fortress; London: SCM, 1986).

(cf. Isa. 47:1-3a). The last lines of Jer. 13:27 are a dirge over dying Jerusalem. The city has become a corpse to be grieved. The corpse is ritually unclean, not a fit habitation for Israel, and certainly not a place suitable for Yahweh.[19] The poem is the passionate nullification of all royal claims, for royal history is relativized and negated by the overriding, nullifying claims of the covenant God who will not brook such defiant disregard.

The loss of royal splendor, the humiliation of proud Jerusalem, and the ensuing grief in the face of death are themes that appear in both vv. 15-19 and vv. 20-27. It may be that all of these verses (vv. 15-27) are one extended poem. I have treated them separately because v. 20 seems to make a new rhetorical beginning. The rhetoric of v. 20, however, may function only for dramatic effect inside a single poetic structure. In either case, the intent of the poetry is clear. The once proud royal establishment that focused on the queen mother is now destined for a deep humiliation and displacement. The first one is on the way to becoming last.

NO RAIN ON THE LAND (14:1-22)

This chapter contains standard conventions of lamentation as they are known in the Psalms of Lament. The lament speeches in vv. 1-10 and 17-22 surround the prose section of vv. 11-16. That prose section presents a controversy between Jeremiah and alternative prophetic voices that are judged to be false. The connection between the grief of lamentation and the practice of false prophecy is one to ponder. Indeed, it is a false discernment of historical reality by the other prophetic voices that causes the grief and loss.

14:1-10 This unit is a lament poem with an answer in the form of a divine oracle. Verses 1-6 are the complaint that portrays the trouble. The situation characterized is a severe drought that causes the land to dry up and creation to wane. The crisis is most immediate for the farmers because the animals depend on grass, which has dried up (cf. 1 Kgs. 18:5-6). The severity of the drought is evidenced in that it now touches not only marginal people but even the nobles, who always have the best water supply. The devastation caused by the drought is sounded in a ringing repetition: "no water" (Jer. 14:3),

---

19. On ritual uncleanness, defilement, and divine absence, see Emanuel Feldman, *Biblical and Post-Biblical Defilement and Mourning: Law as Theology* (New York: KTAV, 1977).

"no rain" (v. 4), "no grass" (v. 5), "no herbage" (v. 6). The asses and jackals, the animals accustomed to foraging, are in trouble. The drought causes the social processes of the community to come to a halt, because now nobles, farmers, cows, asses, and jackals all have something in common. Life is under threat for all of them.

After the articulation of complaint, vv. 7-9 express Israel's characteristic petition.[20] In the liturgy imitated in these verses, Israel assumes that the drought is caused by a failure in relation to Yahweh. For that reason, the complaint begins with a confession of guilt (v. 7). According to this prayer, Judah is willing to accept that drought comes from sin. The appeal is therefore made not to Judah's merit, but to the sovereign way of Yahweh. Yahweh is asked to act not because of Judah but for the sake of God's own reputation ("name"; v. 7).[21] The prayer suggests that Israel now waits on Yahweh and Yahweh therefore cannot let Israel down. Yahweh is indeed the source of hope (cf. Lam. 3:21-24).

The series of rhetorical questions in Jer. 14:8-9a are almost accusations, for they suggest that Yahweh has been a stranger, a sojourner, a man confused, a helpless giant. Notice how the prayer, which opens in an act of trust, is also an insinuation that Yahweh has not been fully effective. While there is an admission of guilt, the focus is placed on what is expected of Yahweh. The attempt to prod Yahweh by praise is crowned in v. 9b with a majestic affirmation, "Thou, Yahweh, art in our midst." In 8:19 a question had been posed about Yahweh's presence. Some doubted Yahweh's presence and the evidence was unclear in that text. But here there is no question of Yahweh's presence. Now that presence is affirmed. The prayer is a statement of boldness that addresses a rather demanding expectation to Yahweh. Yahweh's proper role is to be present in saving ways. Yahweh's presence should be a guarantee of rain, or of whatever else it takes in order to have life. This kind of speech to God is a motivation in the lament form. Its function is to require of Yahweh what is expected of Yahweh.

Jeremiah 14:10 is a crushing response of Yahweh to the complaint. Structurally, Israel expects an answer from God to such a

---

20. On complaint and petition, see the comments of Patrick D. Miller, Jr., *Interpreting the Psalms* (Philadelphia: Fortress, 1986), 48-63. His work is heavily influenced by the seminal work of Claus Westermann.

21. See the forceful use of this motif in Ezek. 36:22-32, and my interpretive comments in *Hopeful Imagination: Prophetic Voices in Exile* (Philadelphia: Fortress, 1986), ch. 4.

prayer. Characteristically, the answer is one of gracious attentiveness. The lament-answer form tends to be facile in conventional religion. As we have seen, however, Jeremiah is not shaped by conventional expectations. The poet departs from the predictable, benign response of the liturgy. An answer is given in v. 10, as the liturgy anticipates, but the prophetic answer is not the one normally expected (cf. Amos 5:18-20). The answer is an unwelcome one, reflecting God's abrasive freedom.[22]

The answer is a clearly structured lawsuit. The indictment in Jer. 14:10a is that Israel has departed from Yahweh. Such a waywardness is the opposite of faithfully "following after" in the way (cf. 2:2; 6:16). The sentence is that Yahweh does not accept Israel or its petition (cf. Isa. 1:15). Yahweh is not prepared to save Israel and instead remembers their disobedience. It is a harsh word, congruent with what we have found elsewhere. In the tradition of Jeremiah, there are limits beyond which Yahweh will not be pushed. Yahweh will not be presumed upon. Israel cannot endlessly violate Yahweh and then expect Yahweh's gracious attentiveness (cf. Jer. 7:8-10). The immediate issue of drought is superseded. Now the issue is survival. Yahweh is willing to let this people die, because they have turned away from the torah. Jeremiah must articulate this bold conclusion against the assumption of established royal religion that Yahweh would never reach such a verdict.

14:11-16 These verses interrupt the lament. The harsh prophetic word of v. 10 must have led to consternation in the community. The covenantal situation is so deteriorated that serious conversation between Yahweh and Judah is not possible. Yahweh withdraws from the conversation, for there is nothing more to talk about. The prophet is forbidden by Yahweh to pray any more (v. 11; cf. 7:16; 15:1). Prophetic intercession keeps the conversation open, but now that avenue of conversation is decisively closed. Israel has reached the limit of Yahweh's patience and the edge of God's graciousness. Now there will be only covenant curse: sword, famine, pestilence (14:12). In these verses we are no longer dealing with drought, but with the entire catalogue of death curses. The curses stand in place of intercession

---

22. James A. Wharton, "The Unanswerable Answer: An Interpretation of Job," in *Texts and Testaments,* ed. W. Eugene March (San Antonio: Trinity University Press, 1980), 37-70, has shown that even in the destabilizing answer to Job in Job 38–41 there is nonetheless an answer. The very reality of the answer is decisive for the faith of Israel.

and come only when the conversation is hopelessly terminated. There is here no qualification or mitigating factor, no chance that Yahweh will speak a different life-giving word. It is indeed the end. The end of the conversation means the end of Israel.

Jeremiah is plagued by the presence of other credible prophetic voices in the community who perceived reality very differently (vv. 13-16). (The best known is Hananiah in ch. 28.) This alternative opinion, rooted in royal-Zion theology, knew there was a judgment. This was never denied. The prospect of judgment was acknowledged even in the foundational royal text of 2 Sam. 7:14-16. According to this establishment view of the covenant, however, the judgment of Yahweh had limits. In due time, because of God's abiding love, the punishment will cease and God will value Israel. There are of course old assertions in the tradition to support this theology. Jeremiah, however, insists that Judah's relation to Yahweh has now vitiated those old assertions.

The issue is joined between the harsh, uncompromising character of torah religion and the buoyant assurances of royal-temple theology. Israel debated God's commitment to Jerusalem. Israel wondered if God's rejection of Jerusalem might go as far as total nullification. For the tradition of Jeremiah, there is no protective line drawn by graciousness against such rejection. There is no guarantee against nullification. This hard-nosed prophetic view is hardly admissable in the religion of anyone, least of all in a religion—like that of king and temple—rooted in the marvelous and unconditional promises of Yahweh.

The opponents of Jeremiah gave assurance of God's *shalom*. They directly contradicted the heavy conclusion of Jeremiah. But according to the Bible (which sides unambiguously with Jeremiah; cf. Jer. 23:9-22), those other reassuring voices are judged to be false and unauthorized. Those prophetic figures are themselves under heavy judgment for misrepresenting reality.[23] We are given no objective norm for weighing the merit of these two prophetic inclinations. The canon, however, votes clearly with the harsh line of Jeremiah and against a religion of easy assurances. The tradition of Jeremiah asserts God's freedom, even from God's partner. It is that

---

23. On the difficult question of "false prophets," see James L. Crenshaw, *Prophetic Conflict,* Beiheft zur Zeitschrift für die alttestamentliche Wissenschaft 124 (1971); and the old but still suggestive statement of Sheldon H. Blank, *"Of a Truth the Lord Hath Sent Me"* (Cincinnati: Hebrew Union College Press, 1955).

very freedom that comes to expression in prophetic faith, in a "theology of the Cross," that is, in the most critical strands of Reformation faith.

When we ask how the canon made its decision for the harsher reading, we can suggest that since Jeremiah was vindicated by the events of 587 B.C.E., the judgment is made, in retrospect, on the basis of historical eventuality. But the biblical canon is shaped finally not by historical observation, but by theological judgment and conviction.[24] The canon-making community found in the words and tradition of Jeremiah something they sensed as true, rightly reflecting the character, will, and purpose of Yahweh. To judge Jeremiah to be true is a theological verdict which allows for something wild, dangerous, unfettered, and free in the character of Yahweh. We cannot accept this literature as canonical without allowing something of its verdict about the inclination of God. To assent, then, to the authority of Scripture is to accept this canonical verdict not only about literature, but also about the character of God. Such a paradigm leads us to think against false prophets who imagine that any particular historical arrangement is immune from God's judgment, or that any established mode of life claims God's unqualified support. None are immune from God's heavy expectations—not in ancient Jerusalem, not now among us.

14:17-22   This unit resumes the complaint of vv. 1-10, only now God does not answer. The opening formula of v. 17 is striking. It is as though the prophet is mandated by God to articulate the lament. The pathos of the poet, in this poetry, is presented as the pathos of God. This lament no longer concerns the drought. It speaks much more comprehensively of a more massive threat. It is tightly organized around three word pairs (v. 18), each of which expresses a totality. The threat is total: "sword and famine." It extends everywhere: "field and city." All leadership has failed: "prophet and priest." The whole community is in death. The cause is failed leadership, which means there is no knowledge of God, no capacity for covenant, no

---

24. On the power and resilience of canon, see Frank Kermode, "The Arguments about Canons," in *The Bible and the Narrative Tradition,* ed. Frank McConnell (Oxford and New York: Oxford University Press, 1986), 78-96. In his *Forms of Attention* (Chicago: University of Chicago Press, 1985), Kermode has considered the power of canon in literature more generally, but the matter applies as well to Israel's normative literature.

inclination for obedience, no attention to torah. Such a total failure can only lead to death. That death, brought on by failed covenant, is the basis for the grief of v. 17, a grief so deep that the tears are unending (cf. 9:1). The poet is moved by what he sees in his prophetic imagination that his contemporaries refuse to see. He grieves as one might grieve in anticipation of a nuclear war, though the leaders do not notice the danger. The poet sees invading armies and the devastation they inevitably bring. He sees a terrible wound for this people he loves. He sees the hurt as inevitable, but complacent Jerusalem does not believe it and does not notice.

The devastation is massive and pervasive. In the country the dead are strewn. In the cities corpses result from starvation. In the midst of all the death, the religious leadership continues business as usual. Jeremiah's poetry is not descriptive. It is evocative and anticipatory. The poet wants his community to look ahead and see where its actions and policies are leading. But official truth looks in another direction. It does not believe that present policy will lead to ruin and devastation. The poet goes on characterizing and articulating while the establishment goes on denying and not noticing. The poet is driven nearly to madness by this poignant vision that is refused and resisted. To the poet, the deathly future is obvious and unavoidable. But the powerful are too sure, too dulled. While the poet can envision a future not yet available, dark in its deathliness, the powerful in Jerusalem numbly assume it will always stay the way it is.

Finally, in 14:19a the complaint again addresses God. The poet wishes the other prophets in v. 13 were correct. But he knows better and does not believe them. On behalf of his desperate people, he addresses God. His address is part honest inquiry, part hope, part reprimand. The question is the same as in Lam. 5:22. The question expects that the answer is "Yes, I have utterly rejected," but it waits eagerly—and perhaps desperately—for a better answer. At last the poet can entertain the terrible possibility long enough to think the unthinkable. Yes, God might utterly reject Judah, might loathe Zion, David, temple.

The experiential evidence supports the theological conclusion of rejection. There is no healing, no *shalom*, no good—only terror (Jer. 14:19b). Israel characteristically expected well-being from God. That is what the Jerusalem religious establishment celebrated. But Jeremiah dared to draw a different conclusion. Jeremiah had to entertain the antithesis. He was able to imagine that God could and would finally reject. The power of the poet, however, is that he will not be satisfied with the answer that God has rejected Judah. The urgent, relentless petition continues. In v. 20, as in v. 7, there is an admission of guilt. In v. 21, as in v. 7, there is appeal to God's self-interest. The full force of the appeal now no longer rests on Judah's guilt or on Judah's merit, or even on God's commitment to Judah. The force of the appeal is the enhancement of Yahweh and Yahweh's throne. The poet urges Yahweh to act only to maintain Yahweh's reputation. Finally, hope against rejection depends on God's own character, because all covenantal grounds have been nullified.[25]

The prayer asks God to remember the covenant (v. 21; cf. Exod. 2:24). That is a dangerous prayer, because in Jer. 14:10 it has been asserted that God will remember. What in fact shall God remember? Shall Yahweh remember Israel's sin (as in v. 10) or God's own commitment (as in v. 21)? One memory leads to death. The other memory yields continued life and possibility. This poem gives no hint of which. Perhaps we wait until 31:34 to see what God will remember and what God will forget. In these laments, however, we do not yet know. The prayer for remembrance is unanswered, but no answer may be preferable to an answer like 14:10. Where there is no answer, there is still possibility as God broods over the options. The poet hopes that God will remember, but the poet does not dare prescribe the memory for God.

At last, in v. 22, there is a return to the theme of rain with which the poem began. It is conceded that only Yahweh can cause rain, and only Yahweh can give life. The sweeping assertion of v. 22 echoes v. 9b. It is an assertion to Yahweh of who Yahweh is, an urging that, in order to be the One in whom Israel hopes, Yahweh must give rain. It is doxology, but not disinterested doxology. Verse 22 is an act of praise that summons God to do what God characteristically and faithfully does.[26] The complaint has moved to doxology, but still God does not answer. We are not given God's response to either complaint or doxology. Indeed, in light of Israel's sin (vv. 7,10,20), the doxology has a hollow sound. Israel cannot endlessly disobey and expect all to be set right by an act of praise (see 7:10). The covenant is more serious than that.

This majestic chapter poses the question of the possible termina-

---

25. On hope when all appeals to covenant have failed, see Brueggemann, *Hopeful Imagination*.

26. On praise as a context for serious petition, see Karl Barth, *Church Dogmatics,* III/3 (Edinburgh: T. & T. Clark, 1960), 265-288. Barth asserts that praise is the beginning and end of prayer, but petition is "the factual order and essence of prayer" (267).

tion of Israel. It is clear that if Israel is terminated responsibility belongs to Israel, not to Yahweh. The literature, however, does not arrive at a conclusion about Israel's fate. It only probes and suggests. Indeed, it is in Israel's interest not to press for a conclusion. Better to leave the hoped-for alternative still available. The answer will come soon enough.

THE FOUR DESTROYERS (15:1-4)

This is a highly stylized unit that announces the finality of judgment against Judah. All four verses pursue this general theme, but there are two quite distinct articulations of it. In vv. 1-2 there is a prohibition against intercession (v. 1) and a summary of traditional curses (v. 2). The prohibition precludes further intercession. It does so by naming Moses and Samuel, the great intercessors in Israel. Since their prayers are now rejected, clearly any lesser intercession is futile. The outcome of silenced intercession is the inevitability of curse. There is now nothing to deter or alter Yahweh's resolve. The fourfold summary of curse is much used in Jeremiah and Ezekiel, though the constituent elements vary. The assertion is that the entire arsenal of covenant curses is now to be executed; there is no hope. That same fourfold catalogue takes on a powerful function in apocalyptic literature as "the four horsemen" (cf. Rev. 6:1-8), though the elements are again slightly changed. The language is as harsh and weighty as the tradition of covenant permits.

In vv. 3-4 we have a related but quite distinct articulation of judgment. Again there are four destroyers, but now they are sword/dogs/birds/beasts. In contrast to v. 2, this set of four elements places most weight on the verbs: "slay, tear, devour, destroy." The verbs make this formulation more awesome and terrifying than the conventions of v. 2. In what must be Deuteronomic rhetoric, the ground of judgment is quite specific (v. 4). In 2 Kgs. 21; 23:26; 24:3 Manasseh is reckoned as the cause of destruction. In Jer. 15:4 the cause of destruction is also assigned to Manasseh, who stands as a paradigm for failed covenant. The beloved city stands under death sentence. Nothing, not even the prayers of this passionate poet, can operate against such a condition.

YAHWEH WEARY OF RELENTING (15:5-9)

These verses constitute a severe judgment on Jerusalem, which begins in the rhetoric of a lament. This is a statement placed in the mouth of God, who speaks in the first person. The rhetorical question of v. 5 is a lament. The expected answer to the question is that no one will pity, no one will bemoan, no one will turn aside. No one will care (cf. 30:14; Lam. 1:12). No one any longer cares about the *shalom* ("welfare") of Jerusalem. *Shalom* was the special gift of Yahweh, and now that Yahweh has ceased to care, no one else can be expected to do it. Kings may pretend *shalom* (Jer. 6:14; 8:11), but in fact no one cares, not even those responsible for caring.

One might expect that this passage portrays Yahweh as rejecting Jerusalem. But 15:6 asserts that Judah rejected first. Yahweh has rejected in response to Judah's terminating activity (see the play of mutual rejection of Israel and God in Hos. 4:6). The matter of who originally rejected is an important covenantal issue. The lament tradition of Israel (cf. Jer. 14:19) could imagine that Yahweh initiated the rejection, but Jeremiah is insistent. It is Israel, not Yahweh, who caused the collapse of covenant. The God who stretched out a powerful hand to save (Deut. 26:8) now extends that same hand to destroy (Jer. 15:6).[27] What began as Exodus is now terminated in an anti-Exodus gesture. The last detached line of v. 6 suggests that Yahweh's patience has come to an end. Yahweh had again and again "relented" (*naham*; cf. 18:8,10; Amos 7:3,6; Jon. 4:2) of a proposed punishment. Yahweh kept changing an announced, justified intention to destroy and making concessions to Judah. Every such change costs God. Yahweh kept delaying the judgment, but now Yahweh is exhausted with such delays and will delay no longer (cf. Isa. 1:14; 43:24). The poem thus articulates not only the current mood of God, but reflects on the long history of frustration that has created this decision of God to reject. The poet builds the case that the rejection which ends in exile and destruction is because of Judah's exhausting conduct.

In Jer. 15:7-9 the series of judgments Yahweh now undertakes is reminiscent of the recital of Amos 4:6-11. In the recital of Amos, Yahweh implements curses in the hope that there would be a change on Judah's part. But the desperate hope of Amos is massively dissapointed: "yet, you did not return." The series in Jeremiah shows Yahweh's strenuous efforts to evoke repentance:

---

27. On the "hand of Yahweh" as a means of rescue and wrath, see Patrick D. Miller, Jr., and J. J. M. Roberts, *The Hand of the Lord* (Baltimore: Johns Hopkins University Press, 1977).

I have winnowed.
I have bereaved.
I have destroyed.
I have made widows.
I have brought destruction.

These past acts are not presented as judgments, but as efforts to save. But God's harsh effort to save Israel did not catch on, "they did not turn" (Jer. 15:7). At the end of v. 9, after a series of verbs of completed action, the last verb looks ahead: "And the rest of them I will give to the sword before their enemies." After each harsh action there had always been a remnant. Now the remnant is also claimed for destruction, so that Jerusalem is fully nullified. Punishment as chastisement has now become punishment as termination. The God of Jerusalem is a God of enormous patience. But now that patience is spent. God is exhausted and will try no more. A people like Israel surely must die at the hand of a God like Yahweh. This God will be taken with singular seriousness. Israel will not practice such seriousness. An end must come.

WHY WAS I BORN? (15:10-14)

This prose unit contains two distinct elements. Verses 10-12 seem to be a reflective lament by the prophet. He reflects that his life is overwhelmingly conflicted, that he is assaulted and maligned on every side. His cry of trouble/woe/misery is a complaint addressed even to his mother, as though he craves intimacy and solace. This bitter statement of self-regard is echoed in 20:14-18, which in turn is reflected in Job 3. The speaker finds himself in quarrels or in litigation on every front, nearly to despair.[28] Jeremiah 15:10b-11 declares that such trouble is indeed unwarranted. First, negatively, Jeremiah is innocent of any wrongdoing, and no valid charge can be brought against him. He has not engaged in the kinds of dealing that ought to evoke such hostility. He has not exploited, abused, or taken advantage of anyone (cf. a like statement of self-vindication in 1 Sam. 12:3-5 and, more generally, Job 31). Indeed, he has not practiced the social exploitation of which he accuses others. His words distin-

---

28. The juridical cast of the argument is easily missed with the conventional rendering "strife." Hebrew *rib* might better be rendered as "litigation." Jeremiah is a man in formal dispute, a fact made evident both in the trial of ch. 26 and in the confrontation of ch. 36.

guish him from his contemporaries, who have violated covenant and now abuse him. Second, positively, he has done something good that matters. He has faithfully executed his ministry of intercession. He has been such an intense advocate of troubled Judah against Yahweh that Yahweh has had to tell him to desist. This statement of self-justification is an assertion that those who afflict him do not know what an advocate he has been. He is a faithful advocate but is treated as though he were an adversary.

The complaint of Jeremiah is a reflection of the costliness of such a ministry of candor and discernment.[29] Perhaps the community has preserved the statement of this text as it became aware that it is Jeremiah's threatening word of Yahweh that evokes the conflict. Jeremiah's many adversaries take issue precisely with his word of threat. The message is so hard that the messenger is at risk. When the message is so formidable, it is easier to focus on the messenger. Such risk is definitional for any who carry the word against established reality.

In Jer. 15:12, however, the speaker seems to recognize that even the effectiveness of his vocation as an intercessor with God is finished and must be given up. The die is cast. God has ordained the assault from the north. In 1:18-19 Jeremiah is made iron and bronze to withstand assault. Now, however, it is the invading army (presumably Babylon) that is the real bronze and iron. Yahweh's purpose is so adamant that none can stop it, not even powerful intercession. No more than Hananiah can break the yoke of exile (28:2) can Jeremiah break Yahweh's relentless purpose. Judah is unable to see that the real danger is Yahweh's relentlessness, not Jeremiah's persistence. Even the prophetic insistence of Jeremiah, which itself is formidable enough, finally must submit to God's resolve. That resolve is more serious, more devastating, more sure than any word of Jeremiah.

One cannot be certain that 15:13-14 is a divine answer to this complaint, but it might be. This oracle is not an oracle of comfort for Jeremiah, who has complained of his trouble. Rather, it is yet another decree of judgment against Judah. All that Judah treasures (cf. 2 Kgs. 24:13-17; Isa. 39:5-7) is now given to Babylon by Yahweh, and no amount of prophetic intercession can stop it. The poet knows about the relentlessness of the historical process over which Yahweh presides. The subject changes from his personal vocation (Jer. 15:10-12) to the destiny of Israel. Finally what counts is

---

29. On candor as a mark of the ministry of Jeremiah, see Brueggemann, *Hopeful Imagination,* ch. 1.

not the prophet, but the sin of Judah and the response of Yahweh. The prophet is quite incidental to the real crisis now to be faced.

The juxtaposition of vv. 10-12 and vv. 13-14 may be evoked by the dual mention of land. In v. 10 the prophet is in conflict with "the whole land." In v. 13 there is spoil taken "throughout all your territory," and now in v. 14 there is exile to another land, one "which you do not know." The sequence thus is a move from the land of contention to the land of exile, in which contention is futile. The displacement is yet another way of seeing God's action against Judah, and seeing that Jeremiah's vocation is about this unthinkable displacement. The role of Jeremiah is lost in the overriding decision of Yahweh against Jerusalem, Judah, and the land. There is not a hint of vindication or comfort for the prophet. It is no wonder that the poet's cry of pain which is disregarded is now followed by another quite personal complaint addressed to God (vv. 15-21).[30]

CONDITIONAL ASSURANCE (15:15-21)

This poetic unit continues the complaint-protest we have found in 11:18-23 and 12:1-6. As there, this poem reflects the shaping influence of the Psalms of Lament in the Psalter. It is likely that the lament form has been appropriated here to make a more personal and specific statement concerning Jeremiah's prophetic vocation as he is placed between the obduracy of Israel and the harsh sovereignty of Yahweh.

The initial words, "thou knowest," are abrupt. As the beginning of the poem, this is a remarkable way of relating to Yahweh. The opening words may be an act of trust and submission to the One from whom no secret can be hidden. But they may also be words of reproach to Yahweh, who knows and yet does nothing on behalf of the one who suffers innocently.

The lament contains three elements: the petition (v. 15b), a statement of innocence and fidelity as a motivation for God (vv. 15c-17), and a statement of complaint (v. 18). The petition consists in four imperative verbs: "remember," "visit," "take vengeance," "do not seize" (RSV "take away"). The imperatives suggest not only a state-

---

30. The juxtaposition of personal pain and public destiny is delicate and complicated. One must not on the one hand excessively focus on the person of Jeremiah; but on the other hand, one must not ignore the lively presence of such a person in the text. Polk, *The Prophetic Persona,* has offered a carefully nuanced treatment of the problem.

ment of strong passion, but also an established relationship that permits bold and candid speech. The one who prays is in a position to make heavy demands on Yahweh, to insist that Yahweh remember and act. This petition is not the beginning of the relation. It rests on promises and previous interactions. The poet expects Yahweh to make good on those previous commitments. The four imperatives are curious because they ask God to be patient and not to "seize" the poet. This abrupt verb "seize" *(lqh)* is used in Amos to describe the prophetic call (Amos 7:15), and in Gen. 5:24 is used with reference to God's seizure of Enoch. Here the term refers to death. The petitioner therefore prays not to have his life terminated. He obviously knows his life to be in great jeopardy.

In Jer.15:15c-17 the poem gives motivations why God should heed the petition. The crisis in which the prophet finds himself is a result of his faith, his unswerving attachment to Yahweh: "for thy sake . . . I am called by thy name." The prophet has not resisted the prophetic mandate, but has delighted in the word entrusted to him by Yahweh. Verse 17 becomes even more specific. Because of his call, he is socially isolated and did not join in the usual social relationships. The statement of innocence is an assertion that the prophetic mandate has been the overriding reality of his life. He has not flinched from it or compromised in any way. Such a claim can rightly expect a positive response from Yahweh. The poet asks only for that to which he is entitled as a faithful partner and obedient servant.

The third element in the prayer (vv. 17c-18) is an accusation against Yahweh. The human sources of conflict (i.e., priests, kings, men of Anathoth) are not the cause of Jeremiah's situation. Yahweh is singled out as the cause of the trouble. The double use of "thou" in this unit places the poetic focus on Yahweh. The rhetoric of v. 18 introduces a new metaphor—sickness and incurable wound.[31] It is useless to speculate on the details of the illness. The sickness metaphor may be only a convention. The oddity for the poet is that sickness follows sin, but he has not sinned. He has in every regard been a faithful servant of Yahweh. For that reason, v. 18b contains an accusation that Yahweh is unreliable and does not honor pledges of solidarity and protection.[32] The imagery shifts from illness to a river

---

31. On the metaphor of "wound" in Jeremiah, see James Muilenburg, "The Terminology of Adversity in Jeremiah," in *Translating & Understanding the Old Testament,* ed. Harry Thomas Frank and William L. Reed (Nashville: Abingdon, 1970), 42-63.

32. This statement of the problem anticipates the poem of Job. In both

or wadi. The image is of a wadi that dries up in times of drought, so that trees planted by it have no chance of life (against 17:8). Yahweh is marked by the indignant poet as an unreliable, untrustworthy stream that will not sustain life (contrast 2:13). The streams of living water have failed.

Jeremiah has been mandated with a burdensome word to his contemporaries. His word from Yahweh is harsh when contrasted with the claims of established religion or the word from other contemporary prophets. That he has evoked hostility is not surprising. What is surprising and disconcerting is that the One who sent him does not stand by him. The prophet turns out to be more faithful than the God who sent him.[33] Jeremiah is utterly alone in the conflict over fated Jerusalem. The isolation from his human companions (15:17) could be overcome by communion with God, but his isolation extends beyond earth to heaven.[34] God does not stand by. God is not with him as was promised (1:8,19).

On two counts we expect an answer from God. First, the lament form characteristically evokes an assuring answer from God.[35] Second, this poignant prayer, if it does not evoke an assurance, should at least provoke God enough to make a self-defense. The Job-like assault of 15:15-18 asks something from God that is congruent with God's promise.

In vv. 19-21 there is an answer from God, but hardly the one anticipated. The conventional answer of the lament form is an assurance of God's presence, power, and compassion. Here, however, the answer is not an assurance, but a condition. The first part of Yahweh's response (v. 19) is a play on the word "turn," which occurs four times:

Jeremiah and Job the problem of theodicy is raised because there is "punishment" for which there is no identifiable sin.

33. In this regard Jeremiah is like Moses, for in the exchanges of Exod. 32–33 it is clear that Moses will stand by Israel after Yahweh is prepared to abandon. William L. Holladay, "The Background of Jeremiah's Self-understanding: Moses, Samuel, and Psalm 22," *Journal of Biblical Literature 83* (1964): 153-164; and "Jeremiah and Moses: Further Observations," *Journal of Biblical Literature* 85 (1966): 17-27, has observed the commonality of the dramatic presentation of Moses and Jeremiah.

34. In Ps. 88:8,18 God is directly responsible for the shunning.

35. Claus Westermann, *The Praise of God in the Psalms* (Richmond: John Knox, 1965), has shown this characteristic form. It is precisely the dramatic power of this characteristic that makes the harsh response of Yahweh to Jeremiah so shattering and noteworthy. This poetic exchange violates the form in which Israel had learned to trust.

If you will *return,* I will *return* you . . .
they will *turn* to you, but you shall not *turn* to them.
(author's translation)

Jeremiah's interactions with Yahweh are not easy and reassuring. They are endlessly demanding so that even the form of "divine assurance" is utilized for the demand of Yahweh. What Jeremiah experiences of Yahweh is exactly how Judah must face Yahweh. The expected assurance for Judah is also rigorous demand.

This carefully constructed statement in v. 19 uses the verb *shub* four times, all of them calling for a reorientation in faithful covenant. The first two uses concern Jeremiah's relation to Yahweh. The turn of Jeremiah is the condition of Yahweh acting on his behalf as a faithful covenant LORD. No specifics are given, but the implication is that Jeremiah has not yet met Yahweh's rigorous expectation. Jeremiah must find ways to be yet more faithful. When Jeremiah does, Yahweh will act in new ways and sustain him. The second pair of uses of the same verb concerns Jeremiah and his human opponents. It is promised that when Jeremiah has turned in new fidelity to Yahweh, Jeremiah's opponents will then yield to him and not he to them. Jeremiah is required to be faithful. Everything depends on Jeremiah's new obedience. When he is faithful, his relation to God and to his fellows will change. God will return him, that is, restore him. His fellows will submit to him.

The continuation of God's promise in vv. 20-21 is more conventional, less demanding, and not stated conditionally. It echoes the initial promise of 1:17-19. God's solidarity with the prophet and readiness to rescue are precisely what is hoped for and not yet experienced. In 15:20-21 Yahweh speaks as the faithful God Israel has always trusted and found trustworthy. But even these assurances are finally governed by the "if" of v. 19. Everything depends on Jeremiah's reliance on and adherence to Yahweh. Everything depends on this for Jeremiah. Everything depends on the same reliance and adherence for Jerusalem. There are no alternatives.

This complaint-response poem can be read at two levels. On one level, it is the prayer of a faithful person in need of a faithful response from God. God does indeed attend to the faithful. Jeremiah's prayer operates on that claim and premise. To that extent, the prayer is simply another use of Israel's patterned speech of complaint, submission, and trust.

The tradition of Jeremiah, however, requires a second level of reading. The poet who protests and yearns is not simply a faithful person. He is a prophet with special words, peculiar mandates, and heavy risks. The issue, then, is not simply God's fidelity toward this one man, but the relation between the sender of a word and the carrier of that word. The word sent by Yahweh and carried by Jeremiah is that Jerusalem must die. It is a burdensome word, not to be spoken lightly. Jeremiah has the sense that he is "out there" alone, abandoned by the God whose word he speaks. The question of the prayer is, will God stand by the carrier of the message? Is the message important enough to God to sustain the messenger? If not, then the message is not to be taken seriously. The seriousness of the message is measured by the credibility of the sender.

Will the sender sustain the carrier of the message? The answer is given in the response of God. The basic assurance is "I am with you." The exposition of that premise is given in four powerful verbs: "save" *(yasha')*, "deliver" *(natsal)*, "deliver" *(natsal)*, and "redeem" *(padah)*. It is indeed a prayer answered. God is trustworthy and stands by the messenger. But the answer is conditional and given only after an enormous price has been assessed from the person of the prophet. That price is integral to the work of the prophet. Because the word is so scandalous, the carrier of the word is inevitably at risk.

A third dimension of reading is also possible. Erhard S. Gerstenberger has suggested that what was originally a personal prayer of the prophet has been processed so that now it becomes a word of assurance to the community after the destruction.[36] Specifically, vv. 19-21 (which parallel 4:1-2) is an assurance given to the community, looking to the repentance and restoration of the community. Thus the prayers of the prophet are taken up into the canonical memory of Israel because the isolation and alienation of the prophet bespeak the status of exilic Israel. The assurances of God are offered to the prophet as a pained person. But they are also offered to the community. The conversation Jeremiah has with Yahweh comes to be a conversation for the entire community. What Jeremiah knows in his prophetic vocation, Israel comes to know in its exile, where it also senses abandonment. As Jeremiah can address God abrasively, so can Israel in exile. As Jeremiah is pressed to more serious obedience by Yahweh, so is Israel in exile. As Jeremiah receives a promise of God's solidarity in trouble, so does Israel in

---

36. Erhard S. Gerstenberger, "Jeremiah's Complaints: Observations on Jer 15:10-21," *Journal of Biblical Literature* 82 (1963): 393-408.

exile. In exile, Israel found Jeremiah's prayer and experience of God to be paradigmatic for its own destiny with God as a people of troubled faith.

YOU SHALL NOT MARRY (16:1-21)

This chapter consists in distinct elements that likely existed independently. They have, however, been brought together in a coherent statement of judgment (vv. 1-13) and hope (vv. 14-21).

16:1-13   The prose passage of vv. 1-9 announces no new themes, but it solemnly and harshly reiterates the unqualified judgment that is to come. In v. 2 the prophet is prohibited from having sons and daughters. The prohibition anticipates the mood of those who so fear nuclear holocaust in our time that they do not want to have any children who might be subjected to the terror. But characteristically, the text does not linger over the personal situation of Jeremiah. This is not simply a prohibition for the prophet, but it concerns all children born in Judah who are subject to the curses that will not be turned away (vv. 3-4). Notice that in these verses we have a triadic emphasis, "this place, this place, this land," in anticipation of judgment and exile. The land itself, along with the people, is under death sentence. The curses of v. 4 are a combination of those listed in 15:2 and 3. By focusing the curses on the children, the prophet attempts to articulate the most extreme case of judgment and pathos. It is an incredibly harsh announcement, reflecting the fact that Judah has come to the end of the road. The entire future is now under assault. In 29:6 the new beginning will concern sons and daughters. But not here. Here there is only an ending.

The second paragraph is structurally parallel to the first. In 16:5, as in v. 2, the prophet is given a personal prohibition which is then interpreted more generally in the verses that follow. In this second personal prohibition of v. 5, the prophet is precluded from acknowledging the death of the community or from participating in the grief. The grief of the end is massive; it is escalated even more by this prohibition against active expression of the grief.

The theological background for the prohibition is given in v. 5b. Yahweh has taken away his "peace" *(shalom)*, his "steadfast love" *(hesed)*, his "mercy" *(rahamim)*. The covenant relation now is over. This triad of words is among the most freighted in the covenantal speech of Israel. The first, *shalom,* may be peculiarly linked to the tradition of Jerusalem.[37] The other two are rooted in the old Mosaic-prophetic tradition reflective of God's deep commitment and powerful pathos.[38] The most fundamental commitments of Yahweh are now exhausted and terminated by recalcitrant Judah. The harshness of this announcement is surely a surprise in biblical faith and must have been a staggering surprise when first spoken. It has been a ready assumption (in ancient Jerusalem and among us) that God's covenant commitment is abiding. Indeed, in 2 Sam. 7:14-15 Yahweh has made an oath never to remove *hesed*. But Yahweh could not have foreseen the unthinkable situation of infidelity that caused all old promises to be under review. In the tradition of covenant, even Yahweh's gracious inclination depends finally on some appropriate response. Having waited so long for a response that never came, Yahweh finally retracts this initial, gracious commitment.

Where there is complete absence of fidelity on God's part, there is death. Israel cannot live apart from God's fidelity. No public grieving, no consolation, no rituals are permitted (vv. 6-7). No acts of consolation are permitted that might mitigate the starkness of the abrupt judgment. Yet not only acts of death are prohibited. The text takes an odd turn in v. 8. The subject of the text has been mourning (vv. 6-7). Now, as though to establish a rhetorical polarity, it is the house of feasting, of eating and drinking, that is prohibited. Verse 9 builds upon the changed future of v. 8. There is to be a cessation of all celebrative life, all new social beginnings. Taken together, "house of mourning" and "house of feasting" mean that all social interaction is now terminated. History stops. Community is over. There is no longer any public life permitted.

Clearly such a massive judgment is difficult for us to fathom theologically. In its first articulation, it is an attempt to say to the contemporaries of Jeremiah how drastic the situation is. God's sustaining presence is now forfeited and public life must experience and embody that forfeiture. As a text available for our subsequent use, this double prohibition is an invitation to ponder God's free sovereignty

---

37. See Norman W. Porteous, "Jerusalem-Zion: The Growth of a Symbol," in *Verbannung und Heimkehr,* ed. Arnulf Kuschke (Tübingen: J. C. B. Mohr [Paul Siebeck], 1961), 235-252.

38. On *hesed,* see Katherine Doob Sakenfeld, *The Meaning of Hesed in the Hebrew Bible,* Harvard Semitic Monograph 17 (Missoula, Mont.: Scholars Press, 1978); and *Faithfulness in Action* (Philadelphia: Fortress, 1985). On *raham,* see Phyllis Trible, *God and the Rhetoric of Sexuality,* Overtures to Biblical Theology 2 (Philadelphia: Fortress, 1978), ch. 2.

that will not be mocked or taken for granted. The other side of that sovereign reality is the recognition that all social, economic, and political systems are provisional and in jeopardy. Both social grief and public celebration are arrangements that endure only by God's gracious leave. If one reads from v. 5 directly to v. 9, one sees that celebrative social life depends on God's steadfast love and mercy. When those gifts of God are withdrawn, more than fellowship with God ends. Life with neighbor is also voided. Social possibilities become as "formless and void" as the darkness of primordial chaos (cf. 4:23-26). The poet moves back and forth between scenarios of cosmic chaos and social dysfunction as he strains for adequate words to express the ending now at hand.

Jeremiah 16:10-13 is a didactic reflection on the painful prohibitions of vv. 2 (3-4) and 5 (6-9). It is another opportunity to state the reasons for the judgment under which Jerusalem stands. Perhaps the threefold inquiry of v. 10 is ironic. The threefold "why, what, what" surely did not need an answer, because the reasons are obvious.[39] Jeremiah's contemporaries are so detached from the claims of Yahweh, however, that they are unable to recognize the realities that the prophet regards as perfectly obvious.

Verses 11-13 answer the inquiry of v. 10, articulating that which Israel should already know. The response is a clear lawsuit speech with indictment (vv. 11-12) and sentence (v. 13). The statement moves dramatically from "because" in v. 11 to "therefore" in v. 13. The reason for the judgment is stated in two stages. First, "your fathers" have forsaken (*'azab*) Yahweh (stated twice) and violated torah. Second, the present generation is worse. The present generation has not listened. The language of indictment is clearly an echo of Deuteronomic theology. The ultimate sins are autonomy and self-sufficiency, which are evidenced in not listening.

The sentence is exile, expulsion, banishment. The final fate is to trust in false gods who cannot save (cf. Deut. 32:37-38). The service of false gods is not only a sin chosen by Israel, but a fate decreed by Yahweh.[40] Judah is to be "out of this land." Yahweh's people are to be in another land, away from all life supports, even away from Yahweh.

---

39. The threefold interrogative is even more powerful in Hebrew, for all three interrogative pronouns are *meh*, thus "why, why, why?"

40. "False gods" as both sin and as punishment is a striking case of the correlation of sin and punishment, on which see Patrick D. Miller, Jr., *Sin and Judgment in the Prophets*, SBL Monograph 27 (Chico, Calif.: Scholars Press, 1982).

The tradition of Jeremiah cannot consistently make up its mind if the sentence is finally death or exile.[41] They are dramatically the same, however, for such radical displacement is tantamount to death. The language of lawsuit is so familiar to us that we miss its bold intellectual claim about the historical process. It is urged that historical, public displacement is not to be understood according to sociopolitical necessities, but according to the sovereign requirements of Yahweh. "Not listening" leads to "hurling." Breaking covenant ends in exile. Judah has chosen for itself to receive "no favor" from Yahweh, who wants to give "favor." This last word of the paragraph falls heavily and decisively: "No graciousness."

16:14-15   The decisive ending of v. 13 makes the abruptness of vv. 14-15 all the more stunning. These verses form a complete contrast to the preceding judgment, for they announce restoration of the people of Israel to "their own land." Critical opinion is unanimous that these verses are a late voice in the tradition. They reflect a later generation of exilic hope, for such hope was not available until after 587 B.C.E. These words may indeed reflect 2 Isaiah and the moment of homecoming evoked by that poetry.

That critical judgment seems secure. However, we should approach the text as it stands and not dissolve the deliberate juxtaposition of Jer. 16:10-13 and vv. 14-15. Both the statement of harsh judgment and of grand homecoming are a part of the canonical text. Both bear witness to God's resolve. Neither cancels the other. Yahweh has two actions to take toward his people (cf. 31:27-28). The first action of Yahweh is displacement. That is not lessened by 16:14-15. Amazingly, however, the second action of homecoming is not precluded by the first act of displacement. There is a homecoming, but dramatically as well as experientially, it does not nullify the pain, shame, and grief of exile that is burdensome and real.

The ground for this second move of Yahweh is found in the Exodus tradition. The generation of the Exodus was also a community of displaced slaves, hopelessly subservient to a ruthless empire that seemed ordained to perpetuity. The Exodus happened because of Yahweh's capacity to invert the historical process and create a new

---

41. The tradition cannot decide which is the actual danger. Thus in v. 3 there is death in the land, but in v. 13 the danger is exile. Seitz, "Theology in Conflict," has suggested that this tension reflects not simply editorial activity, but a conflict in interpretation.

historical possibility that gives life to the marginal. Israel characteristically appeals to the Exodus memories in order to bear witness to the sovereign graciousness of Yahweh against all forms of imperial hopelessness and fatedness. Israel always returns to the Exodus for a "fix" on reality. Jeremiah 16:14-15 does more than return to the Exodus memory, however. This text of new historical possibility dares to say that the Exodus memory will now be superseded because Yahweh is about to outdo that miraculous act by an even greater miracle. This new act bursts out beyond Israel's best memory of liberation. This generation, right before our eyes, now becomes the participant in this new focus of all historical possibility.

The Exodus had been the point of reference from which Israel interpreted all its experiences. Now, in the present moment, there is a new decisive event to which all experience is to be referred. Every other experience is to be understood in terms of this remarkable action of God. Such a claim cannot be made without appeal to the tradition. But the appeal to tradition in these verses is made only to supersede that very tradition. The claim of the tradition is shattered by the new act (cf. 23:7-8; Isa. 43:18-19).[42] There is judgment and there is new possibility. There is exile and there is homecoming. There is death and there is resurrection. Both moves are characteristic of this God. Both moves are definitional for this faith, this people, this God. There is historical shattering, wrought because of infidelity. There is also historical creating in sovereign graciousness. Both belong in tension to Yahweh's character and are the central reality of Israel's life. These two verses do not nullify the "hurling out" of Jer. 16:13, but do assert that after the hurling comes the homecoming.

16:16-18 This unusual statement is difficult to interpret for two reasons. First, it is not clear who it is that is being hunted, fished, punished, and judged. The actual indictment of v. 18 could indeed apply to Judah, which is guilty of inequity, sin, pollution, and abomination. This unit is placed between vv. 14-15 and vv. 19-20. In that context the reference may be to the nations who are to be judged (cf. vv. 19-20), as the countertheme of Israel's rescue (vv. 14-15). But it is more plausible to conclude that these verses refer back to vv. 10-

---

42. A new interpretation of "old things" and "new things" in Isaiah is offered by Ronald E. Clements, "The Unity of the Book of Isaiah," *Interpretation* 36 (1982): 117-129; but I do not believe it touches this contrast in the text of Jeremiah between the salvific tradition and the new act of rescue that is anticipated.

13 and refer to Judah. In that case, these verses assert the coming devastation of Judah from which none can escape.

Another difficult interpretive issue is that the figures of fisher and hunter are not clear. The terms "fishers" and "hunters" refer to agents who will seek out those who are to be judged. Those agents will be so efficient and thorough that none will escape. Such images appear to be metaphors that run toward apocalyptic perspectives. The judgment on the nations here is not unlike the protoapocalyptic images in 25:15-29. While the language is difficult and the references obscure, the verses clearly anticipate the judgment of Yahweh from which none is exempt.

The unit of vv. 16-18 falls into two parts. In vv. 16-17a Yahweh acts through these mysterious agents from whom no one can hide (cf. Amos 9:2-4; Ps. 139:7-12). The second part of the unit (Jer. 16:17b-18) contains more conventional language in which Yahweh acts directly in response to "iniquity." "My inheritance" (i.e., Yahweh's land) is polluted by foreigners—invading armies who bring their religious images and practices with them, thereby making the land ritually unclean. The punishment is not specified, but the penalty is "double," the same language used in Isa. 40:2 against Israel. Judah is to be judged massively by Yahweh for its idolatry and abomination. The passage is elusive in its intent because the metaphors are remarkably open and lacking in specificity. The comprehensiveness of judgment, however, is abundantly clear.

16:19-21   This unit begins in a statement of trust. Such an initial statement of trust characteristically provides a basis for a prayer of complaint. Only here the statement of trust is not followed by a complaint. It is, rather, an anticipation of the time in the future when the nations will submit to Yahweh. The poem thus expresses the anticipation that, in due time, the nations will recognize and admit their failure and the inadequacy of their gods. This will be expressed as a confession of sin on the part of the nations, who will finally embrace Yahweh as the true God. The nations will confess that their gods are "false" (*sheqer;* RSV "lies") and "worthless" *(hebel),* that their gods are really "no gods." The affirmation that Yahweh is "strength," "stronghold," and "refuge" contrasts with the failure of the gods who are not reliable and cannot save. A covenantal prayer of trust is used for a polemic against false religion. This is a stunning admission, because it is tantamount to conceding the illegitimacy of the imperial political enterprise as well. The inverse point is made in v. 21. As the idols are seen to be false and worthless, so the true God,

Yahweh, is now shown to be powerful and mighty. The nations will concede Yahweh's power and might as they become obedient to Yahweh's kingdom.

Chapter 16, as it now stands, seems to be composed of a variety of fragments. As the chapter is now ordered, it is organized into two parts, the two parts we expect in canonical shaping. Verses 1-13 are a statement of judgment, in which God will remove all marks of covenant concern (v. 5). Verses 14-21 consist in three quite distinct elements, but they form a secondary unit of hope and new possibility. The three original units, respectively, affirm that:

(1) Israel will come home (vv. 14-15),
(2) the nations will be judged (vv. 16-18),
(3) the nations will turn to Yahweh (vv. 19-21).

All three reflect a situation of "planting and building," which presumes the judgment has gone before and has been completed. The important affirmation is that Israel's history is now alive in a new way. That new life depends on the assertion of Yahweh's power and might, and the knowledge of Yahweh as the LORD of covenant (v. 21). Where God is known, history can begin again, even after massive judgment. These verses concern the new historical beginning made possible by Yahweh's sovereign resolve.

JUDAH'S SIN ENGRAVED (17:1-4)

This passage offers one more intense and solemn lawsuit speech against Judah. The indictment (vv. 1-3a) establishes the unbearable, undeniable guilt of Judah. The substance of the sin, expressed in quite stereotypical language, is worship of other gods—violation of the main claim of the torah. No details are given, for they are already known. Judah's idolatry has been adequately explicated elsewhere. The "bill of indictment" (i.e., the record of guilt) is permanently engraved so that it is irreversible, not to be changed, denied, or forgotten. It is written in the ultimate places of memory, on the heart and on the altar. This record on the heart is the very antithesis of the torah on the heart (31:33). Something will be written on the heart, either sin or torah. The mention of the altar in 17:1 may anticipate the more polemical mention of altar in v. 2, but here it is a public place of record.

The sentence of vv. 3b-4 consists of two elements. First, an unnamed enemy will seize the wealth and treasure of Judah (cf. 2 Kgs. 20:12-15). This was indeed accomplished by the Babylonians, who seized the temple and the related objects which constituted public wealth (cf. Jer. 52:17-23).[43] Second, the announcement is again made of loss of heritage and subservience in a foreign land (cf. 16:13). Violation of the torah (in this case, worship of other gods) results in historic displacement. The structure of prophetic thought (which Klaus Koch terms "metahistory")[44] refuses to relinquish either theological claim or historical eventuality. Prophetic faith insists that the two are held together in Yahweh's sovereignty and at enormous cost to the people of Yahweh.

The separation of theological claim and historical eventuality is a perennial temptation and even a commonplace among us, with one or the other being prized to the neglect of the other. In this text the theological claim concerns *disobedience* of Yahweh. The historical eventuality concerns *destruction* by Babylon. The claim of Jeremiah is that the theological reality of *disobedience* and the historical actuality of *destruction* can only be understood together. Disobedience without an historical settlement is a misunderstanding of Yahweh's sovereignty. To explain destruction apart from disobedience is equally a wrong perception of Yahweh's rule. They belong together. To be sure, the prophetic, poetic tradition is aware that God's rule is not a mechanical management by fiat, nor a despotic absolutism. The prophets do not entertain such a naive supernaturalism. They know there is slippage, anguish, ambiguity, and human initiative. But the poetry is singleminded in witnessing to God's resilient presence in all such ambiguity. This insistence is not naive, simpleminded, or innocent, but it is indeed a relentless insistence. An untenable separation is made by "spiritualists" who choose theological claim over historical eventuality, or by "secularists" who choose historical eventuality and shrink from theological claim. Such a separation in either direction completely misunderstands the intent of biblical faith. Prophetic thought permits no such choices, no escape from the overriding tension of this linkage. *Disobedience ends in displacement.* A split between historical eventuality and theological claim may separate disobedience from displacement, but the prophets countenance no such illusion.

---

43. See Peter R. Ackroyd, "The Temple Vessels—A Continuity Theme," *Supplements to Vetus Testamentum* 23 (1972): 166-181; and "An Interpretation of the Babylonian Exile: A Study of 2 Kings 20, Isaiah 38–39," *Scottish Journal of Theology* 27 (1974): 329-352.

44. Klaus Koch, *The Prophets,* vol. 1: *The Assyrian Period* (Philadelphia: Fortress; London: SCM, 1983), 70, 144-156.

LIKE A TREE PLANTED BY WATER (17:5-13)

This is one of the more unusual sections of the tradition of Jeremiah. It contains four distinct elements. The first three appear to be sapiential sayings, while the fourth (vv. 12-13) is a doxology of judgment containing echoes of other Jeremiah texts. The unit no doubt has a complicated editorial history, but we have no access to that process.

17:5-8   These verses are a sapiential instruction which articulates "the two ways" of life and death. The language has close parallels to Ps. 1, but the metaphors are more consistently developed and in tighter parallel here. Moreover, the invitation and threat in this context are drawn close to the crisis of Judah in Jeremiah's time. The form is conventional, with a single subject, "the man." The condemned man is the one who trusts in human power, whether military, economic, technological, or whatever (cf. Isa. 31:3). "Trust in man" may mean to trust human wisdom or human armaments, as the kings of Judah were wont to do. Both wisdom and armaments are ways in which a monarchy sustains itself apart from the requirements of covenant. The contrast to such might and power is found in Yahweh, who practices justice and authorizes covenantal relations (cf. Jer. 9:23-24; cf. 16:21). A person (or a community) who trusts falsely is surely headed toward death, expressed in the metaphor of a dried-up shrub. John Calvin suggests that this particular shrub is not simply dead but gives the "appearance of life," even though the root system is gone.[45] Calvin's interpretation suggests that while Jeremiah saw death, his contemporary situation still had "the appearance of life." It is the stark contrast between what is and what appears to be that evokes such pathos in the poet.

The poem contrasts such a person (or community) with one who trusts in Yahweh and who stays free of false reliance on either human power or human wisdom. The alternative choices offered in this metaphor are very much like the preaching of Isaiah, who appealed to kings to trust in Yahweh and not in foreign agents (Isa. 31:1-3; cf. 36:4-10,13-20). The one who trusts only in Yahweh is destined for life, like a green tree with plenty of water. A destiny of either life or death is determined by the object of one's trust. False trust has important policy implications in Jeremiah's time, as in our own. This summons to singular faith is not a mere religious proposal, but re-

---

45. John Calvin, *Commentaries on the Book of the Prophet Jeremiah and the Lamentations,* vol. 1 (repr. Grand Rapids: Baker, 1979), 351-352.

quires policy decisions. The metaphor of withered shrub or watered tree is more intense and more compelling when it is remembered that the poem emerges in a culture that characteristically is desperate for water. The metaphor of water in such a context makes clear that trust is a life-and-death matter.[46] No tree or shrub can survive without water. There are no viable substitutes. Likewise, Judah will find no viable substitute for a genuine trust in Yahweh. Every alternative will lead to withering and death.

17:9-10 These verses are another wisdom saying, placed now as a commentary on vv. 5-8. The teaching contains two affirmations, which together assert an awful judgment. The first affirmation (v. 9) is that the human heart is fickle. The RSV rendering, "deceitful," recalls that this word (*'aqobh;* cf. Ps. 49:6; 2 Kgs. 10:19) is the term from which comes the name "Jacob," the one who "overreaches, deceives, exploits, takes advantage of." In Jer. 17:5 the heart is condemned for turning from Yahweh. This observation in v. 9 is not carefully formulated theology, but is a sapiential observation that human persons are characteristically untrustworthy and unfaithful. The statement about human character in v. 9 is matched by an affirmation concerning Yahweh in v. 10. Yahweh is the God from whom no secret can be hidden (cf. 16:17), who deals with human persons according to their just desserts. Human fickleness and divine accountability together lead to an inevitable judgment. The poem is not interested in theological speculation, but simply narrates what is evident in Jerusalem. The outcome of destruction is inevitable because the human heart will not change, and Yahweh will not cease to search the mind and heart to locate loyalty and fickleness. The juxtaposition of themes on human obduracy is paralleled in Gen. 3:1-8; 6:5. Here, as there, the overreaching human person seeks to hide and cannot. Yahweh outlasts every attempt at concealment.

17:11 This verse is an odd, isolated statement which, as is common in wisdom instruction, offers a lesson from an observed natural phenomenon. A partridge hen gathers little chicks that are not of her brood. That is, she collects what does not belong to her. One

---

46. See Amos 8:11-12 on the power of the metaphor. Critical judgment has often kept a separation between Jer. 2:13, for example, and this sapiential poem. Taken together, they articulate the conviction that Yahweh is the only source of life.

reading of this figure is that partridges are scavengers who take what is not theirs. Another is that the hen is so lustful that it will abandon any egg for the sake of a new venture. In her lust, the hen works against nature to create a false brood (cf. 8:7). In either case, the hen is cited to warn those who take what is not theirs (cf. 2 Sam. 12:1-4; Matt. 25:24). The poem does not pursue the metaphor very far, but turns it to the subject of riches gotten unjustly. In the end, unjust riches cannot be retained but will surely be lost. When wealth is gotten through injustice (cf. Jer. 22:3-14), it is no more proper than when a chick is seized by a scavenger hen. Such wealth is improper, a violation of natural relations, and will surely be lost. The greedy rich are under judgment. Again, the teaching—as is typical of wisdom sayings—is detached from any context. In Jeremiah, however, the context in which that saying is heard is against the system of royal wealth. Such wealth will be lost and those who have it will be forsaken. It is as sure as a partridge not being able to keep what is not hers. The prophet skillfully takes up what must have been a conventional wisdom observation and transforms it into another harsh critique of an avaricious city.

17:12-13 These verses articulate a doxology of judgment. The brief poetic unit juxtaposes a hymn addressed to Yahweh and an indictment against those who do not embrace Yahweh. In v. 12 Yahweh is celebrated as enthroned. In v. 13 this exalted one is Israel's only hope. The remainder of v. 13 is built around the double use of "abandon" *('azab)*, which now is linked to the use of the same verb in v. 11 concerning chicks who "leave" *('azab)* the hen. Yahweh is Israel's only hope. Israel in its stupidity has abandoned the only hope. As in 2:13, Israel has forsaken the only resource of life and so is destined to death by thirst and starvation. While 17:12-13 are originally unrelated to vv. 5-8, they are now brought together in the traditioning process. Taken together, they pursue the motif of water and life, of drought and death. In the marginal topography of Judah, where there is no water, all life will die (cf. Amos 4:7-8). The terrible incongruity is that Judah had a sure source of the water of life, and now has rejected it. The only outcome is death. This utilization of the theme of water and life illuminates the juxtaposition of Jer. 17:12-13 and 5-8. In both cases, water permits life (cf. John 4:10). In this prophetic rendering, "water" is taken to be covenant fidelity.

In sum, Jer. 17:5-13 contains an odd assortment of themes and rhetorical elements. John Bright suggests this section is "Jeremiah's 'miscellaneous file.'"47 While the several elements are from different sources, they now form something of a unit, in which Yahweh's saving power (vv. 10,12-13a) is contrasted with Israelite waywardness (vv. 9,11,13). Yahweh's sovereignty constitutes the offer of life. In these images, Yahweh does not intervene in judgment. Rather, life works its own destiny, and where there is no water (here, Yahweh) death is certain.48 Yahweh's sovereignty and Israel's waywardness juxtaposed in this way present to Judah a limited range of possibilities.

The positive alternative is to turn to Yahweh in trust. Then Israel may live. The logic of the argument is the same as the "turn" summons of Amos: "Seek me and live" (Amos 5:4), or the Deuteronomic instruction to "choose life" (Deut. 30:19). The poetic rendering of Jeremiah, however, is much more subtle, requiring imaginative decisions more elemental than simple changes in behavior. The passage is bounded in Jer. 17:5 and 13, however, by the verb *sur* ("turn away from"), indicating that Judah has rejected the only way of life, and so comes death.49 Israel must finally deal with Yahweh, the only source of Israel's future. Yahweh is the source of well-being (v. 8), the hope of Israel (v. 13a), the source of life (v. 13c). If Yahweh is rejected by the one who "trusts in man" (v. 5), like the deceitful heart (v. 9), like the greedy partridge (v. 11), like the ones who leave the living well (v. 13), death comes.

The context in which these wisdom sayings appear places them in the service of the harsh prophetic judgment over Jerusalem. The address of these sayings toward Jerusalem is not explicit, but clearly wisdom is now used to make the case that Jeremiah's Jerusalem has violated normal natural relations. Judah has as much chance of living as a shrub in the desert, a wanderer without water, a partridge taking a chick, a greedy one keeping wealth. The chance is nil, for "forsaking" leads to death. "Turning away" and "abandoning" are Israel's way of rejecting Yahweh and Yahweh's gift of life.

---

47. John Bright, *Jeremiah,* 2nd ed., Anchor Bible 21 (Garden City, N.Y.: Doubleday, 1978), 119.

48. See Klaus Koch, "Is There a Doctrine of Retribution in the Old Testament?" in Crenshaw, *Theodicy in the Old Testament,* 57-87.

49. The double use of "turn aside" is reminiscent of 1 Sam. 12:20-21, a central text for the tradition of covenant which seems to lie behind the tradition of Jeremiah.

BE NOT A TERROR (17:14-18)

These verses resume the prayers of complaint and petition we have noted in chs. 11, 12, and 15. It is not clear why or in what way they are related to the immediate circumstance of ch. 17. Perhaps these verses provide a counterpart to the harsh lawsuit speech of 17:1-4, with the reflective sapiential materials of vv. 5-13 leading to this passionate, needful prayer. The lawsuit announces a harsh future. Verses 5-13 suggest the common sense grounds (artistically wrought) about why this judgment is natural and inevitable. This rendering leads to the prayer, which may be both personal and public. The prayer then is a response of faithful, needful speech in the midst of a people that has not been faithful and does not know it is needful.

The brief prayer contains elements familiar in the Psalms of Lament:

(a) petition (v. 14a),
(b) motivation (vv. 14b-16),
(c) petition (v. 17a),
(d) motivation (v. 17b),
(e) petition (v. 18).

The initial petition is a personal one, asking for healing and deliverance. The poet throws himself utterly on Yahweh as the only source of healing. The poet's stance is therefore precisely opposite that of indicted Judah. The second petition (v. 17a) is the negative counterpart to the petition of v. 14a: "Be a healer . . . be not a terror." The poet has already known terror from God (cf. 20:10 on "terror on every side"). Now God is asked to change from terror to healing. The third petition, like the first, is also a personal one. It includes two personal requests: "Let me not be put to shame, . . . let me not be dismayed." These requests appeal to the standard assurances given in a salvation oracle (cf. 31:19; Isa. 54:4). The lament seeks to guide Yahweh into making such an assurance.

The main petitions in Jer. 17:18, however, are four requests for punishment of the poet's enemies: "put to shame . . . be dismayed . . . bring the day of evil . . . destroy . . ." This petition is the other side of the positive hope for self in vv. 14a and 17a. What the poet asks against his enemies is precisely what he himself wants to escape. It may surprise us that the prayer is so hostile. Such hostility bespeaks the courage and candor of prayer that is characteristic in Israel. Jeremiah prays against his adversaries knowing that God knows the heart and gives what is due (v. 10). The poet now asks that God give just due to the enemy, that is, punishment commensurate to the offense. The poet expects this of God and urges God to be faithful to those expectations.

The prayer offers several alternative motivations in an attempt to move God to act. First, in v. 14b the motivation is a statement of praise: "Thou art my praise." In v. 17b it is a statement of needful trust: "Thou art my refuge." The first seeks to enhance God. The second asserts Jeremiah's dependence and reliance on God. Both the praise and the plea seek to draw God into involvement with the situation of need, so that God should make Jeremiah's crisis God's own cause.[50]

Two other rhetorical features may be noticed. First, the prayer concerns the coming day of judgment. In v. 16 the poet asserts that in the past he has not wished such judgment on his enemies. He has not been preoccupied with retaliation. But in an abrupt change of mood, he does exactly wish for vengeance (v. 18). The poet believes that God's judgment is sure, he wants it soon, and he does not doubt who deserves judgment. The poet trusts in God's decisive sovereignty.[51] Second, three times in the poem a strong pronoun is used for God: "*thou* art my praise" (v. 14); "*thou* knowest" (v. 16); "*thou* art my refuge" (v. 17).[52] The threefold strong "thou" is matched by the threefold use of "*I*" (vv. 16,18), also a strong pronoun.[53] Both pronouns are used for the sake of heavy emphasis.

The repeated use of such strong pronouns indicates that this relationship is one of intense communion. The relation in this moment of poetry is at a point of critical urgency. The one who prays is filled with hurt and rage, and entrusts vengeance to God. Such complaints are characteristically answered by an oracle of assurance.[54] In this

---

50. Jeremiah prays out of the boldness characteristic of Israel's tradition since Moses. On the bold act of prayer that makes human need into an "interest" of God, see Greenberg, *Biblical Prose Prayer,* 10-18.

51. On vengeance as an act of sovereignty of a legitimate government, see Mendenhall, *The Tenth Generation,* 69-104.

52. The Hebrew verbal system has pronominal suffixes to indicate the subject of the verb. It also has a set of independent suffixes which may be used for additional emphasis. It is that "strong pronoun," "thou," which is used three times in this poem for special emphasis.

53. Parallel to the "thou" noted in the previous note, this unit also uses the strong pronoun "I" three times for emphasis. The juxtaposition of these two sets of pronouns is remarkable for the rhetoric of the unit.

54. On the oracle of assurance, see the recent study of Edgar W. Con-

poem, however there is no answer. The intensity of the moment and the dread of the situation break the conventional form. This faithful poet prays an unanswered prayer. The hostility he faces from human agents is matched by the silence of God. No theological explanation is given for this silence on God's part. It is simply a reality in this anguished life of faith. God's silence to the poet corresponds to the absence of God announced to the whole people. God is no longer available, either to Israel or even to the poet. The poet experiences the very absence that is the destiny of Israel.[55]

REMEMBER THE SABBATH (17:19-27)

This prose passage is most unexpected in Jeremiah. The subject matter of sabbath is of course rooted in the old tradition of the Decalogue (cf. Exod. 20:8-11; Deut. 5:12-15).[56] The sabbath emerges as a matter of intense religious concern, especially after the Exile (cf. Isa. 56:4-5; Neh. 13:15-22).[57] For that reason, this prose unit is commonly regarded as later. We do know, however, that Jeremiah utilized the tradition of the Decalogue (cf. Jer. 7:9). Reference to the sabbath, therefore, is not necessarily alien to the tradition of Jeremiah and in itself is no reason to regard the passage as later.

The unit is divided into two parts, both concerning the sabbath. In 17:19-23 fidelity to sabbath is urged. Verses 21-22 urge obedience to the sabbath commandment with strong imperatives. Verse 23 follows as an indictment, indicating that Israel did not listen and did not obey, but violated the sabbath. This unit is dominated by the verb "hear" *(shemaʿ)*. In v. 20 there is a summons to listen, not unlike the classic Deuteronomic imperative of Deut. 6:4. In Jer. 17:23

---

rad, *Fear Not, Warrior,* Brown Judaic Studies 75 (Chico, Calif.: Scholars Press, 1985).

55. On the dramatic power and significance of the absence and silence of God, see Andre Neher, *The Exile of the Word* (Philadelphia: Jewish Publication Society, 1980).

56. On the cruciality of the sabbath commandment for the Decalogue, see Patrick D. Miller, Jr., "The Human Sabbath: A Study in Deuteronomic Theology," *Princeton Seminary Bulletin* New Series 62 (1985): 81-97; and, more generally, Walter Harrelson, *The Ten Commandments and Human Rights* (Philadelphia: Fortress, 1980), 79-92.

57. The sabbath emerged as a crucial mark of Israel's distinctiveness in the exilic and postexilic periods, and had something of a polemical character to it. See Gerhard von Rad, *Old Testament Theology,* vol. 1 (New York: Harper & Row; Edinburgh: Oliver & Boyd, 1962), 79-84.

the same verb is used twice to indict Israel. "Not listening" is the final disobedience. Life is not submitted to the will of Yahweh.

In the second half of the unit (vv. 24-27), the indictment of v. 23 strangely is ignored. In these later verses Judah is given a fresh chance. These verses are presented as a double "if . . . then" construct, in turn positive and negative. According to this text, Israel can decide afresh to keep covenant by way of keeping sabbath. The first "if . . . then" construct presents the positive option (vv. 24-26). If the community listens, it can be safe under a king and all Israel can be engaged in religious pilgrimage. The picture presented in these verses is of a great religious homecoming. The Jerusalem so much assaulted and critiqued by the covenant tradition is now the joyous goal of celebration. The negative option quickly follows in the second "if . . . then" construct (v. 27), however. If Israel violates sabbath and so breaks covenant, there will be massive destruction. Everything hangs on the sabbath, because the sabbath is the most dramatic sign that the will of God is honored and the life-giving power of God is trusted. To break sabbath means to violate God's will and to distrust God's gifts.

The pivotal role of the sabbath commandment in the future of this community may strike us as severe and peculiar. We must remember, however, that the sabbath becomes the identifying mark for the covenant community. Sabbath observance is understood as a deep rejection of imperial patterns of exploitation. It is the dramatic act whereby this people asserts to itself and announces to the watching world that this is Israel, a different people with a different way in the world, who will not behave according to the expectations of the imperial world. In the purview of covenant, the stability of political life (v. 25) and the effectiveness of worship (v. 26) depend on sabbath, an act that hands life back to God in trusting obedience.[58] If life is not handed over to God regularly, with discipline and intentionality, then the entire political-religious system will end in destruction.

This passage, like much else in Jeremiah, stakes everything on the centrality of God. It does so by distinctive appeal to the centrality of sabbath. Sabbath-keeping is taken as a measure of obedience to

---

58. See Matitiahu Tsevat, "The Basic Meaning of the Biblical Sabbath," in *The Meaning of the Book of Job and Other Biblical Studies* (New York: KTAV; Dallas: Institute of Jewish Studies, 1980), 39-52: "Every seventh day the Israelite renounces his autonomy and affirms God's dominion over him" (48).

Yahweh. While this focus on sabbath may link the passage to the concerns of the exilic or postexilic community,[59] the main claim is the same as the dominant tradition of Jeremiah. Obedience leads to life, though the specific form of obedience takes a different shape in each new generation and circumstance. In this case, sabbath asserts the cessation of destructive self-reliance, which is Judah's predominant temptation. We have seen that self-reliance is a central pathology of this people. Sabbath fidelity is one surrender of such self-reliance.

THE POTTER AND THE CLAY (18:1-23)

This chapter contains diverse materials that must have had different contexts of origin, but in their present arrangement there is a discernable logic to the chapter. After the indictment (vv. 1-12) and the sentence (vv. 13-17), we have an expression of the opposition the poet had evoked (v. 18) and his prayer for help in the face of that opposition (vv. 19-23).

18:1-12 The narrative indictment of vv. 1-12 begins with a command to Jeremiah. He is instructed and he obeys. He goes as sent, and the result is a divine oracle. His observation in v. 4 prepares the way for the oracle that follows (vv. 6-12). Jeremiah observes that the potter completely controls the clay, can reshape it, and is not committed to any particular form for the clay (v. 4). The potter will completely reshape the clay until the potter has it the way he wants it.

The interpretation of this observation is rooted in the parallel drawn in v. 6. God can do to Israel whatever Yahweh chooses, just as the potter can the clay (cf. Isa. 45:9-11). Israel is not autonomous or independent, but is completely in the control of Yahweh. The oracle asserts Yahweh's complete sovereignty and Israel's complete subservience. That is the nature of the relationship, which finally cannot be avoided or denied.

The metaphor of potter and clay leads us to expect an unambiguous assertion of Yahweh's sovereignty. The argument that follows, however, is much more subtle. Jeremiah 18:7-10 are organized according to a double sequence of "if . . . if . . . then."[60]

---

59. See Robert P. Carroll, *From Chaos to Covenant* (London: SCM; New York: Crossroad, 1981), 215.

60. This sequencing is constructed from the rhetoric of the passage. The actual propositions do not all occur in the text, but this clearly represents the structure of the argument.

A. 1. *If*... I declare ... that I will pluck up ... (v. 7),
   2. *if* that nation ... turns from its evil (v. 8)
   3. *(then)* I will repent of the evil that I intended to do to it (v. 8).
B. 1. *If*... I declare ... that I will build and plant it (v. 9),
   2. *if* it does evil in my sight ... (v. 10),
   3. *then* I will repent of the good which I had intended to do to it (v. 10).

The first "if" (A.1, B.1) concerns God's decree. The second "if" (A.2, B.2) refers to a fresh decision on Israel's part. The "then" (A.3, B.3) expresses Yahweh's readiness to act in new ways in response to Israel's new behavior. In both sequences the first "if" is God's initial decision either to plant or to pluck up. The second "if" celebrates Israel's freedom. Israel is not fated but can act in new ways.

This mode of argument affirms, first, that God is free and can respond and, second, that Judah's obedience is of decisive importance. In light of both these affirmations, Judah is exhorted to choose carefully how it will act, for its future depends on its action. Yahweh's responsive sovereignty and Judah's determinative obedience are both constitutive of Judah's life.

In v. 11 an appeal is made that Israel should decide afresh. God has made a decree (the first "if," in v. 7), but that decree can be changed by Judah's action (the second "if," in v. 8). The argument asserts Yahweh's full sovereignty, consistent with the ability of the potter to control the clay. But the second theme, that Israel can take an initiative, violates the metaphor, for Israel has freedom that the clay does not have. The clay cannot challenge the potter, but Israel can act so that Yahweh will change. The narrative both uses the metaphor (to assert sovereignty) and violates the metaphor (to assert Judah's zone of freedom).

In v. 12, however, the prophet dismisses all of the freedom Israel seemed to have in vv. 8-11. Now Israel's chance to change is nullified. The clay now can take no action free of the potter. There is no more time for turning. Judah has waited too long. Judah of course had had freedom of choice. But that freedom has now been forfeited through sustained resistance and stubbornness. The text is not interested in a theoretical question of free will. Rather, it addresses the pastoral reality that resistance to God practiced so long eventually nullifies the capacity to choose life. Israel's long-term resistance left it no longer able to choose life. Jerusalem's judgment is sealed because Judah has been too stubborn. Judah rejects God's plan which is for covenant obedience and chooses its own alternative plan that opts for autonomy and disobedience. Judah resolves to act autonomously, without reference to Yahweh.[61] Judah's plan is a plan of stubbornness which refuses the reality of God's sovereignty. Such a refusal ends in death. The narrative entertains a playful freedom out beyond the metaphor, but by v. 12 that freedom is ended and the potter completely controls the clay. Eventually the potter will quit on the clay because the clay will never turn out right. As the potter shapes clay (v. 4), so Yahweh shapes evil for Judah (v. 11).[62] The potter is not endlessly committed to working with this clay, if the clay is finally recalcitrant. The potter will finally quit, which means that the clay has no future.[63]

18:13-17 This poetic unit is nicely placed after the prose verdict of vv. 1-12. We have just been told that Israel will follow its own plan, against the plan of Yahweh, and that plan will lead to death. This poetic unit surely had no initial link to the preceding. Because of the editorial formula of judgment at the beginning of v. 13, however, this unit now functions to pronounce judgment after the harsh verdict of v. 12. The two units are connected by words which are rough homonyms. In v. 12 the RSV renders one term as "stubborn" *(sh-r-r)*; in v. 13 the RSV has "horrible thing" *(sh-ʿ-r-r)*. Stubbornness and obstinate autonomy are Judah's "horrible thing." In this poem the "horrible thing" is done by the virgin, who should be completely devoted to her husband (cf. 2:2).

Jeremiah 18:13-14 appeals to natural phenomena to understand the grotesqueness of Judah. In v. 14 snow does not "leave" *(ʿazab)* the mountains of Lebanon. It is always there. It belongs there. The

---

61. As in other cases, the prophet places in the mouths of his opponents self-indicting words which are a polemical construction that would never have been uttered, but they are words reflecting actions and attitudes. We have seen a cluster of such alleged quotes in ch. 2.

62. Notice the reiteration of the word *yatsar* ("form") in vv. 4,11.

63. The metaphor of potter-clay has an important and sustained use in the tradition, and Jeremiah's use should be understood in relation to other uses of the same metaphor. In 2 Cor. 4:7 the metaphor is used positively for a community of faith fully reliant upon and responsive to God. Between the deathly use of the metaphor by Jeremiah and the affirmative use by Paul stands the use of Isa. 45:9-10, which asserts that God's sovereignty over Israel (the potter over the clay) will cause Israel's rescue, even if the rescue takes a form that Israel would not prefer. All three uses stress God's sovereign power over the community of faith, whether in judgment or in mercy.

crags of Sirion are the natural habitat for snow. Indeed, the snow of Lebanon cannot be snow anywhere else; it will disappear and cease to be snow if it is moved. The second metaphor of mountain stream reiterates the same claim. The metaphor affirms that as snow belongs in the mountains, Israel belongs with Yahweh, is always with Yahweh, cannot be Israel anywhere else. Yahweh is Israel's natural habitat, and to try to be Israel anywhere else will lead to disappearance. Elsewhere we have seen the verb *'azab* for Judah's leaving of Yahweh (2:13,17,19). Abandonment of Yahweh is the fundamental issue. Nobody ever heard of snow leaving the crags of Sirion. Nobody ever heard of Israel leaving Yahweh and still being Israel. Israel, like snow, will melt into oblivion if it leaves. When Israel leaves Yahweh, it ceases to be Israel.

The contrast to faithful, predictable snow which stays in its proper place is stated in 18:15-16, as the poem moves from nature to human behavior. Judah has forgotten Yahweh the way snow cannot forget the mountains. Verse 15 identifies the modes of forgetting as false worship, departure from tradition, and disobedience. The outcome of forgetting is that the land has become a ruin (v. 16). This outcome is inevitable. When the way of the LORD is abandoned, the land itself loses its life-giving capacity, because the capacity for life is in the gift of Yahweh, not in the character of the land itself. Baalism believed the land itself contained the gift of life. Israel's covenant faith knows that it is only Yahweh who causes the land to give life.

Forgetting Yahweh reduces the land to vulnerability and the people to deep humiliation. Verse 17 announces the specific form of judgment. It is like scattering before the wind—that is, exile. Israel will be blown away. Judah will be scattered the way the wind scatters chaff (cf. Ps. 1:4). Along with displacement, Judah will experience the absence of God (Jer. 18:17b). More precisely, Judah will experience God's "back" *('oreph),* not God's face (cf. Ps. 13:1; 27:8-9). Where God's face is not seen, God's power is not available, and there is death. The removal of God's face likely asserts the nullification of the cultic apparatus in Jerusalem, which is designed to ensure God's presence.

This little poetic unit has a clear structure. It begins with a statement of judgment (Jer. 18:13). It then asks a rhetorical question which focuses on the fidelity of creation (v. 14). From the image of clinging snow and flowing streams, the poem moves from indictment to sentence, from "forgetting" (v. 15) to "scattering" (v. 17).

18:18 No doubt the harsh tenor of the prophetic message evoked hostility. Verse 18 suggests how pervasive and massive the opposition is. To "make a plot" ("devise a plan") suggests that the opposition to the prophet and his fearsome word is not simply an irrational, emotional response, but it is opposition that is formidable and intentional, that has developed a strategy for silencing this treasonable voice (cf. Mark 3:6). To "devise a plan" uses the same language as Jer. 18:12. As Judah is indicted for making its own recalcitrant plans (v. 12), so now we see those "plans" aimed both against Yahweh (v. 13) and against the prophet of Yahweh (v. 18). The plans of the opposition are an embodiment of the recalcitrant autonomy against which the prophet speaks.

Like the opponents of Jesus, the leadership "takes counsel." The triad mentioned (priest, wise, prophet) represents the power structure, the knowledge industry, and the religious authority of the establishment. That triad is matched by the three modes of authority that ordered the community: torah, counsel, word.[64] Jeremiah is perceived to be the enemy of all of these modes of authority. All of these established agents of public authority make common cause against this "voice of disorder." Those public leaders are adamant to maintain the status quo, immune to the notion that it is the very arrangement they defend which will result in exile and/or death. They perceive Jeremiah as a disruption, but they do not notice Yahweh, who sent Jeremiah as the unavoidable disrupter.

To "smite with the tongue" suggests public speech against the prophet. This is likely more than slander or gossip. Most probably, it means taking the prophet to court and filing public charges, with the hope of marking him as an enemy of the state (cf. 26:8-11). The word entrusted to the prophet has indeed made him a public enemy (cf. 38:4) and has isolated him from the main sources of public authority (cf. 15:17). As we shall see later, there were those who still supported him, perhaps at risk to themselves (cf. 36:19). It is worth noting that the support for the prophet comes not from the religious leaders but from civil authorities, perhaps those who themselves were increasingly alienated from the self-serving ideology of the royal-priestly apparatus.

18:19-23   The prayer of the prophet in these verses likely is an independent piece, but it has an appropriate place here in response to

---

64. On these modes of leadership and the corresponding modes of knowledge, see Walter Brueggemann, *The Creative Word* (Philadelphia: Fortress, 1982).

the conspiracy of v. 18. The prayer follows the general pattern of lament psalms and is dominated by petition. The verbs of petition articulate a series of requests:

> give heed, hearken (v. 19),
> deliver up,
> give over (v. 21),
> forgive not,
> nor blot out,
> deal (v. 23).

The petitions are reinforced by a series of jussives:

> let their wives become,
> may their men meet,
> may their youths be slain (v. 21),
> may a cry be heard (v. 22),
> let them be overthrown (v. 23).

The objects of this petition are not named, but the context suggests that they are the opposition identified in v. 18. Two things are clear in the petition. First, Jeremiah continues to trust in and look to Yahweh for well-being. His problematic situation drives him to more passionate faith and urgent prayer. Second, Jeremiah never doubts that he is entitled to good from Yahweh and is not embarrassed to seek good and insist upon it (v. 20). He prays as a righteous one who is entitled to God's intervention (cf. 12:1).[65] Jeremiah's petition is for God to implement covenant curses against his enemies, including the standard triad of famine, sword, and pestilence (18:21). The language of v. 22a moves beyond convention, however, and presents a visceral image of Yahweh's visitation. Jeremiah prays finally that justice should be done without forgiveness (v. 23).

Jeremiah provides two groundings for this petition. The prophet has done good even for his adversaries (v. 20). He has acted as intercessor (cf. 7:16; 15:1) and does not warrant their hostile response. His second ground of appeal is a theme recurrent in the prayers of lament: "Thou knowest" (18:23). This is an act of praise, but also a statement of profound trust. Jeremiah trusts the justice of God and is willing to entrust to God the response to his opponents. Jeremiah

---

65. This prayer of vengeance which is rooted in and expresses confidence about one's own righteousness and the wickedness of one's opponents has a close parallel in Ps. 109:8-19. Again Jeremiah apparently utilizes a standard tradition of speech.

is completely confident that he will be vindicated and that his opponents will be found guilty.

The prayer begins with reference to "my plea" (v. 19). The language is juridical. It suggests that Jeremiah is in court, stands accused, and now turns to Yahweh for vindication. The ground of vindication is that he has faithfully spoken the word entrusted to him. He has acted faithfully as intercessor. He has practiced obedience, even if it was an unwelcome obedience. He asks no special mercy for himself and wants none shown to the others.[66] Already in 12:1-6 Jeremiah is troubled that God is not just. Here he pleads simply that God will be just and deal righteously with him because he is righteous, and deal appropriately with the wicked conspirators, who should be treated wickedly.

This chapter serves two different concerns. In vv. 1-17 the text concerns the obduracy of Judah and its coming exile and death. In vv. 18-23 we are concerned with the hostility evoked against the person of Jeremiah for speaking such a harsh word. The trouble experienced by Jeremiah and his harsh prayer (vv. 18-23) can only be understood in relation to the public issues of vv. 1-17. Finally, the issue is not the well-being of the prophet, but the validity of the judgment against Jerusalem. The evil "plans" made against Jeremiah (v. 18) match the evil "plans" made in resistance to Yahweh (v. 12). When Yahweh's "plan" is rejected (v. 11), death will come. No amount of hostility against the messenger will modify the message. The clay finally will have to submit to the potter or be discarded. Jeremiah is clear that Judah has had options, and equally clear that Judah has chosen infidelity.

THE BROKEN FLASK (19:1-15)

We have considered the metaphor of potter and clay in 18:1-12. The same image is used again in 19:1-15 with much more sustained and devastating effect. Jerusalem will be nullified so that it "can never be mended" (v. 11).[67] The passage falls into two unequal parts. In vv.

---

66. The juridical cast of the argument is much like that of Job, on which see Claus Westermann, *The Structure of the Book of Job* (Philadelphia: Fortress, 1981). Westermann shows the delicate interweaving of lament and lawsuit.

67. The RSV has "mend," which renders the Hebrew *rapha*, most often translated as "heal." That Hebrew term reflects a correction of the text that is conventional and universally accepted.

1-13 we have a long summons from Yahweh to Jeremiah, instruct-
ing him in what he shall say and do. Then in vv. 14-15 we have a narrative of the prophet's actual actions. The long instruction to
Jeremiah from Yahweh has as its counterpart a very terse narrative of
compliance. The disproportion makes clear that the weight is borne
not by anything Jeremiah says or does, but by the commanding
word of Yahweh, which is the decisive element in this text. The
speech of God dominates the text. Jeremiah's own words are only
derivative from the words of God and bring those words of Yahweh
to fruition.

19:1-13 The long speech of Yahweh here is organized around the
two simple acts depicted in vv. 1-2 and v. 10. In vv. 1-2 the prophet
is ordered to take an earthen flask and speak to the elders and senior
priests. That is, he is to address the power structure. In v. 10 he is
ordered to break the flask and speak again to the same representatives
of the establishment. In both cases the earthen flask provides an occasion for an extended word of judgment. The initial act of vv. 1-2 leads
to the long speech of vv. 3-9, and the act of v. 10 to the speech of vv.
11-13. The initial instruction assures that Jeremiah's effort is a quite
public act, legitimated by the priests and elders who accompany him.
The history-making word of Yahweh is not a secret matter; it happens
in the midst of the public community.

The speech of vv. 3-9 is an extended lawsuit speech in three parts.
The first brief element (v. 3) announces the main accent of the
speech: Yahweh is now bringing evil upon Jerusalem, a judgment so
severe that it will evoke a stunned, shocked response from all who
hear of it.

The second element (vv. 4-5) is the indictment, which sounds
themes we have frequently encountered and which echoes Deuteronomic phraseology. The dominant verbs are "abandon" and "pro-
fane." The first verb *('azab)* continues the dominant metaphor of
marital infidelity, which we have seen frequently in the Jeremiah
tradition. The second verb *(nakar)* means "to make alien or foreign."
Jerusalem has been made alien. It is so abused that it has become an
unwelcome, inhospitable place for Yahweh. The particulars referred
to by these powerful verbs include wrong cultic practice ("burn incense") and wrong social practice ("innocent blood"). The reference
to "burning sons" (v. 5) may be an allusion to Assyrian distortions,[68]

---

68. On the relation of this practice to Assyrian practices, see Morton
Cogan, *Imperialism and Religion: Assyria, Judah and Israel in the Eighth and*

but the phraseology is quite stylized and perhaps should not be taken too concretely. The general point is that all of life in Jerusalem is now ordered in ways that are alien to Yahweh.

The third extended element (vv. 6-9) has a "therefore" which corresponds to the "because" of v. 4. The lead sentence of the judgment asserts that coming events in the valley around Jerusalem will necessitate a new name for the valley. It will be called "the valley of Slaughter," for the killing done by Yahweh will be massive and unavoidable. This prediction of the fate of the city is made more specific in vv. 7-9, all of which culminates in the horrendous vision of v. 9. The rhetorical power of the verdict against the city is evident in the series of first person verbs in the mouth of Yahweh:

> I will make void
> I will cause to fall
> I will give (v. 7),
> I will make (v. 8),
> I will make (v. 9).

The action is sure, incontrovertible, and directly from the hand of Yahweh. There is here no mediating agent, such as the Babylonian army. The first person verbs make clear that it is Yahweh alone who takes these destructive actions.

The actual substance of the judgment appeals to the old covenant curse tradition. What now befalls Jerusalem are not novel acts, but the very threats which the torah tradition had long mediated.[69] There will be death by sword (presumably Babylon, but not specified). The simple announcement of death, however, is not rhetorically adequate. We are offered a picture of bodies piled up as food for birds (v. 7). The bodies will be uncared for, unprotected, and dishonored. The city, envisioned as a pile of ruins, will be a place of mocking (v. 8). The famine will be so great that people will

---

Seventh Centuries B.C.E., SBL Monograph 19 (Missoula, Mont.: Scholars Press, 1974). Cogan has persuasively argued that in this period Assyrian practices may have been attractive and seductive, but they were not systematically imposed. John W. McKay, *Religion in Judah under the Assyrians, 732-609 BC*, Studies in Biblical Theology, 2nd series 26 (Naperville, Ill.: Allenson; London: SCM, 1973), has argued in a fashion parallel to Cogan.

69. On prophetic use of the old covenant curses, see Delbert R. Hillers, *Treaty-Curses and the Old Testament Prophets*, Biblica et orientalia 16 (Rome: Pontifical Biblical Institute, 1964).

desperately act as cannibals against neighbors and their own children (v. 9).

This judgment of God is no doubt stereotypical and hyperbolic. Its massive, relentless force is necessary to penetrate the complacent self-assurance of Judah that "it can't happen here." This prophetic speech makes the harsh claim: it can and it will. We are not sure what to make of this picture. It is a poetic scenario. The vision is one of rhetorical overkill in an attempt to suggest something comparable to the unthinkable death of a nuclear holocaust (cf. 8:1-3).[70] This picture is beyond historical realism, because the fate of Jerusalem falls outside such civil expectations. The rhetoric must match the passion of God, who has been provoked beyond any convention. The rhetoric runs beyond convention, because the social realities are beyond anything yet known in Jerusalem.[71]

After that intense scenario, the action of 19:10 is terse, and powerful because of its terseness. The verse is dominated by the stark word "break" *(shabar)*. The act evokes a second passionate comment (vv. 11-13). Verse 11 draws together the claims of this text in the most unambiguous way possible: like this earthen flask, so this city and this people will be broken. This narrative does not report sympathetic magic, as though the broken flask enacts the broken city.[72] "Sympathetic magic" is the notion that a dramatic act like the breaking of a pot may *cause* the destruction to which it alludes. While it is, in my judgment, too much to think the people in this text believed in such causation, there is no doubt that the dramatic act opened up a field of fertile imagination filled with dread and fresh discernment. The broken flask is a parabolic assault on imagination. The coming judgment is a firm resolve on the part of God. That resolve is all the more ominous because "it can never be mended" (v. 11). This is the point of no return. This destruction is not for chastening or for dis-

---

70. As Richard L. Rubenstein has argued ("Job and Auschwitz," *Union Seminary Quarterly Review* 25 [1969-1970]: 421-437), it cannot be claimed that the destruction of Jerusalem can be compared in scope, magnitude, or significance with the holocaust. I refer only to the rhetorical force with which the poet seeks to anticipate the judgment in the event. That rhetorical force is comparably present, even if the historical reality and significance is much less.

71. The extreme rhetoric utilized for this event suggests a case of using "limit language" to help Israel experience a "limit experience." See Paul Ricoeur, "Biblical Hermeneutics," *Semeia* 4 (1975): 107-128.

72. Against John Bright, *Jeremiah,* 2nd ed., Anchor Bible 21 (Garden City, N.Y.: Doubleday, 1978).

cipline. There is no invitation to repent. It is not intended to "teach a lesson." There is no escape clause. The judgment is final, massive, decisive, unarguable.

What an incredible word for this prophet of the covenant tradition! Jeremiah is utterly a child of the tradition of Moses. He takes to its conclusion what has been implicit all through the tradition. Since Exod. 19:5-6 the whole of Israel's life with Yahweh has been governed by this uncompromising "if." The whole enterprise is finished. There is in the purview of the prophet no hint of continuing care, no second thought on Yahweh's part, no yearning or wistfulness. This is the end of the tradition, the end of all things sacred.

Jeremiah is confronted by a royal establishment (and we may believe public opinion) that relied on the abiding continuity of God's covenant commitment. Against that, Jeremiah is a faithful interpreter of the Mosaic tradition. This outcome in destruction had been proposed from the beginning in this tradition of "if." Moreover, the prophet also offers a correct reading of historical events. Jerusalem is indeed destroyed! This really is an ending, whatever theological verdict one may render. Thus a *correct reading of public events* and a *faithful reading of the tradition* converge in this shocking and ominous text. The city now faces the very end that the covenant tradition had anticipated for the disobedient. God has not made an unconditional commitment to any historical construct—not even to Jerusalem. The tradition illuminates what is happening. The outcome of history vindicates the tradition.

Jeremiah is intensely immersed in both tradition and historical events. They come together in a stunning, almost unbearable verdict. Jeremiah 19:12-13 serves to expand the verdict of v. 11. The city has been rendered ritually unclean, a place where Yahweh cannot abide. As Yahweh finds the place uninhabitable, so the power for life departs. Where God's power for life is absent, death comes quickly.

19:14-15 Chapter 19 thus far is a decree from the mouth of Yahweh. Only now do we have narrated the speech of the prophet. It is striking that in this recounting of the prophet's response there is no mention of the earthen flask, no breaking of it, no travel with elders and priests. It is as though the prophet does not take the specifics of the command seriously. He simply stands in the temple and speaks. He goes to the heart of the city, the temple court, to speak his word. One may wonder about the reduction of all of Yahweh's words and command to act in vv. 1-13 to the simple statement of v. 15. Perhaps Jeremiah is not as enthusiastic about this heavy word as is Yahweh. Perhaps he does not want to engage in such rhetorical overkill. Perhaps he wants to soften the dramatic effect. Perhaps he believes the harsh judgment does not need to be voiced yet again with such eloquence.

For whatever reason, v. 15 gives only the essentials. The threat from Yahweh is an echo of v. 3: "I am bringing evil." Nothing is specified. Both the indictment and sentence of v. 15 lack specificity. The climactic indictment is "You did not listen." Everything depends on listening. Everyone suffers when there is no listening. Out of the tradition of Deuteronomy, not listening is the fundamental act of autonomy and bad faith. Not to listen is not to belong, not to concede sovereignty. Not listening is to claim one's own place and take one's own counsel (v. 7). It is to imagine one is free to order life as one wills, which leads to forsaking and making alien. Even Jerusalem in its splendor and dignity is not so free, so autonomous. Such a mistaken pretense leads only to death. That death is now at hand, says the poet.

JEREMIAH IN STOCKS (20:1-6)

This passage appears to be a straightforward narrative report of an event in the life of the prophet. It offers a different form of rhetoric from the preceding chapter and perhaps is not originally related to it. However, the canonical juxtaposition of the two is not inappropriate. Jeremiah 19:1-15 is one of Jeremiah's most devastating speeches of judgment, leading to the conclusion "it can never be mended." Such a harsh word surely would evoke criticism and hostility from his hearers. We observe that criticism and hostility in 20:1-6, in which the administrative officer of the temple establishment treats Jeremiah to public abuse as an enemy of the establishment.

The leadership that is threatened by Jeremiah and that responds to him is embodied in Pashhur, who administers the temple. The confrontation of Jeremiah and Pashhur is not unlike that of Amos and Amaziah (Amos 7:10-17). Two views of reality clash and there can be no compromise. The action Pashhur takes on behalf of official truth is not a personal act of revenge, but is the public, "legitimate" procedure which deals swiftly and harshly with dissent. The temple complex claims to be the embodiment of God's presence and purpose, and therefore it cannot countenance the notion that Yahweh is against that very institution. Jeremiah is taken a political prisoner. The priest seeks to intimidate the prophet, hopefully to silence him.

Jeremiah is not intimidated or cowed. In response to this public punishment (Jer. 20:2), the prophet responds boldly and vigorously (vv. 3-6). Jeremiah's scathing response, rather than his punishment, is the point of the text. Jeremiah comes to see that the resistance he meets is not simply personal. The agents of the temple are enemies of God's word, and that word must therefore be uncompromising and unrelenting. (On the relation of personal opposition and opposition to the very purpose of God, see 1 Sam. 8:7.)

Jeremiah is not penitent or apologetic. He is immediately back on the attack against the baseless pretensions of the royal-temple establishment. His response is in three parts. First, he dramatically renames the temple administration (Jer. 20:3). A changed name witnesses to a changed reality. The temple was to bring *shalom,* but it brings *terror* (cf. 6:25). The administrative head of the temple is renamed "Terror on every side," or "Surrounded by trembling."[73] The temple (represented by Pashhur) and the city are now marked by terror and not peace. The temple cannot keep its promises. The system is under judgment and has failed. It may mouth *shalom,* but it embodies terror. It is therefore subject to God's terror.

The prophet is not especially interested in Pashhur, however. Second, he is focused on the city and temple, enmeshed as they are in self-deception (20:4-5). The whole company of Pashhur—his associates, friends, accomplices—is under judgment. They are under a death sentence. Jeremiah appeals to the standard twofold form of judgment/sword and exile. (It is never clear when the invading armies will kill and when Israel will be deported. Rhetorically, the two futures of death and exile are treated as parallel.) The decisive statement in the mouth of Yahweh is, "I will give all Judah . . . I will give all the wealth . . . into the hand of their enemies." The word "all" is repeatedly used. The punishment is complete. There will be no escape. The Babylonian armies simply enact the decree of Yahweh. The priests are helpless against the resolve of God. The imperial seizure of temple treasury is narrated at the end of the book of Jeremiah (52:17-23). The critique of the temple apparatus serves to delegitimate the royal-temple ideology and its particular definition of the world.

---

73. On this phrase, see William L. Holladay, "The Covenant with the Patriarchs Overturned: Jeremiah's Intention in 'Terror on Every Side' (Jer. 20:1-6)," *Journal of Biblical Literature* 91 (1972): 305-320. Holladay sees the phrase as a subtle announcement of an inversion of all old covenant reliances.

Third, the oracle returns to Pashhur at its close (20:6). His personal destiny is exile, and finally death in exile. The judgment applies to the man, his family, and all his allies in the temple apparatus who have participated in the deception. (This destiny is not unlike that pronounced by Amos in Amos 7:17.) The final word of the verse is "false" *(sheqer)*. The temple has not embodied the truth of God. The personal references to Pashhur (vv. 3,6) form an envelope around the more public announcement (vv. 4-5). All three parts have the same aim, however. All of vv. 3-6, the personal and public words, announce the great historical reversal that is now decreed. Those at the center of the temple, the focus of well-being and security, are the very ones displaced and exposed to death. The very place that is to guarantee life has become the very seat of death. The symbolic world of Jerusalem is now effectively dismantled. The physical dismantling is still to be accomplished by Babylonian arms, but the dismantling is primarily accomplished by this prophetic word with its power to expose, indict, and displace.

I HAVE BECOME A LAUGHINGSTOCK (20:7-18)

This final, most pathos-filled complaint of Jeremiah now is placed to follow the prophet's extraordinary challenge to established religion (vv. 1-6). In 18:1–20:6 Jeremiah speaks a massive word of judgment. He does it boldly and unflinchingly, full of confidence, certain that he speaks the very truth God has entrusted to him. Such speech is costly, however, not only because of the external hostility and resistance that his word evoked (20:1-6), but because of the intense, personal toll of speaking against the very reality that must have been his own spiritual home. In announcing this harsh judgment of Yahweh, Jeremiah is not speaking only against the world of "the others" who are his adversaries, but against the very symbolic world he himself inhabits. The cost of such a harsh judgment is that the prophet predictably arrives at pathos, hurt, and despair.

The new rhetorical unit that begins in v. 7 stands in stark contrast to the preceding. Jeremiah is unflinching in his public speech (vv. 3-6). But after this defiant proclamation, we are permitted access to his conversation with Yahweh, which has a quite different tone. Now he joins issue with Yahweh over the cost of his public work. This poetic struggle with God is divided in two distinct parts—vv. 7-12 and vv. 14-18. Between them comes a curious doxological break in v. 13.

20:7-12   The prayer in these verses bears all the marks of a psalm of lament. While the poet uses that familiar genre, the personal poignancy of the poem corresponds to our general understanding of the pathos of Jeremiah. The poem opens with a powerful complaint against God (vv. 7-10). Although the lines complain about human hostility ("I have become a laughingstock"), the focus is on the ways of Yahweh, who seems not to be faithful and trustworthy. The complaint begins with an accusation that Yahweh has seduced him (v. 7). The verb rendered "deceived" could be rendered more strongly as "harassed," "taken advantage of," "abused," even "raped." Jeremiah finds himself helpless before Yahweh's power, which is overwhelming and irresistible, even if not trustworthy. Jeremiah admits the power of God, but concedes nothing else (cf. Job 9:19-27). The complaint only asserts Yahweh's raw, primitive power that overwhelms even the one who seeks to serve him. The words of the poem anticipate Job.

Yahweh's power is beyond challenge, and that places the prophet in an unbearable, "no-win" situation. On the one hand, Jeremiah is mandated to speak against Jerusalem, but his speaking evokes deep hostility (Jer. 20:8). On the other hand, when he does not speak (in order to avoid the hostility) he is even more troubled, for the word of Yahweh is a burning compulsion to him (v. 9). The prophet has only two alternatives, and neither one works. When he speaks, Yahweh does not support him. When he is silent, Yahweh does not console him. He has this awesome burden from Yahweh, but without the accompanying power or presence of Yahweh. Yahweh has mandated him but has given him no visible support. The only way this awesome task could be endured is with Yahweh's reliable solidarity, and that is withheld.

Jeremiah's message has evoked a "whisper campaign" against him (v. 10). He is maligned by those who cannot bear his word and who want to dismiss him as an irresponsible dissident. In v. 3 Jeremiah had labeled his nemesis, Pashhur, as "Terror on every side" (i.e., he is a bundle of trouble and disturbance). But now the phrase is turned against Jeremiah himself. He is made the butt of attack and criticism. He now is the one who is accused as the bringer of trouble and terror. He is the object of harsh criticism and perhaps a conspiracy (cf. 18:18). In the face of his own fidelity and in the face of the weighty opposition he evoked, Jeremiah prays an urgent prayer. He asserts that he is in real danger (20:10), that he is in trouble because he has been faithful to Yahweh (v. 8). He insists that his danger is Yahweh's responsibility, that Yahweh must care and act. Jeremiah is without resource against his friends and associates who want to do him in (v. 10). He relies completely on Yahweh's advocacy.

A second characteristic element of the lament is the assertion of trust in Yahweh (v. 11). This statement of trust is almost contradictory to the complaint. Whereas Yahweh earlier had been accused of infidelity (v. 7), now Yahweh's powerful steadfastness is celebrated.

Jeremiah's assertion of confidence in Yahweh serves two functions. First, it is a statement of genuine trust. He has come to know that Yahweh's power is reliable and can be counted on. Second, it is a motivation addressed to Yahweh, reminding Yahweh of Yahweh's character and responsibility. Already in the call narrative of ch. 1, Yahweh had issued a "do not fear" to Jeremiah (1:8), much as a general might give to his troops. Yahweh promised to be with and for Jeremiah in the battle to come (1:17-19). Now Jeremiah, in his prayer, appeals to that metaphor to assert what Yahweh can do and to remind Yahweh of what must be done. Because Yahweh is such a warrior, Jeremiah is confident that the threats made against him will disappear, because they cannot stand against the mobilization of Yahweh.

The third element in this prayer (20:12) is a petition to Yahweh. The introductory lines echo 17:10. In that prayer it is affirmed that God tries the heart and gives people what they deserve. Here the prophet appeals to that same sure reality. Jeremiah does not ask for free grace, but only for an equitable settlement. He asks to be rewarded for his relentless obedience. The petition is lean and pointed: "let me see thy vengeance." He prays for the very vengeance for which the enemies ask (v. 10). Jeremiah does not take vengeance in his own hands. He only prays that Yahweh should enact the vengeance that is appropriate to Yahweh's own character.[74]

This prayer is an act of weakness and of power. Jeremiah is aware that he is weak and helpless. He cannot prevail, but he is confident that Yahweh can and will prevail. Michael Fishbane has seen how the word "prevail" dominates the poem.[75] The Hebrew word *yakal* occurs four times: "thou hast prevailed" (v. 7), "I cannot (prevail)" (v. 9), "we can overcome him" (v. 10), "they will not overcome me" (v. 11). Jeremiah prays about overcoming and being overcome. His

---

74. See the discussion of vengeance in Mendenhall, *The Tenth Generation,* 69-104. This vengeance is not arbitrary and undisciplined, but is the embodiment of the rule of law. See Susan Jacobi, *Wild Justice* (New York and London: Harper & Row, 1983).

75. Michael Fishbane, *Text and Texture* (New York: Schocken, 1979), 91-102.

only hope is that Yahweh will be his ally and not his enemy. When Jeremiah is alone, he is lost. He cannot withstand the enemy. But if Yahweh were to be his advocate, he is very sure of vindication, both because he is innocent and because Yahweh is powerful (2 Cor. 11:30; 12:9). Otherwise, he is hopelessly defeated by an alliance of Yahweh and his human adversaries. Either way it will be unequal. Without Yahweh, he is unequally weak; with Yahweh, he is unequally triumphant.[76] Everything depends on Yahweh. That is why the prayer is so urgent and passionate. Jeremiah must have Yahweh on his side. Only his prayer can summon and evoke Yahweh to stand with him.

20:13 This verse is problematic and may not be a part of the original poem.[77] David J. A. Clines and David Gunn have shown, however, that the verse is the culmination of vv. 7-12, and is a fourth element of the lament psalm, resolution in praise.[78] Such a reading would suggest that the speaker is so confident of Yahweh's answer, of Yahweh's intervention, and of his own innocence that he anticipates a resolution as though it is already wrought. Thus the prayer moves dramatically, as Israel characteristically does in prayer, in four steps: complaint/trust as motivation/petition/praise.

Jeremiah cannot find satisfaction in the public arena, nor in social relations. He is finally driven to face the theological reality of his life and vocation. He is driven to God as his "only source of comfort and strength." In the face of God he is made aware of the deep, inescapable problematic of his life. Through its long history, Israel had found Yahweh to be sufficient solace in every threatening situation. In this verse Jeremiah turns to praise of God because he has found Yahweh to be adequate, reliable, present, decisive. Such a certitude

---

76. The attempt of Jeremiah to draw Yahweh into solidarity against a common enemy is illuminated by the analysis of "triangling" in family dynamics. See Murray Bowen, *Family Therapy in Clinical Practice* (New York: Aronson, 1978).

77. Robert P. Carroll, *From Chaos to Covenant* (London: SCM; New York: Crossroad, 1981), 128, notes that v. 13 contains common hymnic elements. That in itself is not sufficient grounds for concluding it is an addition. It does in any case perform an odd function between vv. 7-12 and vv. 14-18.

78. David J. A. Clines and David M. Gunn, "Form, Occasion and Redaction in Jeremiah 20," *Zeitschrift für die alttestamentliche Wissenschaft* 88 (1976): 390-409; and "'You Tried to Persuade Me' and 'Violence! Outrage!' in Jeremiah XX 7-8," *Vetus Testamentum* 28 (1978): 20-27.

was not anticipated by the poem, but Jeremiah is characteristically Israelite in arriving at this doxological conclusion. The God who was experienced as fickle at the beginning of the poem is forced by the prayer to become his powerful ally and advocate. Such a one as Jeremiah cannot hope for or expect more than that. But he can indeed expect and receive that much. The truth spoken even in the face of establishment hostility permits praise and solidarity with God. Jeremiah's lonely voice is a voice of truth. He finds himself allied with the God of all truth. Jeremiah does not find himself "prevailing" either with God or with his fellows, but the move from complaint to praise is itself a form of prevailing, finally the only form of prevailing that is available to Israel.[79]

20:14-18   After the bold, confident conclusion expressed as praise in v. 13, we are shocked and taken aback by vv. 14-18. It is quickly clear that Jeremiah's complex and troubled life leaves more to be said even after triumphant praise. Verses 14-18 form a strange disjunction after the trust of vv. 11-12 and doxology of v. 13. It is as though the theological resolution and well-being expressed in vv. 11-13 cannot be sustained, because life is too raw. This does not make such trust and praise false, but they are not the whole truth. The full truth of Jeremiah includes a harsh counterpart. This bold and obedient prophet found himself in this moment of candid poetry alone, abandoned, hopeless, full of despair. Perhaps he is an unstable personality. No doubt his contemporaries found him so. The poem, however, gives us no warrant for a psychological analysis. We face a crisis of reality deeper than that. The measure of the crisis is that this cry, this curse, is not addressed to God or to anyone (vv. 14-15). The poet is bereft of anyone to whom address can be made, utterly alone with only shrillness against a hostile abyss.

The poetry moves abruptly from praise (v. 13) to the poison of assault upon everything that is near and dear. We are given no clue as to what might have evoked this poem of violent rejection and self-hatred. Perhaps this outpouring is triggered by the massive resistance Jeremiah encountered in his poetic vocation, or perhaps he is aware—in spite of the doxology—that God is not overly attentive. Or perhaps the poem is less focused and intentional than that. The

---

79. That the petition should culminate in an act of trust (vv. 11-12) and in a hymn of praise (v. 13) is characteristic of Israel. Thus again Jeremiah follows the practice of Israel. On such statements of trust in times of distress, see Ps. 27:1; 73:25.

curse speech may be an undifferentiated act of both deep exhaustion and a sense of futility about his vocation.

In any case, the verses are a cry from the depth (cf. Ps. 130:1). It is a cry so personal in character and so urgent that it lacks the focus of address. It is a wish hardly formed, not yet ready to be cast as a prayer. It is a yearning for "nonbeing," and in that regard is closely paralleled to the longer poem of Job 3. The poet wishes the day of his birth had never happened (Jer. 20:14). He knows of course that times of birth are awesome, specific, and irreversible (cf. 8:7), but he dares to imagine that his birth was not necessary and need not have been. The main assault in 20:15-17 is against the bearer of the news of his birth. He imagines the day of his birth. His father waited while the midwives worked. Then the news. Then rejoicing. But the waiting, the news, the rejoicing are all rejected. If only the news had not been brought. Jeremiah has made entry into this community only when the news of his birth is announced by the messenger. If the news had not been announced, he might have been unnoticed, unvalued, unassaulted, uncalled. The bearer of the message is rejected by Jeremiah because he did not need to bring the news. He could instead have suppressed the news and killed the baby. Perhaps there is subtle irony. As Jeremiah himself is rejected as a messenger, so Jeremiah would reject the messenger who caused him to be present and known in the world. Jeremiah knows all about messengers being rejected, and he wishes his birth message had never been delivered.

The poem ends with the great "why" question of human existence (v. 18); but it is not a general existential probe. The question is quite concrete. His urgent inquiry is more than simply the "why" of human existence. It is the "why" of being given a burden of "plucking up and tearing down," a message completely (and predictably) resisted. The issue is not existence, but vocation that shapes existence. Jeremiah's dread-filled question lingers unanswered, as we might expect. We do not know why, as Jeremiah does not know— because the ground and reason are hidden in the purposes of God.

Two facets of this poetic unit may be considered. First, how honest the Bible is! It does not deny or deceive about how costly the truth of God's word is. Such deep faith as Jeremiah's does not lead neatly to well-being, but to recurring crisis. The Bible knows about troubled, bitter faith that is left unresolved. Second, never does the poet finally curse God. While the poet seems to have gone berserk with curse, he also knows where the boundaries of faith are and how they must be honored. In a euphemism, Job's wife urges the cursing of God (Job 2:9), which Job will not do. Nor does Jeremiah. Nor does the poet curse his parents, who caused him to be. Indeed, there is no word uttered that would be a dishonoring of parents (cf. Deut. 5:16). In the bitterness and sense of abandonment that is experienced, that much of the relation still holds.

We must be aware of the odd (and, I judge, deliberate) juxtaposition of Jer. 20:7-13 and 14-18. These two poetic units are utterances of faith in tension. The second (vv. 14-18) does not cancel the first (vv. 7-13). One might imagine they should have come in reverse order, so that the doxology comes after the curse. But that is not how they are given. We do not know how to adjudicate between them. They are both given us as witnesses of this powerful, troubled faith. They both belong to this prophetic life of vitality and fidelity.[80] Such faith as Jeremiah's has seasons of trustful resolution and of bitter alienation. The two moods here in juxtaposition perhaps echo God's way with Jerusalem, which also knows about judgment and promise, about alienation and resolution. The alienation never quite reaches nullification.[81] The resolution seems never to be total. Both speeches of reassurance and of harsh protest are on the way. It is a troubled way, but it is the only way available to Israel.

There can be little doubt that this entire piece of poetry (vv. 7-18) partakes in *conventional forms* from the life of Israel, in turn lament and curse. There also can be little doubt that the poem reflects the *personal intensity and passion* of Jeremiah. The recognition of those two factors, however, still leaves us with the hard question of the public character of this poem. In what way or sense can the poem be the voice of public Israel? If the cry is only from the person of Jeremiah, then the poem has no larger or enduring interest. If, however, the poem is about the unwelcome, unbearable power of

---

80. The antithesis of "vitality" and the "embrace of death" that Jeremiah approaches here is greatly illuminated by the subtle discussion of Robert J. Lifton, *The Broken Connection* (New York: Simon and Schuster, 1980), esp. chs. 12-15. Lifton (153-154) reviews a case study of a person who "swung between total submission and violent image-feelings." Jeremiah seems to swing precisely between "total submission" (vv. 11-13) and "violent image-feelings." Lifton observes that his subject experienced "the absence of an in-between capacity for anger and rage." I suggest that Jeremiah's poetic outbreak in vv. 14-18 is for him (and characteristically for Israel) the "in-between capacity for anger and rage" that limited the destructive force of images of violence.

81. On "nullification" and the capacity of God to work a newness in the "null-point," see Walther Zimmerli, *I Am Yahweh* (Atlanta: John Knox, 1982), 111-133, esp. 115, 133.

the Word, about the seductive way of God with the messenger, about the capacity to praise the God who sends the Word, about the despair evoked among those who embrace the Word, then the poem is a theological disclosure which concerns the whole community of the Word. In this way, I submit, the poetry of the person may be appropriated and appreciated by the canonical community which continues to reflect on the message to the community. In the long run the message is of more interest to Israel than is the personal anguish of the messenger. While they cannot be separated, it is only interest in the message that lets this poetry of the messenger be taken up into the awareness and memory of the community.

JUDGMENT AND HOPE
Jeremiah 21:1–25:38

We group these several chapters together largely as a matter of convenience, because it is difficult to detect an intentional ordering. These chapters do cohere, however, around two themes: judgment and hope. The assertion of judgment is heavy, consistent, and nonnegotiable. Beyond the judgment, these texts offer important hints of hope. Chapter 21 is a general statement of judgment; chs. 22:1–23:8 more specifically indict the kings, and 23:9-40 is a specific judgment against the prophets. The materials on kings and prophets are not in the first instant related to the general indictment of ch. 21, but the theme is common enough to make sense out of the placement of the materials. Chapter 24 issues a powerful, if surprising offer of promise, and ch. 25, in language that is extreme in the Jeremiah tradition, sounds both judgment and hope. These five chapters together assert that God is doing something radical concerning Judah and Jerusalem which is marked by an awesome and frightening discontinuity.

THE FIRE NEXT TIME (21:1-14)

This passage, like much of the text, is set in the midst of the Babylonian threat. The first invasion by Babylon in 598 B.C.E. has left Jerusalem crippled and fearful, with the uncertain Zedekiah on the throne. The yet-to-come disaster of 587 is only vaguely anticipated, but not so vaguely as to avoid profound anxiety. The king is troubled. The chapter is arranged as a question to which four answers are given. The first two answers, in vv. 3-7 and 8-10, are prose and are stylistically congenial to the question of vv. 1-2. The second two answers (vv. 11-12, 13-14) are poetic units that are intentionally placed here, though probably not originally articulated for this context.

21:1-2 The question posed to Jeremiah by the king and priest here is an urgent one asked in the face of a grave political threat. Judah knows that such political questions cannot be separated from the reality of God and God's purpose. The text intends high irony that the king and priest, leaders of the establishment which has resisted Jeremiah, are finally driven to the prophet as a last resort. Conventional forms of strategy and policy have failed. Finally the sovereign word of Yahweh must be taken into account (cf. ch. 37). Babylon is on the move. The king has no recourse except the prophet. The prophet has been perceived as an adversary of the throne, but now everything short of this adversary has failed. The imperative "inquire of the LORD" is not simply a directive to acquire factual data. The request includes a search for information, but it goes beyond information to urge a fresh commitment of loyalty to Yahweh (cf. Amos 5:4,6; Isa. 55:6). The issue concerns a restored, trusting relation that goes beyond any new data. The question is to discern whether Yahweh is reliable and faithful in this crisis.

Jeremiah 21:2 contains a marvelous rhetorical tension. The appeal is to "Yahweh's wonderful deeds," that is, the old memory of saving deeds that focuses on the Exodus. The inquiry is to find out if that economy of historical support is still operative. If the God who defeated Pharaoh is still available, then there is hope. That powerful appeal to the old saving traditions is undermined by "perhaps," however, which makes appeal to the tradition of mighty deeds tenuous at best. The question yearns and hopes that the prophet will give assurance that the old categories are still at work and that God will do one more "wonderful deed" to save, against rapacious imperial power from Babylon.

21:3-7 Jeremiah's answer, however, is not to the liking of the king, nor does it provide any ground for certitude. The first response is addressed directly to the king. It is dominated by a series of first person verbs: "I will turn back, I will bring together" (v. 4), "I will fight" (v. 5), "I will smite" (v. 6), "I will give (deliver)" (v. 7). The rhetorical pattern of this response is shaped by the old modes of faith. The same powerful verbs that have resounded in Israel's life are still operative. Yahweh still acts and still takes decisive initiative. Yahweh is still the subject of the great active verbs.

The astonishing surprise of the answer in vv. 3-7 is that the old rhetoric is now inverted, so that the great verbs of the tradition are now used precisely against Judah, and therefore in favor of Babylon. Jeremiah has reversed the credo tradition of Judah to use against Judah. It is Judah who will now be without weapons, utterly vulnerable, completely helpless (v. 4). The most telling inversion is in v. 5, which uses the particular language of the Exodus. The notion of "outstretched arm and strong hand" is an old formula (Deut. 26:8; Ps. 136:12), now used against Judah by Yahweh, who has become Judah's enemy.

Jeremiah 21:7 seems to be added in case the preceding is not quite clear. The initial invasion was to cause pestilence, sword, and famine, a conventional recital of curses. Verse 7 adds the proviso that if any do not succumb to these curses, they will nevertheless face the direct power of Babylon. This oracular statement envisions no escape. It is addressed to the royal dynasty and to the entire city. The climactic statement uses the old harsh formula originally enlisted to resist Canaanite ensnarement: "no pity, no sparing, no compassion." Zedekiah's inquiry is answered, and the answer is not ambiguous. As much as any text in the tradition of Jeremiah, this one announces the nullification of all of God's old commitments to this special arrangement. The pathos of the announcement is intensified because it is envisioned as a result of Yahweh's "wonderful deeds."

There is important and intentional irony in the juxtaposition of Zedekiah's request and the prophet's answer. Zedekiah had asked for assurance about Yahweh's "wonderful deeds" (v. 2). The prophet, especially in v. 5, answers in Exodus language, thus alluding to "wonderful deeds," only now inverting them so that they are deeds *against* Judah and not *for* Judah, as anticipated by the king.

21:8-10 The second answer is addressed to the people, not the king. While the first response drew on the tradition of the Exodus, the second answer draws on the tradition of the Deuteronomist. Interestingly, the judgment is not massive or ruthless. Yahweh offers an invitation parallel to Deut. 30:15-20. Whereas 21:3-7 announced only death, these verses allow a chance for life. The way of death is to stay in the city and resist Babylon. To stay in the city means sword, famine, and pestilence (v. 9a). This part of the second response is parallel to vv. 3-7. The announcement is ideologically pure, offers no reservations, and is experientially probable. An occupied city is likely to foster famine and pestilence after the sword.

Verses 8-10, however, move beyond the vision of death with which vv. 3-7 end. These verses offer life, hope, an alternative possibility. To be sure, "this city" is under Yahweh's resolve for evil and cannot be saved (v. 10). Included in the reference to "this city" are the social ideology and policy of the throne and temple, and the power arrangements that sustain that ideology and policy. But individual persons need not go down with the city. The inhabitants of the city can escape. The judgment is against the arrogant temple and the self-serving monarchy. It is as though a distinction is made between "people" and "government," as we often do with reference to "the Russian people," or "the Cuban people." The oracle provides an out for the "people of Jerusalem." That is why vv. 8-10 are addressed to people, unlike vv. 3-7, which are addressed to the king. The alternative possibility is to "go out" to Babylon, to submit and find life.

It is worth noting that the verb "go out" (v. 9) is *yatsa,* the primary word for "exodus." Perhaps the usage is an accident, as it is a quite ordinary word. But in light of the explicit Exodus language (v. 5) and in light of the yearning for "wonderful deeds" (v. 2), it may be suggested that Judah's hope now is an exodus away from the "bondage" of Jerusalem to an odd "freedom" under Babylon. Perhaps this conclusion simply reflects the Deuteronomic bias in favor of Babylon. In any case, there was a lively, difficult, and urgent debate in Jerusalem about the possibilities still available. Some wanted to stay and fight. Others (including Jeremiah) saw surrender as a way of survival. While that must have been an ambiguous question for the contemporaries of Jeremiah, the book of Jeremiah insists upon a convergence between Babylonian policy and the will of Yahweh. Response to Yahweh now implies submission to Babylon. Because this convergence is now established in the canon, it cannot be explained simply on grounds of political calculation. The convergence is asserted on the basis of theological conviction. God wills submission as the door to a future community life.

21:11-12 The third answer is again addressed to the monarchy. It is probable that this is a free-standing prophetic oracle, with no particular reference to the question of vv. 1-2, nor to the immediate quandary of Zedekiah. It is a conventional urging about the covenantal character of the dynasty and could have been uttered in many contexts. The address in v. 12 is formal and impersonal— "house of David." This word is addressed to any Judean king in any context. It is the voice of the old covenant urging a covenantal, obedient shaping of royal power and policy.

The structure of the passage is a double imperative: "execute justice," "deliver," followed by a "lest" of avoidable consequence (v. 12). The same structure of multiple imperatives followed by "lest" is found, for example, in Deut. 8:11-17 and Amos 5:6. The double imperative (Jer. 21:12a) articulates the insistence of the Mosaic, prophetic tradition that the purpose of the monarchy is to assure justice for the marginal, weak, and helpless. This insistence on the priority of social well-being is offered against the monarchy's temptation to self-seeking and self-serving. Only a commitment to justice will secure the monarchy.

The threat introduced by "lest" (v. 12b) is equally conventional. It introduces the standard threat of the royal apparatus being burned in judgment (cf. Amos 1-2). Its placement in this location may have been suggested by the reference to fire in Jer. 21:10. The tradition relentlessly asserts that concentrations of power (i.e., monarchies) that are inattentive to the weak will surely end in disaster. It is assumed by the poem that no strategy of state, no matter how wise or strong, can be a substitute for the simple connection of justice and well-being that is foundational to all social reality. Justice prevents destructive fire. Conversely, injustice brings destructive fire. No substitute for justice can preclude destruction, even though every established power imagines the linkage can be broken. There is a moral coherence to the political process, and that moral coherence is guaranteed by Yahweh, who finally cannot be ignored.

Verses 11-12 are lean and clear. They reiterate an old prophetic claim that the practice of justice is the source of well-being. Placed in this chapter, however, the two verses give a surprising answer to the question of vv. 1-2. In verses 11-12 there is still time and opportunity to avert the Babylonian fire. The chance for escape that is offered is drawn from the essential covenantal character of Israel. The possible escape from judgment in these verses does not come by submitting to Babylon, but by doing what is most characteristic for Israel, namely justice. Verses 1-2 asked for a "wonderful deed." There is need for a new wonderful deed, for the old wonderful deed of the Exodus has now been forfeited. There is still a chance for life, but the chance depends on justice from the royal establishment.

The first three answers to Zedekiah's inquiry of Yahweh are of very different kinds:

vv. 3-8: inescapable destruction of the whole,
vv. 9-10: a chance for escape by surrender and exile,
vv. 11-12: a chance to save the whole by the practice of justice.

The three alternatives may represent different perceptions in response to different circumstances, but they also reflect different theological traditions. The first (vv. 3-8) asserts that Yahweh's only mighty deed will be to destroy. The second (vv. 9-10) believes that the mighty deed of saving will be mediated through the painful process of submission to Babylon and exile. The third (vv. 11-12) makes social justice a prerequisite for a saving deed, which is still an available option. This third is most powerfully rooted in the Mosaic tradition and least concerned to accommodate present circumstances.

21:13-14 The fourth answer is not in any direct way related to the preceding. It is a poetic fragment that lacks even the specificity of vv. 11-12. It apparently has no reference to either Zedekiah or Babylon. Its substance is most congruent with the first answer of vv. 3-7, though there is no specific link even to that statement.

The opening address to "inhabitant of the valley, rock of the plain" completely lacks a concrete reference. The oracle ostensibly is given against and in response to the question in v. 13b, "Who shall come down against us?" Perhaps the question is a request for information. More likely, it is a statement of defiance: that is, none would dare come against us; none would possibly succeed against us.

While the address of the oracle is unclear and the question is somewhat ambiguous, there is nothing unclear or ambiguous about Yahweh's answer (v. 14): "I will punish." Yahweh directly and personally will intervene in Judah's history. There is no mediating agent. Yahweh does not utilize Nebuchadnezzar. History is governed and judged by none other than Yahweh, who is able to intervene and can indeed enter any habitation. None are safe from Yahweh. The response of Yahweh contains elements of lawsuit. The sentence is fire; the indictment "the fruit of your doings." Judah's deeds evoke Yahweh's fire. The situation is not remote from that of vv. 11-12, but now Judah's circumstance is greatly deteriorated and therefore more hopeless.

It is difficult to know why vv. 13-14 are included here. The most likely reason is the mention of "fire," which coheres with vv. 10 and 12. Thus the latter three units all speak about a terrible destruction by fire. The notion that the city will burn reflects the deep antithesis of the prophetic tradition to urban monopolies of money, power, and religious pretense. God finds such self-serving concentrations of power deeply inimical to the covenant and to the possibility of humaneness. The image of fire evokes a harsh and total destruction.

If, as the text now stands, all four units are answer to the question of vv. 1-2, the king probably wishes he had not asked. The first answer (vv. 3-7) and fourth answer (vv. 13-14) offer no hope. The second answer (vv. 8-10) gives hope in exile, and the third answer (vv. 11-12) gives hope through radical social reorientation. None of these answers is bearable for the king and his company. The desperation of the situation had driven King Zedekiah to Jeremiah and to Yahweh. But no solace is given by the prophet. The question was asked with a hopeful "perhaps" (v. 2). At most, the response is a tenuous possibility, so tenuous that the king was unable to seize upon it. Zedekiah can only wait for "the fire next time."[1]

ORACLES ON THE KINGS (22:1–23:8)

The Jeremiah tradition is concerned with Jerusalem as a comprehensive social reality. But more particularly it is the king (and the dynasty) that embody the entire urban establishment. The conduct of the king is decisive for the weal or woe of the entire social system. The prophetic critique of kingship in this chapter has a double focus. On the one hand, as an embodiment of a self-serving ideology, the monarchy in principle is critiqued as disobedient and irresponsible. On the other hand, particular kings are handled in relation to specific items of conduct and policy. The tradition of Jeremiah takes a critical view both toward specific kings and toward the foundational claims of the institution of monarchy. Chapter 22 asserts that the trouble coming upon Jerusalem is trouble caused by the monarchy. While the entire chapter concerns the monarchy, a division may be usefully made between vv. 1-9 and vv. 10-30.

THE ROYAL HOUSE (22:1-9)

In vv. 1-9 we have a very general poetic unit concerning the Davidic house. This unit lacks contextual clues. Its pronouncement concerns the general attitude of prophets toward kings. The oracle is not dated, and the king is not named. It is a free-floating oracle which could have been used and placed in various contexts.

22:1-7   These verses consist of a quite stylized speech plus a poetic fragment. The address is formal, "King of Judah." Verse 3 lays down the main program of a covenantally-instituted monarchy. It begins with Israel's primary words addressing social responsibility, "justice and righteousness." These two words are found in the program of Ps. 72, in the royal coronation oracle of Isa. 9:7 (and its antithesis in Isa. 5:7), in the celebration of Solomon in 1 Kgs. 10:9, and in the sapiential rationale for kingship in Prov. 8:20. The two words taken together characterize social power and social practice in which there is strong support and care for the socially weak and marginal. (The critical statement of Ezek. 34:1-10 characterizes royal power that re-

---

1. The phrase derives from the ominous formulation of it by James Baldwin, *The Fire Next Time* (New York: Dial, 1963).

neges on this central mandate.) The remainder of Jer. 22:3 gives details of what justice and righteousness entail, the language of which closely parallels the prophetic summons of 7:5-7. The entire program is care for the marginal and powerless. That is the business of kings.

Jeremiah 22:4-5 contains a quite symmetrical statement concerning the assured gains and losses related to the imperatives of v. 3. This unit is arranged in two parallel "if . . . then" structures, one positive and one negative. The positive promise of v. 4 indicates that if the monarch "listens," all dimensions of royal power, including horses and chariots, will be guaranteed. The negative counterpart in v. 5 is that if the king does not attend to justice and righteousness, the "house" (i.e., the temple and dynasty) will be leveled. The "if . . . then" structure of these verses is remarkable, for this rhetoric makes the monarchy explicitly conditional.

The question of conditionality is the subject of a very old dispute in Israel.[2] The Mosaic community knew the covenant was based on the fragile condition of obedience (cf. Exod. 19:5-6), but the royal ideology of Jerusalem regarded God's commitment as unconditional (2 Sam. 7:14-16; Ps. 89:24-37). Various articulations can be identified that fall between these two alternative interpretations.[3] The options in Jer. 22:4 and 5 may formally be symmetrical, suggesting that the monarchy still has a choice. But judgment for the monarchy is announced, because the monarchy has not and will not meet the requirements of justice and righteousness.[4] While this "if . . . then" argument may be a statement under the influence of the Deuteronomist, it is also consistent with the old Mosaic covenant tradition which we expect Jeremiah to articulate. The net effect of the "if . . .

---

2. Jon D. Levenson, *Sinai and Zion* (Minneapolis: Winston, 1985), has in general resisted the bifurcation in the OT between conditional and unconditional aspects. However, I do not see how these tendencies when expressed concretely in the text can be harmonized.

3. See Walter Brueggemann, *David's Truth in Israel's Imagination & Memory* (Philadelphia: Fortress, 1985), esp. ch. 4, for the continuing theological power of the David tradition. The split between conditional and unconditional is no doubt an ideal construct which permitted many different nuances in concrete expression.

4. This text is like 18:1-12, in that it announces a theoretical possibility of change but then the realistic conclusion is drawn that Judah is at the point of no return. The theoretical possibility is acknowledged, but is no longer available. On this strategy, see A. Vanlier Hunter, *Seek the Lord!* (Baltimore: St. Mary's Seminary & University, 1982).

then" formula is to subordinate the monarchy to the torah, its requirements, and its sanctions.[5] This subordination deabsolutizes the monarchy and makes the king, like everyone else, subject to the demands of torah.

By themselves, vv. 4-5 suggest that Jerusalem still has a chance, if it will obey. The positive choice is still available. As the text stands, however, vv. 6-7 close off that option and announce judgment. Verses 6-7 are marked off rhetorically as an independent poetic piece. In their present context after vv. 4-5, however, they function to deny the possibility vv. 4-5 seemed to have offered. The time for a positive choice has passed. Judah and its kings are at a point of no return.

Verses 6-7 present a great reversal, in which the high one is brought low and there is no more chance for rectification.[6] The metaphor is that the dynasty is high, great, and majestic, like the fertile land of Gilead or the powerful cedars of Lebanon (cf. Isa. 2:12-17). Yet such height will not deter Yahweh. Yahweh will turn the fertile land into wilderness (Jer. 22:6b; cf. the contrast in Isa. 35:1-2). Agents of destruction will be dispatched by Yahweh (Jer. 22:7b). The best cedars will be cut and used only to fuel a fire of destruction. The poem moves at various levels of power. It moves in the direction of an apocalyptic conflagration. It also hints at the overthrow of a despised regime in which the oppressed sack and ravage all that remains when the power is gone. Faithful to the poetic and imaginative idiom, the destroyers are not named, but in the name of Yahweh they will commit massive destruction. The dynasty is under severe judgment, without invitation to repent. The live options given in vv. 4-5 are completely nullified. The monarchy has created for itself a situation of hopelessness.

22:8-9 These verses appear to be a prosaic clarification of what has preceded. In the poetry of vv. 6-7 no specific reason is given for the harsh judgment. These verses supply the reason with a simple "why . . . because" structure of question and answer. The answer is that they have forsaken "the covenant of the LORD their God." The punishment matches the affront. Israel "forsook" *('azab)* the

---

5. The Deuteronomist also struggles with the relation of torah and king. The primary inclination of the Deuteronomist is to subordinate the king to the torah. See, e.g., Deut. 17:14-20; 1 Sam. 12:13-15,25.

6. On the devastating reversal, see Isa. 2:9-22; 47:1-3, which is the antithesis of the positive reversal of 1 Sam. 2:6-8; Ps. 113:7-9; Luke 1:51-53. The Jeremiah tradition is fully informed by both modes of inversion.

covenant, and is now a forsaken people (cf. Isa. 54:6). Again the decisive term *'azab* is used, in parallel with worship of other gods. The harshness of judgment derives from the most fundamental violation of Yahweh's covenant. The contrast of this judgment with the condition of Jer. 22:3 is important. In v. 3 the conditions for continued covenant are ethical, without explicit theological reference. In v. 9 the reason for destruction is theological without ethical specificity. One may argue that the two different reasons reflect different theological traditions and different editorial layers. Or one may credit the tradition with understanding that the ethical conditions of v. 3 and the theological reason of v. 9 are in fact synonymous, a point made clear in vv. 15-16.

For all of vv. 1-9, the main point is that even such a powerful institution as the monarchy must meet elemental requirements of human compassion and responsibility in order to survive. The fulfillment of these requirements is glaringly absent in Jerusalem. The consequences are unavoidable and should not come as a surprise. Again, the text provides an unambiguous and remarkably disciplined conclusion. The text is an invitation for each new generation to reflect on the uncompromising condition Yahweh has set for historical well-being. The way of a people in history cannot, by any strategem, circumvent the elemental requirements of humaneness. The historical process is finally and inescapably a moral process. The judgment of God is not "supernaturalist," but is worked out in the discerning dynamics of power transactions in social relations.

THE FAILURE OF MONARCHY (22:10-30)

The remainder of the chapter now explicates these general statements through reference to specific kings. This section reads like a chronicle of kings during the years of Jeremiah and the last days of Judah.[7] A general review and critique of kings evidences the claim that kings are subject to assessment by the prophets, who represent

---

7. See John Bright, *Jeremiah,* 2nd ed., Anchor Bible 21 (Garden City, N.Y.: Doubleday, 1978), 144-146. The important point is that the chronicle is subjected to a very particular criterion of assessment, namely justice and righteousness. For a critical historical assessment of these kings, without the particular theological norm of justice and righteousness, see J. Maxwell Miller and John H. Hayes, *A History of Ancient Israel and Judah* (Philadelphia: Westminster; London: SCM, 1986), 391-415.

the real governance of Yahweh. The prophets speak of Yahweh's rule which stands in tension with the rule of the Jerusalem regime (cf. Isa. 6:1). Such a prophetic review has the dramatic effect of destabilizing or delegitimizing absolute royal claims made by Davidic kings. The tradition of Jeremiah is preoccupied with the authority of the prophetic word as a decisive mode of God's governance, which inherently threatens the monarchy. That preoccupation in Jeremiah can be traced back to the call narrative of Jer. 1:4-10. Kings are assessed by their response to this strange governance of Yahweh.[8]

22:10-12 In these verses the first reference to a specific king includes a general poetic statement and a specific prose comment. The contrast in the poetry of v. 10 is between Josiah ("him who is dead") and Jehoahaz ("him who goes away").[9] Josiah was an effective king who died in a military action and is much celebrated by the traditions of Jeremiah and the Deuteronomist (cf. 2 Kgs. 23:25). At his death, his son Jehoahaz was placed on the throne by a popular movement, but was immediately deposed by the Egyptians, who carried him into exile in Egypt (2 Kgs. 23:30-33). There he died (cf. 2 Kgs. 23:34). The poetic verse of our unit suggests that the real weeping in grief should not be for dead Josiah (Jer. 22:10). Josiah has escaped the trouble through his death and is now better off. It is his son in exile who faces the real problem and needs to be grieved, for exile is more cruel than an honorable death.

The refrain is constant in all three verses:

never return (v. 10),
never return (v. 11),
never see the land (v. 12).

The unit asserts the dread and finality of exile. The king himself is of little interest to the tradition. He is, however, a sign of the failure and the judgment of the monarchy. The kings in Jerusalem, of which Je-

---

8. As the Jeremiah tradition is now constructed, the word is addressed "to the nations and to the kingdoms" (1:10). Among these, clearly the first nation/kingdom addressed is Judah, i.e., the kings of this chapter. The claim of the tradition is that Yahweh's work of "plucking up and tearing down," of "planting and building" is the way in which Yahweh presides over the kings. Jeremiah is party to the notion that the monarchy, like the temple establishment, finally must answer to the God of the torah. Torah is a more elemental theological construct than is monarchy.

9. The king, Shallum, is mainly referred to elsewhere by his throne name, Jehoahaz. Cf. *A History of Ancient Israel and Judah,* 402.

hoahaz (Shallum) is a sorry case in point, are unable to cope either with internal threat or with the resolve of God. Monarchy is no barrier against God's ultimate nullification of Jerusalem. Royal ideology and pretension are quickly dismissed. Grief for the king is in fact grief for Jerusalem, now under certain death sentence.

22:13-19 This unit has two parts. In the second part, Jehoiakim is named (v. 18) and vv. 18-19 are a funeral lament for him. The poetry is an anticipation of his death, in which he will be mocked, scorned, and dishonored. The poet skillfully discredits and dismisses the failed kingship of Jehoiakim by portraying a death in which there is no adequate funeral and no serious grief.

Verses 13-17 lack specificity, but the reference to a king and his father (v. 15) parallel the identity of father and son in v. 18. We may therefore understand this unit to be a contrast between the well-respected father, Josiah, and the contemptible Jehoiakim, who is the real subject of this unit. Josiah is simply a foil to this pitiful son Jehoiakim, who succeeded his brother Jehoahaz on the throne in 609 B.C.E. and lasted until 598. It is an irony of Judean history that Jehoiakim engaged in dangerous political exploitation and adventurism, evoking the wrath of Babylon, but died well and comfortably before the Babylonian Empire responded (2 Kgs. 24:5-7). The biblical tradition judges him to be contemptible. He brought upon his people costly trouble, which he himself did not experience.

The poetry of Jer. 22:13-17 has three elements. First, vv. 13-14 are a radical critique of the false use of power. The "woe formula" is an announcement that death will come. The formula anticipates a funeral for a governance whose death is already underway. This formula is not spoken in harshness, but in grief, concerning the inevitable outcome of long-term systemic irresponsibility on the part of the king. This critique is expressed in the verbs following the woe—"who builds," "who makes," "who says," "who cuts." All four verbs concern economic exploitation, rendering others subservient for the sake of self-aggrandizement. The key concern of the poem, stated at the outset, is injustice and unrighteousness (v. 13), precisely the antithesis of the imperative of v. 3. This king, apparently Jehoiakim, has violated the most elemental responsibility of covenantal kingship. He has violated what it means to be king in order to enhance his own prestige by his conspicuous consumption.

Second, vv. 15-16 are a stunning act of social criticism, the most poignant of its kind in the entire Bible. The poet raises the question of what constitutes legitimate social power. He asks with disdain if it is visible luxury that constitutes kingship. That rhetorical question is answered in vv. 15b-16 by comparison to Josiah, who "did justice and righteousness." Again the key terms, "justice and righteousness," occur, placed in contrast to the seductions of cedar and vermillion, marks of affluence. "Justice and righteousness" are a precise contrast to the base, self-serving values of Jehoiakim. As a result of his social policy of caring for the weak and needy, Josiah prospered and had secure rule. Josiah is characteristically regarded as the king who executed policies according to the covenantal requirements of the Deuteronomist. He is portrayed as the embodiment of the best of Moses' covenantal dream.

The final line of v. 16 is one of the most remarkable in Scripture. It equates "knowing God" with doing justice to the needy.[10] The equation needs to be seen in its full claim. It is not asserted that knowledge of God leads to justice, nor conversely is it claimed that social justice leads to knowledge of God. They are the same. One might, on the basis of this text, conclude that the practice of justice is the very reality of Yahweh. In this text we are very close to the contemporary conversation about *praxis* as the mode of faith. In the most radical terms, this poetry anticipates John Calvin's judgment that right knowledge of God comes through obedience.[11]

The third element in this section (v. 17) brings the two previous ones together. On the one hand, v. 17 reiterates the judgment of vv. 13-14. On the other hand, it continues the contrast of Jehoiakim with Josiah, for Josiah would never practice oppression and violence. Josiah had not succumbed to a self-serving royal ideology, but still understood that the king exists for the people. Jehoiakim is thus exposed as one who imagines he is autonomous and does not need torah. Such autonomy destroys its practitioner, and destroys society at the same time. Josiah is offered as a norm by which Jehoiakim is

---

10. Jose Miranda, *Marx and the Bible* (Maryknoll, N.Y.: Orbis, 1974), 44-53, has most clearly grasped the radical subversiveness of this poetic unit.

11. John Calvin, *Institutes of the Christian Religion,* I, vi, 2 (Library of Christian Classics [Philadelphia: Westminster; London: SCM, 1960]). See also Charles M. Wood, "The Knowledge Born of Obedience," *Anglican Theological Review* 61 (1979): 331-340. Daniel W. Hardy and David F. Ford, *Praising and Knowing God* (Philadelphia: Westminster, 1985), argue and indicate by their title that knowledge of God comes through praise of God. Calvin, I think, would not disagree, for he would not make a deep distinction between praise and obedience, which are the two submissions through which God is known.

to be judged. No wonder the first word is "woe" (v. 13), as is the last word (v. 18; RSV "Ah!"). It is the only word the poet has for this king. Death is destined to come, and when death comes, the king not only dies but brings his city down with him.

Four possible statements of grief are suggested in v. 18, and all four are rejected: "ah . . . ah . . . ah . . . ah."[12] It is astonishing to have the death of the king envisioned, and then to have public grief precluded. The poet wants the utter shame and humiliation of this king to be clear. The poem is a dramatic act of delegitimation for a king who merits no honor. The dishonor is extended in v. 19. The king is to be treated in death as any other worthless animal carcass, simply disposed of in order not to disrupt the city. The scenario is a remarkably harsh one, appropriate for this most ignoble king. The ground of shame is named at the beginning of the unit in vv. 13-14—injustice and unrighteousness.

That Jehoiakim apparently died a routine death with a routine royal burial (2 Kgs. 24:6) indicates that the poet's anticipation did not in fact occur. That does not detract, however, from the powerful assertion of this poem that kings as agents of injustice are sure to be dismissed as ignoble, irrelevant, and not grieved or remembered. In the world of royal ideology all kings are honored at death, no matter how bad they have been. But the poet constructs another world, a world of covenantal truth, in which the rule of kings is assessed differently. Through poetic imagination, faithful listeners are invited to break with the make-believe world fostered by royal interest and join the poet's world. The poem fights for the imagination of Israel, to wean Israel away from excessive fascination with the visible power in Jerusalem. The disgrace envisioned for Jehoiakim cuts through the facade of self-serving and self-righteous monarchy which flourished in self-deceiving Israel.

22:20-23   In this long poetic collection on kings the small unit of vv. 20-23 is an intrusion, but it is not inappropriate. Whereas the context asserts judgment on individual kings, these verses assert a harsh judgment on the whole community. We may observe four rhetorical factors that disclose the thrust of the poem. First, the

---

12. The term rendered in the RSV four times as "ah" is Hebrew *hoi*, which is a cry in prospect of or in the midst of death. The use of the term summons Judah to an imagined death scene and an appropriate response of grief. The point of the poem is that in a situation where grief is appropriate there will be no grief, because the king will not be lamented.

poem begins and ends with "Lebanon" (vv. 20, 23). Lebanon as a geographical reality refers to a far boundary; as a metaphor it refers to pride and security. The poem addresses the community in its strength and prosperity (v. 21). The prophet identifies the crisis while Judah still thought there was no crisis. Second, there is a double "cry out" (v. 20), perhaps echoed in v. 23 with "groan." The cry is a desperate cry for help from someone who is vulnerable, weak, and abused. The juxtaposition of Lebanon and "cry" bespeaks an inversion. The strength of the establishment has been reduced to weakness, its competence to vulnerability and desperation (cf. Exod. 11:4-6). Third, in Jer. 22:21 there is a double use of *shemaʿ*, "I will not listen . . . you have not listened." The decisive failure of Israel is that they did not heed Yahweh, from whom comes their life. Fourth, the verb and noun "shepherd" is *raʿah/roʿeh*, which is matched by the word "wickedness" (*raʿ*, v. 22). These homonyms indicate the connection between the wickedness of not listening and the judgment of being cast to the wind, that is, blown away in exile. The poem ironically asserts that the wind that "scatters" will replace the shepherds that "gather." The once gathered community will be scattered in exile.

The poetic unit of vv. 20-23 begins and ends with reference to "Lebanon." However, this reference is in fact a reference to Israel. The metaphor "Lebanon" is applied to Israel because Israel under Jehoiakim has imitated Lebanon and now is trapped in the same destructive values as Lebanon.[13] Those values are symbolized by "cedar" (cf. vv. 14,23). The community that relies on the commerce and affluence embodied in cedars is doomed for death as a community that denies covenant (cf. Isa. 2:6-8).

This poetic unit also announces the scattering of a community once powerful. The poetry means to lead reality, to construct for Israel a scenario of an exilic future, even while Judah imagined itself safe. While the subject is different from that of Jer. 22:18-19 and the judgment is much more massive, the primary announcement of exile and death is congruent with the preceding. A harsh, inescapable ter-

---

13. For the capacity of Israel's poets to handle metaphors in powerful, subversive, and imaginative ways, see Carol A. Newsom, "A Maker of Metaphors—Ezekiel's Oracles Against Tyre," *Interpretation* 38 (1984): 151-164. See also Paul A. Porter, *Metaphors and Monsters: A Literary-Critical Study of Daniel 7 and 8,* Coniectanea Biblica, OT Series 20 (Lund: C. W. K. Gleerup, 1983; repr. Downsview, Ont.: Reproduction House, 1985).

mination is coming, a hurt like birth pangs (v. 23), only now they are the pangs of death.

22:24-30 The last king mentioned in this unit is Coniah, better known as Jehoiachin (vv. 24-30). He is the son of Jehoiakim, grandson of Josiah. It is his destiny to ascend the throne in 598, just in time to reap the bitter benefits of his father's deathly policies. Within a year of his ascension he is deported to Babylon, where he endures a long captivity (cf. 52:31-34; 2 Kgs. 25:27-30). Jehoiachin receives two distinct treatments in biblical tradition. On the one hand, he bears the hopes of this people and keeps the thread of the royal promise alive; on the other, he is clearly helpless and historically impotent, as he has no chance to act on the hopes he embodies. In this passage Jehoiachin is not a figure of hope. He is only an object for deep pity.

This unit concerning the last king is divided into prose (Jer. 22:24-27) and poetic elements (vv. 28-30). In the prose of vv. 24-27 Jehoiachin is identified as Yahweh's "signet ring"; the embodiment and sign of dynastic hope, and one of the few assurances of any thinkable future (cf. Hag. 2:23; Zech. 3:8). Nonetheless, he is "torn off" (Jer. 22:24). God is portrayed as an indignant lover who removes a precious ring from his finger and throws it away, nullifying all the hopes and promises that the ring symbolized. The king is rejected. With him the royal line beginning with David is ended and the royal promise nullified. The king and his mother, the bearers of royal identity, are abandoned by God, given over to Babylon.[14] There they died a lonely, disgraced death (v. 26). What was asserted of Jehoiakim in vv. 18-19 is now enacted with his son. This boy-king will be thrown out of Jerusalem, even as the corpse of his father was envisioned as rejected. The royal history of temple and throne is now terminated, albeit only in an imaginative scenario. The historical reality of this poetic scenario became visible a few years later.

The poetic counterpart of vv. 28-30 is one of the most poignant and pathos-filled units in the Bible. The poet articulates the deep anguish of this humiliating rejection of the boy-king. The poet wants

---

14. The mention of the queen mother (v. 26) strikes us as odd. Christopher R. Seitz, "Theology in Conflict: Reactions to the Exile in the Book of Jeremiah" (Ph.D. dissertation, Yale University, 1986), 164-171, has persuasively suggested the cruciality of the queen mother for royal power, and derivatively why she should be expressly mentioned in this context. See also note 16 on p.125 above.

his listeners to focus on this boy on whom the whole Jerusalem establishment has staked its future. Now he is rejected, forgotten, disgraced. The metaphor is a broken pot not valued (v. 28; cf. 19:10-11). In the metaphor of potter and clay (already employed in 18:1-4), the potter could reshape and finally reject. Of course it is Israel and not the king who is the clay of Yahweh in chs. 18-19. Here the clay is handled with greater specificity. He is rejected as worthless. His rejection is echoed in Ps. 118:22. Jehoiachin is indeed a rejected stone.

The pathos, however, is not merely over the boy. Where the king is jeopardized, the whole land is vulnerable. The poet articulates a larger grief over the land, which now must die as well (Jer. 22:29). This dirge is lean and stark, and therefore powerful. The poet utters only three bold words: "land, land, land." The dirge is not even couched with the initial "O," which is added in the RSV. It is like the tears and sobs of one who can only name the deceased's name over and over and over. It is important to note than in v. 29 this lean cry of grief belongs to Yahweh, who weeps over land and king. The death is so unbelievable. This good land (cf. 3:19) is now brought to death. Jeremiah 22:30 brings no relief from the death. Perhaps the pathos is not unlike that of a fourth-generation farmer in middle America who watched with choked tears while the bank foreclosed and auctioned the land for the mortgage. One can only say, "Land, land, land," when what has been home is now forfeited.

In Ps. 72 it is the justice of the king that brings prosperity in the land. Where there is no king the land cannot function. The dynastic promise rooted in 2 Sam. 7:13-16 is now terminated, albeit with grief and pathos. Not only is there no visible heir, but Yahweh has been pushed to a point of no return. There will be no heir. That great royal promise of 2 Sam 7:13-16 had appeared to be absolute and unconditional. It was in fact rigorously conditional (cf. Ps. 132:11-12). There would be an heir if the torah were obeyed. No obedience, no heir.

The "if" of Ps. 132:12 is consonant with the "if" of Jer. 22:4-5: the royal mandate is not unconditional. If one asks "why" about the fate of Jehoiachin in v. 28, or "why" more generally in v. 8, the answer is given in v. 9. The answer is the "because" of covenant violation. The invitation in v. 3 is premised on justice and righteousness. The indictment in v. 13 is precisely injustice and unrighteousness. Out of that wickedness of not listening (vv. 21-22), Jehoahaz (vv. 10-11) and Jehoiachin (vv. 24-30) are grieved; Jehoiakim is rejected (vv. 13-19); the city is dismissed (vv. 8-9), and the land is left wretched (v. 29). What could have been according to the promise of Yahweh now cannot be.

The poet gives speech to the coming tears of Jerusalem. We dare think they are the tears of God (v. 29; cf. 9:1-2).

A RIGHTEOUS BRANCH (23:1-8)

These verses bring to completion the general comment about kings. This unit continues the theme of ch. 22. It is organized around one very general indictment of monarchy and three quite unexpected promises.

23:1-2a The indictment in these verses is a general statement about kings ("shepherds"), parallel to the indictment of Ezek. 34. The "sheep" refer to Judah. There has been a scattering of the sheep (exile) because the shepherds have been inattentive to the sheep (cf. Mark 6:34). The shepherds have been remiss, because they have been preoccupied with themselves and their own well-being. The compelling metaphor of sheep and shepherd makes a powerful political statement. Mismanaged royal power is the single cause of exile. Neglected sheep will predictably be scattered.

The three promises of vv. 2b-4, 5-6, and 7-8 each begin with "behold." The placement of such promises in the Jeremiah tradition is unclear, especially when the promises are explicitly dynastic. The conventional judgment of scholarship has been that the hope passages are late and the dynastic promises are intrusive.[15] Whatever the historical and literary problems concerning these promises, the theological truth is that the tradition of Jeremiah asserts that the God who can nullify Judah can also work a new thing. Thus on theological grounds, these promise passages articulate Yahweh's resolve to work a newness in the face of historical realities and in spite of dynastic failure. The hope of God is not nullified because of Judah's failure. In the long run, and through anguish, God's hope overrides that historical, covenantal failure.

23:2b-4 The first promise asserts that God will act through no

---

15. The assignment of these promises to a later hand is characteristically not based on internal evidence, but on a more general theory of the prophetic literature. Cf. Robert P. Carroll, *From Chaos to Covenant* (London: SCM; New York: Crossroad, 1981), 147-48. A case is made by Bright and William L. Holladay for the assignment of these promises to Jeremiah in his later period. What is overlooked in both of these scholarly conclusions is the place of hope and promise in the tradition.

human agent, but will directly cause a homecoming. The verb "gather" is a precise resolution of "scatter" in vv. 1-2a, and stays with the metaphor of sheep. The gathering of sheep (as in John 10:1-18) refers specifically to the ending of exile. In our text, it is only after the gathering that new "shepherds" will be established, kings who will do what shepherds are supposed to do. The gathering from exile will be God's own action. Nonetheless there will be human shepherds who are the restored Davidic kings.

The double image of Yahweh as shepherd and of human shepherd reflects a tension (also seen in Ezek. 34:23-24) concerning the role of the Davidic dynasty in the Exile and beyond. There was surely dispute in exilic Judah about the cruciality of the Davidic house for the future. It is clear that the powerful claims for the Davidic house continued to be voiced in exile with a yearning for a restored kingdom. But there must also have been an alternative position among exiles which believed that no monarchy was needed when God reconstituted the community. With or without a human king, Judah's hope in exile concerns restoration of an ordered political life in which people are to be cared for, even as they have more recently been neglected. As with all these promises, this one holds together the power of God to create a newness and actual historical possibility. The new community which God gathers is regarded as a real historical possibility. The hope of Israel is concrete, this-worldly, and offered against the despair of present circumstances.

23:5-6 The second promise is the most explicitly Davidic promise in the tradition of Jeremiah (cf. also 33:14-16). The notion of a royal Branch is more appropriately expected in the tradition of Isaiah (cf. Isa. 11:1). The promise is so powerful and pervasive, however, that it also shows up in the tradition of Jeremiah. The usage asserts the conviction that God has not finally abandoned a commitment to the Davidic house. The Davidic possibility is envisioned as a king who will practice righteousness as was required in 22:3 and rejected in 22:13-14. In the days of this promised king (23:6) there will be a royal obedience which will make public life possible. One can see here exilic anticipations for the restoration of a valid public life, the very anticipations that the Christian community has found embodied in Jesus of Nazareth.[16] The new shepherd

---

16. It is worth noting that the promise articulated here is taken up in the "Common Lectionary C" in the use of Jer. 33:14-16 during Advent. Quite clearly, the Church has handled the text with reference to Jesus.

of the Davidic line is to implement a very old promise to "dwell securely" (v. 6; cf. Lev. 26:5; Ezek. 34:25).

This king will embody righteousness, to which his very name will attest. It is perhaps intentional and ironic that the "real king" anticipated is called "Yahweh is our righteousness" *(Yahweh tsidqenu),* while the last king of the line up to 587 is Zedekiah ("Yahweh is righteous"). The coming king will be genuine "righteousness" *(tsedaqah),* whereas the remembered King Zedekiah is not at all an embodiment of righteousness. That king bore the name; the coming king will embody the reality. The proposed name for the new king indicates a governance that brings well-being through justice.

23:7-8 The third promise asserts that the homecoming out of exile will be more dramatic than the initial Exodus. Liberation from Babylon will be so overwhelming that liberation from Pharaoh will be superseded and therefore not be remembered or spoken of. In 21:2 Zedekiah had asked about Yahweh's doing a new "wonderful deed." We have seen how ch. 21 employs exodus language negatively. In this promise the question of Zedekiah is answered. There will be a new wonderful deed which will displace the Exodus memory. Israel's hope outdistances even its powerful memory. The great gathering of liberated Judeans evidences that Yahweh is faithful and powerful. The land so grieved (22:29) now is a functioning homeland again.

We have seen that the old cannot be mended (19:11). Now God will work a newness (23:7-8). The newness is wrought precisely by God, and precisely in exile. There will be no newness by the operation of the old apparatus, and no newness prior to exile. Life will be lost—and then given again. This God presides over both loss and gift. Notice that the blessings announced are not guarantees of continuity. Rather, they bear witness to the deep discontinuity and imagine that God has power and will to assert the newness again, newness underived from what has gone before.

ORACLES ON THE PROPHETS (23:9-40)

The traditioning process has brought together in this passage a number of originally independent materials which deal with the general theme of prophetic authority. We may divide the unit into three sec-

---

Such a use requires an interpretive posture that recognizes that the text "does and does not" run toward Jesus.

tions, though even these are likely formed from smaller literary fragments (9-22, 23-32, 33-40).

Jeremiah lived midst a variety of competing "truth claims," each of which purported to be a disclosure of Yahweh's will. In that dispute, there were no objective criteria by which to adjudicate the various claims. Jeremiah is one of the parties to that dispute. In these verses he makes his clearest argument for his version of reality, and makes it against the "truth versions" of others whom he dismisses as false.[17] While the vindication of Jeremiah came through the anguish of the historical process, in the dispute itself it was not clear who was telling the truth and who had in fact discerned God's will and purpose. Jeremiah, against the other prophets, announced the end of Judah's "known world." The prophets who opposed him tried in various ways to soften the massive judgment he anticipated. Despite their protestations, that world did end as Jeremiah had announced. The tradition deduced from this outcome that Jeremiah had indeed stood in the council of the LORD. The canonical process that legitimated Jeremiah and excluded the other prophets with their rival message is a recognition of the truth of Jeremiah's perception.

23:9-12   Verses 9-22 are a general assault on prophetic voices that contradict Jeremiah.[18] Verses 9-12, however, are a more general indictment of religious leaders, both priests and prophets. The poet characterizes his deep consternation over the contrast between the words of Yahweh and the betrayals of that word. In vv. 10-11 he makes a connection between the wickedness of the leadership and what that wickedness does to the land. The tradition of Jeremiah is deeply concerned for the future of the land.[19] The land of Judah is so overburdened with evil that it cannot function. The linkage between bad leadership and the condition of the land is a powerful, imaginative assertion (cf. 22:28-30). Because of political abuse, the

---

17. On conflict between prophetic voices, see James L. Crenshaw, *Prophetic Conflict*, Beiheft zur Zeitschrift für die alttestamentliche Wissenschaft 124 (1971); and Simon J. DeVries, *Prophet Against Prophet* (Grand Rapids: Eerdmans, 1978).

18. See Robert R. Wilson, *Prophecy and Society in Ancient Israel* (Philadelphia: Fortress, 1980), 249-251.

19. See Walter Brueggemann, "Israel's Sense of Place in Jeremiah," in *Rhetorical Criticism*, ed. Jared J. Jackson and Martin Kessler, Pittsburgh Theological Monograph 1 (Pittsburgh: Pickwick, 1974), 149-165; and Peter Diepold, *Israels Land*, Beiträge zur Wissenschaft vom Alten und Neuen Testament 95 (1972).

land is driven to grief and mourning, which take the form of drought. The land is reduced to deathliness because religious leadership is unprincipled and self-serving. Perverted religion produces public crisis. The conclusion of 23:12 is that religious leadership cannot hide in its sanctity, but will be punished.

23:13-15 These verses become more specific. Now the priests are not mentioned. The subject is the prophets, and by v. 15 it is specifically the "prophets of Jerusalem," whom we may take to be the hirelings of the royal-temple establishment. In 3:6-11 we have seen the comparison of Israel and Judah at the expense of Judah. The same contrast is made here with the same result. The poet is not in fact interested in northern prophets. They are mentioned only as a foil to get at the southern prophets, whose disobedience is more profound than their northern counterparts. The Jerusalem prophets are morally unprincipled. They strengthen the hands of evildoers, that is, they support, endorse, and legitimate public policy that violates covenant (23:14). The verb "strengthen" is noteworthy, for it contrasts with the indictment against Jeremiah—that he "weakens" the hands of the leadership (38:4). The poet understands well the enormous power of religion to legitimate public policy. The religious leadership which opposes Jeremiah legitimates public policy uncritically, and in so doing it generates more wickedness. The outcome is that "all of them" (i.e., the entire population) are like Sodom and Gomorrah: worthy of destruction (cf. Gen. 19:1-29).

The indictment in Jer. 23:15 is not specific. The references to Sodom and Gomorrah and to adultery in v. 14 could suggest that the sins under indictment are sexual. These references do not stand alone, however. The adultery is paralleled by lies (v. 14), so that in all likelihood what is under indictment is a destructive, disobedient, noncovenantal way of ordering *every* aspect of community life. The poet understands that perverted sexuality goes along with a general distortion of public life that touches every phase of economic and political policy. In Ezek. 16:48-52 the metaphor of Sodom is used again with the contrast of Israel and Judah. There the sins of Sodom are "pride, surfeit of food, and prosperous ease," and lack of aid for the poor and needy. If that reference illuminates our poem, then the indictment is a general disregard of Yahweh's purpose of justice and righteousness. Jeremiah 23:15 summarizes the indictment and promises judgment on the distorting prophets.

23:16-17 These verses give more specificity to the conflict over the claims of the prophets. Jeremiah's opponents give assurance of *shalom* ("It shall be well with you"), and assert that no evil can come upon Jerusalem. These opponents are to be credited with some sophistication. They are surely not simply liars, or indifferent to moral matters. They may be quite conscientious, but are able to perceive reality only through the lens of Jerusalem ideology. Their commitment to divine sovereignty and moral sensitivity is filtered through a deep conviction about God's enduring commitment to king and temple. They trusted God's unconditional commitment to the Jerusalem enterprise. Jeremiah, however, dismissed their religious posturing as self-serving ideology which perverts reality and mocks God's truth. Jeremiah sees that Israel's faith is distorted to be a rationale for a particular political claim.

According to Jeremiah, the message of unconditional well-being *(shalom)* is false *(sheqer)*. The prophets' message of *shalom* misreads the historical situation and misrepresents the character of Yahweh, who is uncompromising about the concerns of justice and righteousness. As the message is false, so also the source of the message is false. Reliable prophetic announcement is given from God, but this message comes from the imagination of the prophets, not from God. That is, what claims to be truth is fantasy and wishful thinking. The "visions" of these prophets are not simply the result of personal idiosyncrasy, however. The minds and hearts of the other prophets are shaped by and in the service of the royal ideology. Their words are not private daydreaming, but systemically determined distortion.[20] Thus the contrast in v. 16 between "their own minds" and "the mouth of Yahweh" can be understood as a contrast between royal-temple ideology and the harshness of the covenant tradition. Those whom Jeremiah critiques offer only "vapor" for truth. Their "vain hopes" are not reliable and cannot be acted upon.

23:18-22 These verses reiterate the contention that the establishment prophets speak their own self-serving, uncritical message, unauthorized by Yahweh. These verses appeal to the "council of the gods," which meets to decide their will for the earth.[21] That council

---

20. On systemic distortion, see Jürgen Habermas, *Legitimation Crisis* (Boston: Beacon, 1975). Habermas writes of the problems of modernity, but his analysis is helpful for our interpretive work, for Jeremiah was facing precisely the systemic distortion of reality done by the royal-temple enterprise.

21. Patrick D. Miller, Jr., *Genesis 1-11: Studies in Structure and Theme,*

is presided over by Yahweh. When a decision is reached, the council dispatches a messenger (sometimes a prophet) to announce the decision of the gods on earth (cf. 1 Kgs. 22:19-23; Isa. 6:6-8). The messenger who is dispatched has no freedom to give his own opinion, but can only give the verdict reached by the government in heaven.

Jeremiah claims to have stood in that council and been present when the decision about Jerusalem was made (Jer. 23:18). His message, authorized from heaven, is that Jerusalem will be destroyed (vv. 19-20). His claim of authority is expressed in the formula that is repeated throughout the tradition, "Thus says the LORD." That is, the message is from another source and it is not mine. The opponents of Jeremiah cannot legitimately say, "Thus says the LORD," because they have not been given a heavenly message, have not been present when the decree on Jerusalem was announced, have not been authorized or dispatched (v. 21). They have invented their own word and their own authority for the word (v. 22). Thus the dispute is not only about the substance of competing prophetic announcements, but also about the authority that lies behind and justifies those competing announcements. The contrast between Jeremiah and the other prophets can be traced back to the initial statement of Jeremiah's call. The words of 1:7 evoke the image of the messenger dispatched by the divine council:

> To all to whom I send you you shall go,
> and whatever I command you you shall speak. (1:7)

These claims about Jeremiah's vocation are precisely contrasted with the dismissal of his opponents:

> I did not send the prophets, yet they ran;
> I did not speak to them, yet they prophesied. (23:21)

Jeremiah is sent. They are not. Jeremiah is commanded. They are not.

JSOT Supplement 8 (Sheffield: University of Sheffield Press, 1978), has explored the rootage of the "divine assembly" of the gods. In "The Sovereignty of God," in *The Hermeneutical Quest,* ed. Donald G. Miller, Princeton Theological Monograph 6 (Allison Park, Pa.: Pickwick, 1986), 130-31, 135-37, Patrick D. Miller, Jr., has explicated the theological significance of the divine assembly. It is noteworthy that he places the imagery of "divine council" under the rubric of Yahweh's sovereign authority. That is exactly what is at work in this text. See also E. Theodore Mullen, Jr., *The Assembly of the Gods,* Harvard Semitic Monograph 24 (Chico, Calif.: Scholars Press, 1980).

Against this background of the divine council, the final adjudication among these various voices is made on the actual substance of the message. The verdict of the council is negative concerning Jerusalem, and any announcement to the contrary cannot have been generated in the divine council. It is a fantasy to announce well-being when the real verdict is judgment, wrath, and death. God decides God's own mind (in Hebrew, "heart"; v. 20), which is in contrast to the mind (heart) of the false prophets (v. 16). God is not simply a human projection. The reality of God's heart and God's decision (v. 20) contrasts with the heart and fantasy of Jeremiah's opponents (v. 16).

Beyond the dismissal of the false messengers who do not tell the truth because they have had no access to the truth, this unit makes three additional assertions. First, the judgment against Jerusalem has now been mobilized and will not be deterred. It is sure to come (v. 20). Second, the talk of the earlier prophets had been a call to repentance. Genuine prophetic announcement should have wrought a change.[22] The poem presents a play on the theme of "turn." In v. 20 the anger of the LORD will not turn; in v. 22 people "would have turned." But now there will be no turning, either on the part of God or on the part of his people. Neither will turn. Third, in v. 20 the poet places a most ominous and dread-filled assurance at the center of this unity: "in the latter days." Presumably the latter days are after the destruction, perhaps in exile. Because the prophets have not had a true word, they have not turned Judah from evil. Because they have not turned Judah, God's judgment will not be averted. The awesome reality of God's sovereign rule will be evident as God's anger is implemented. The future of Judah, deathly as it is, is linked to the failure of prophecy.

23:23-32   The critique of false prophets continues in the prose of vv. 23-32. Verses 23-24 assert the sovereign freedom of God. God is not near and available (v. 23).[23] God is unavoidable (v. 24). That God should be "near" is a promise from the temple cult. The assertion that God is distant thus stands over against the temple ideology.

---

22. Hunter, *Seek the Lord!*, has shown how the prophetic summons to repent is always a previous summons that is no longer possible. The previous summons is characteristically referred to in order to set a context for the present articulation of judgment.

23. See Werner E. Lemke, "The Near and the Distant God: A Study of Jer. 23:23-24 in its Biblical Theological Context," *Journal of Biblical Literature* 100 (1981): 541-555.

God's distance enacts God's freedom, and if God is distant from the temple cult, God is also distant from these domesticated prophets. The claim about God in v. 24 also stands against the dominant ideology. Jeremiah resists the temptation to make God an uncritical patron of the establishment. False prophets always seek to draw God too near to favorite arrangements and so minimize God's sovereign freedom.

After this introduction which focuses attention on the character of God, the text turns again to the theme of false prophets. These verses do not state the content of the prophetic lies, though we may assume they are a continuation of v. 17. The text contrasts "lies" (vv. 26, 32) with truth (v. 28). The prophets opposing Jeremiah are false, but they could speak faithfulness. The substance of lies and falseness is that Yahweh's name is forgotten (v. 27), the word of Israel's God is distorted (v. 29), and God's name is taken in vain (v. 31). The effect of all such dreams, fantasies, and distortions is that Judah is led astray, away from God's will into a death-dealing disobedience (v. 32).[24]

We are not told what the specific point of acute conflict is. Verses 23-24 suggest, however, that in the name of the royal-temple apparatus the sovereignty of God has been reduced to uncritical patronage, and the mandate for justice and righteousness has been translated into security and order. God's word is like fire that burns and a hammer that smashes (v. 29). Every other prophetic word that is accommodating and anemic is recognized as an alien word and is not Yahweh's legitimate word. These other prophetic voices have become so perverted, so self-serving in their rejection of Yahweh's true character, that Israel's discernment of God is distorted. The judgment is upon the perverting prophets here, but the terrible end which eventuates will be upon the entire distorted community that can no longer discriminate between the truth of Yahweh's purpose and the falseness of futile attempts at control and self-securing (cf. Isa. 5:20; Ezek. 13:8-16).

Jeremiah 23:23-32 is indeed a dispute between rival prophetic voices which appeal to competing theological traditions. Behind the dispute concerning true and false prophets is a dispute about the character of God. The ideological prophets of the establishment cele-

---

24. This passage has important connections to Deut. 13:1-3, wherein it is asserted that prophets and dreamers will lead Israel away from Yahweh and into disobedience. In our text, Jeremiah locates this religious seduction with the prophets, on the one hand, and with the public political crisis of Jerusalem, on the other hand.

brated and affirmed God's nearness and God's abiding commitment to and presence within the Jerusalem establishment. God had become a part of that social arrangement. In sharp contrast, Jeremiah bears witness to a God who is "afar off"—free, sovereign, and not a mere appendage to the established religion. The issue in the dispute is not about the content of a particular announcement, but about God and God's relation to Judah. Until Judah is clear about the character of Yahweh, it will never be clear about the discussion in the divine council, about whom the council may send to Judah, or what the message will be. Jeremiah is unambiguous about the message, because he knows clearly about Yahweh who will govern by his uncompromising will for justice and righteousness. The dispute begins and ostensibly concerns what the other prophets say and do. As the unit is completed, however, it becomes clear that the question of prophetic vocation is secondary to the foundational question of the reality and character of God. In this articulation of Yahweh's character, we are close to the central concern of the tradition of Jeremiah from which all else follows.

23:33-40   These verses are an appendix to the material concerning false prophets. The text appears to be a play on the word "burden" *(massa)*, the meaning of which is obscure. The term "burden" has a double meaning. It can mean an oracle that purports to be a disclosure from Yahweh (vv. 33,35-36,37-38). In this text the word also has a second meaning: a weight which Yahweh must carry and which leaves Yahweh exhausted (v. 33).[25]

The text is framed by vv. 33 and 39-40. In both the opening verse and the closing verses, the ones who speak "the burden" are threatened with exile. In v. 39 the threat of being "lifted up" *(nasa)* is linked to the "burden" *(massa)*. An additional wordplay is thus operative. The one who burdens *(massa)* will be lifted up *(nasa)*.

Within this frame, the text is highly problematic. Verses 34-38

---

25. Scholarship has not found a helpful explanation beyond the rather obvious point that the word is used in a double way as a homonym and that the power of the text depends on this double meaning. For critical attempts to establish linguistic grounds for the wordplay, see Henry S. Gehman, "The 'Burden' of the Prophets," *Jewish Quarterly Review* New Series 31 (1940/1941): 107-121; and William McKane, "משׂא in Jeremiah 23,33-40," in *Prophecy: Essays Presented to Georg Fohrer on His Sixty-Fifth Birthday,* ed. John A. Emerton, Beihefte zur Zeitschrift für die alttestamentliche Wissenschaft 150 (1980): 35-54.

seem to revolve around the relationship of the religious profession-
als to the word, the "burden," of God. There is a rhetorical pattern
of alternation between assertion and question. Thus in v. 34 the
assertion of Yahweh's "burden" is prohibited, but in v. 35 the question about Yahweh's word is legitimated. Again in v. 36 the assertion
of burden is prohibited, but in v. 37 the question is permitted. In
v. 38 the assertion of the burden is again placed under judgment.

This rhetorical pattern suggests the following conclusion about
the proper function of the religious leadership. The prophets and
priests seem to presume that they can answer for God, and such presumption is summarily rejected in this text (vv. 34, 38). One can ask
about Yahweh's burden, but one cannot presume to know it (vv.
35,37). Presumptuous knowing, which closes one to true knowing
(cf. vv. 23-24), results in being lifted up and cast out into exile. As
elsewhere in the Jeremiah tradition, the religious leadership stands
under indictment for attempting to curtail and control God's free
and full sovereignty.

THE TWO BASKETS OF FIGS (24:1-10)

This text is dated by the editors between the first deportation of 598
B.C.E. and the second, decisive deportation of 587 (v. 1). During
that time, the exiled boy-king Jeconiah (Jehoiachin) was head of the
exilic community in Babylon. After the people of Judah were exiled
and away from their homeland, they came to be called "Jews." Thus
we may refer to this exiled community as the "Jewish community."
That reference, however, refers to the same covenanted community
which concerns the whole of Scripture, the people of the covenant.
It is only because of geographical displacement that the particular
word "Jew" became useful and necessary. The community included
prominent citizens and skilled artisans (v. 1; cf. 22:24-30). During
the same period, the Jews who remained in Jerusalem were presided
over by Zedekiah, uncle of Jehoiachin and the third son of Josiah.
Zedekiah's status is unclear. Perhaps he is legitimately king (as in
2 Kgs. 24:18), or perhaps he is only regent for Jehoiachin. The uncertainty of his status is no doubt commensurate with the ambiguity and tension between the two communities.[26]

---

26. The dispute between the two communities is well documented and
explored by Seitz, "Theology in Conflict." Seitz shows that the historical
situation of the two communities evoked very different theological perceptions and conclusions.

The reality of two Jewish communities, one in exile and one in Jerusalem, is peculiarly important for this passage. There must have been rivalry and conflict between a community in exile and a community at home. On the face of it, one would imagine that the ones left behind (even if they are not the leading citizens) must have felt themselves fortunate for not having been deported. It must have been obvious to them that they were God's chosen—not only especially loved, but protected and entrusted with God's future. Given that self-understanding, it would be equally obvious to the ones in Judah that the Jews in exile were not in God's favor. Because they were the ones who suffered the punishment of exile, they must be rejected and judged by God.

This discernment of the historical process and the assignment of roles of favored and judged is the logical discernment. It must have been obvious to both communities, so obvious that it produced respectively a sense of arrogance in Judah and of dejection in exile. The Jerusalem community seemed to have ground for pride, even as the exilic community in Babylon had ground for despair.

The surprise of Jer. 24 is that it does not participate in that logical and obvious discernment. This text proposes a bold alternative interpretation of God's actions and the significance of these two Jewish communities.[27] This text is a polemic against what seems the obvious reading of God's intent in terms of affirmation and rejection. The text presents its alternative reading of historical reality through a vision, through which the prophet sees as others had not seen.

24:1-3   These verses report the vision of two baskets of figs.[28] The baskets of good figs and rotten figs suggest to the prophet communities of "good" and "evil." The oracle does not return to the figs, but instead moves away from the vision to the prophet's interpretation of what he has seen.

24:4-7   These verses explicate "the good figs," who are the exiles

---

27. See Walter Brueggemann, "A Second Reading of Jeremiah After the Dismantling," *Ex Auditu* 1 (1985): 156-168; and David Noel Freedman, "The Biblical Idea of History," *Interpretation* 21 (1967): 32-49.

28. On the phenomenology of visions, see Susan Niditch, *The Symbolic Vision in Biblical Tradition*, Harvard Semitic Monograph 30 (Chico, Calif.: Scholars Press, 1983). The motif of a vision of figs is taken up in the OT elsewhere only in Jer. 29:17. Clearly the tradition is not interested in the phenomenology of vision.

in Babylon. The exiles are regarded as "good" by Yahweh. That is against the more conventional, obvious reading given by Jews in Judah that the exiles are objects of God's judgment. This oracle asserts instead that the exiles are the objects of Yahweh's special favor. Their goodness does not rest in themselves, but in sovereign assertions of Yahweh, who announces them to be good (cf. Deut. 9:6). The freedom of Yahweh in making such a dramatic assertion parallels that of Gen. 15:6, in which Yahweh "reckons" (*hashab*) Abraham to be righteous.[29] This is one of the most stunning theological claims in Jeremiah. The community in exile is the wave of God's future. Such a claim may indeed be self-serving propaganda, or it may simply be pastoral consolation for displaced people. It is nonetheless presented to us in the Bible as a theological verdict by this God who is now allied, by free choice, precisely with the community that the world thought had been rejected. It is indeed an act of free grace which creates a quite new historical possibility. The text thus bears witness to the conviction that this God can and will create a new community from among those rejected.

These exiles now are presented as the object and recipient of God's gracious intervention. God "set my eyes" upon them for good (v. 6). God resolves to return them from exile and to permit them to resume life in the land. In v. 6 the narrative utilizes the powerful verbs of 1:10. Now the positive verbs "plant" and "build" are operative. Indeed, "tearing down and plucking up" have already happened, and now God restores.

In 4:4 the poet had hoped for a change in Israel's heart. Now, however, the solution is more radical. Yahweh will give Israel a new heart (24:7). It is as though the narrative knows Israel can never change its inclination (cf. 13:23). The only chance of newness is due to God's radical and underived action. The gift of a new heart (see also 31:31; Ezek. 36:26) is done by God, because Israel cannot change its heart. Newness out of exile is wrought by God's powerful graciousness.

The purpose of the new heart for Israel is for the sake of a restored covenant with Yahweh: "They shall be my people and I will be their God" (Jer. 24:7). The covenant formula indicates that Israel's autonomy has now been happily displaced by an embrace of covenant. There is no hint that Israel has changed. Rather, God has simply

---

29. On the term in Gen. 15:6, see Gerhard von Rad, "Faith Reckoned as Righteousness," in *The Problem of the Hexateuch and Other Essays* (1966; repr. London: SCM; Philadelphia: Fortress, 1984), 125-130.

overridden former realities by his power to "regard" the situation afresh (v. 5). That sovereign "regard" makes covenant newly possible. Israel will now embrace its rightful character and live willingly in this relation with Yahweh: "They shall return to me" (v. 7). Israel is now to be who Israel finally must be, the people of Yahweh. God gives Israel "a heart to know" (v. 7a), and so Israel will return with "their whole heart" (v. 7b). Israel with a new heart can now live faithfully and joyously in covenant.

24:8-10 This last part of the speech looks at the other half of the Jewish community. The bad figs are those who were not in Babylonian subjugation but remained in Jerusalem. This is a radical, polemical reading of historical reality. Remaining in Jerusalem or fleeing to Egypt is now regarded as resistance to God's intent and therefore makes one subject to judgment (cf. 42:9-17). The practical effect of this judgment is to delegitimate the rule of Zedekiah. The ones in Jerusalem are not the real Israel of the future, and the one who governs there (Zedekiah) is not the real king of Yahweh's people. Here as elsewhere, the book of Jeremiah operates on the firm conviction that the history ruled by Yahweh has a decidedly Babylonian flavor to it. Those who do not submit to the Babylonian reality are in fact in rebellion against Yahweh's purpose.

The sentence pronounced against the Jewish communities in Jerusalem and in Egypt includes language out of the old curse tradition (cf. Deut. 28:37). Those who refuse Babylon shall be subject to keen ridicule and are to be abandoned and hopeless (Jer. 24:9). The sentence includes the standard threefold curse that is pervasive in the tradition of Jeremiah: "sword, famine and pestilence" (v. 10).

The vision and oracle of this chapter are of particular interest at two levels. First, one may observe how the *claims of a partisan community* come to be regarded as a *normative theological position*. There is no doubt that this text comes out of and reflects the community of Babylonian exiles.[30] The text is a partisan claim concerning who would exercise leadership among Jews and who would take initiative in the coming reconstruction of Judaism after the homecoming. That is, what is cast as religious reality is surely the mobilization of political opinion in a power struggle. While this partisan struggle may be the life setting for ch. 24, the Bible no longer presents this text as a self-serving claim. The rereading of history in ch. 24 is pre-

---

30. See Ernest W. Nicholson, *Preaching to the Exiles* (Oxford: Blackwell, 1970), 110-111.

sented as a verdict rendered by God. The God of the Bible does indeed take sides in the midst of difficult historical conflicts. The passage may be very close to the cynical notion that winners write history, but we take the claim of this text as much more than that.

Second, we can see how drastic and astonishing are God's judgments in the historical process. The exiles devalued by the world are here identified as the bearer of God's future. This revaluation of the world's rejects is the surprise of the gospel, echoed in so many places. This revolution is evident in God's decision to choose "rabble" to form Israel (Exod. 12:38; Num. 11:4), in Jesus' decision to be friends with sinners (Luke 7:34), in the choice of the lowly, not the wise and the powerful (1 Cor. 1:26-27), in the choice of the stone that the builders rejected (Mark 12:10-11). This God seems indeed to *make* the future with those whom the world judges to be *without* a future.

THE CUP OF WRATH (25:1-38)

This is an odd and unexpected unit in the Jeremiah tradition. We have encountered nothing like it heretofore. It is a sustained and relentless announcement of God's judgment upon all the nations of the earth—even upon Babylon, who is regarded in most of the Jeremiah tradition to be God's agent. Now the one who has been God's agent stands under God's judgment. Judgment in Babylon, moreover, is inevitably news of rescue for Judah.

25:1-14   The first part of this peculiar chapter opens with familiar, conventional language. The passage is plodding prose, and surely is heavily influenced by the thought of the Deuteronomist. This chapter is rooted in the foundational assumptions of Israel's prophetic tradition, but moves beyond that tradition in articulating a very shrill philosophy of history. The first oracle is dated precisely to 605 B.C.E. (v. 1). That year was a pivotal time in the world of Jeremiah. In the geopolitics of the Near East that year, Babylon emerged as the victor in the battle of Carchemesh and the primal power of world politics.[31]

Verse 3 gives the date of 626 (thirteen years after 639). This date is reckoned by many scholars as the beginning of Jeremiah's ministry, though others take it to be the date of his birth.[32] Verses 3-7 pres-

---

31. See a summary of the data by Miller and Hayes, *A History of Ancient Israel and Judah,* 403.

32. On the chronology as it bears upon this date, see H. H. Rowley, "The Early Prophecies of Jeremiah in Their Setting," in *A Prophet to the*

ent a view of the history of Judah from a prophetic-Deuteronomistic perspective (see also 2 Kgs. 17:7-18 and Zech. 1:2-6). This view asserts that (a) the prophets are sent by God, (b) the prophets called Judah to "turn," and (c) Judah refused in its stubbornness to turn. The entire history of Judah is presented as a long history of disobedience and resistance. Such a reading is extended and expanded in Ezek. 16, 20, and 23.[33]

This dismal verdict leads to the harsh sentence of Jer. 25:8-11, which is a summary of the anticipations that have been sounded in the tradition of Jeremiah. The dramatic rhetorical introduction of "Therefore . . . because . . . behold . . ." indicates that we are now at the battle line. The astonishing assertion which opens the argument is that the entire land will be given over into Babylonian control. We are now familiar with this Jeremianic judgment. What is new is that Nebuchadnezzar is explicitly referred to as "my servant" (v. 9).[34] Even alien rulers are utilized to work out Yahweh's purpose. Such a prophetic judgment is an act of theological courage and must have been galling to Judeans. A more palatable, positive counterpart is found in Isa. 45:1, which refers to Cyrus, king of Persia, as "my messiah." Even with such a positive prospect, however, Isa. 45:9-13 reports hostile resistance. If the positive notion that God uses Gentiles to save evokes hostility, we can only guess what was evoked by the announcement that God uses Gentiles to judge. The implicit claim is that God governs gentile history as well as Israelite history (cf. Amos 9:7).

The dominant motif then is that God's sovereignty and governance is massive, irresistible, all encompassing. Yahweh's sovereignty

---

Nations, ed. Leo G. Perdue and Brian W. Kovacs (Winona Lake, Ind.: Eisenbrauns, 1984), 33-61; and William L. Holladay, "The Years of Jeremiah's Preaching," *Interpretation* 37 (1983): 146-159.

33. See Moshe Greenberg, *Ezekiel, 1–20,* Anchor Bible 22 (Garden City, N.Y.: Doubleday, 1983), 270-306, 360-388. Such negative recitals are an inversion of the old recital of God's mighty deeds of rescue. For a juxtaposition of the old recital and the inverted recital of disobedience, see Pss. 105–106.

34. On the theme of Nebuchadnezzar as the servant of Yahweh, see Thomas W. Overholt, "King Nebuchadnezzar in the Jeremiah Tradition," *Catholic Biblical Quarterly* 30 (1968): 39-48; and Werner E. Lemke, "'Nebuchadnezzar, My Servant,'" *Catholic Biblical Quarterly* 28 (1966): 45-50. Overholt accepts the theological claims of the phrase, "Nebuchadnezzar, my servant," but Lemke has reservations on both critical and theological grounds.

is now turned against Judah. The concrete result is that the old curses will be implemented (Jer. 25:9; cf. Deut. 28:37; Jer. 24:9) and communal life will cease (25:10; cf. 7:34). It is noteworthy that in 25:9 the judgment is said to be "forever" *('olam)*. However, the word *'olam,* which we translate "forever" (RSV "everlasting"), does not mean an absolute, timeless future. Rather, it refers to all thinkable, foreseeable future. That future, however, is always left open for God's new and transformative action. God is not fated even by what is said to be "forever." The Bible asserts that in every circumstance God can work a newness which subverts and astonishes all that we regard as closed, settled, and absolute. At the end of the verdict (v. 11) the subservience to Babylon is for seventy years. The tension between "forever" and seventy years suggests redactional activity.[35] The first statement about "forever" is probably a prophetic verdict, unencumbered by historical specificity. It means "for all forseeable future." The subsequent "correction" of seventy years may reflect the beginning of historical specificity. That is, either it intends to tone down the horror, or it means to keep the verdict in the realm of historical realism. It may also reflect the actual end of exile and the return of deportees to the homeland.[36]

The reference to seventy years begins to take the poison out of the "forever." It suggests that the harsh judgment is not final and is not to perpetuity. It begins to look beyond judgment to new God-given historical possibilities. Such a move does not lessen the harshness of the judgment. It is rather a disclosure of another dimension of this God who governs the historical process. This God does not "keep his anger forever" (cf. Ps. 103:9). This God chooses different possi-

---

35. It is exceedingly difficult to know what is intended with "seventy years." It could be simply a traditional number which is appropriate for some matters, such as the duration of a destroyed city; it could be a reference to one generation span as a way of reckoning time, or it could be intended to refer to concrete dates. Cf. Avigdor Orr, "The Seventy Years of Babylon," *Vetus Testamentum* 6 (1956): 304-306, who argues that the apocalyptic tradition of "seventy years" began with a concrete chronological intention.

36. My propensity is to take the number as a limiting factor, but there is no doubt that the reference to "seventy" provides a source from which prophecy begins to move in apocalyptic directions. On that general problem see Michael A. Knibb, "Prophecy and the Emergence of the Jewish Apocalypses," in *Israel's Prophetic Tradition,* ed. Richard Coggins, Anthony Phillips, and Michael A. Knibb (Cambridge and New York: Cambridge University Press, 1982), 155-180.

bilities and gives new gifts. On that basis, the figure of seventy years is a first whisper of hope in the midst of exile. This reference at the edge of Israel's thinking affirms that Israel is now facing Yahweh's second season, a season of new life.

In Jer. 25:12-14 we encounter a quite new move in the tradition. While the seventy years is not usually taken literally, the reference suggests that the hated Babylonian hegemony has its limits and its end point. The text moves on with a *waw* consecutive, rendered "then" (v. 12). God turns against Babylon. According to this philosophy of history, the very empire dispatched by God (v. 9) is now harshly judged by God. The judgment of God against the empire is because of the "iniquity" of Babylon (v. 12). Isaiah 47 provides a more detailed account of this same theological verdict. God did indeed authorize Babylon against Judah (Isa. 47:6). But Babylon, without mercy and with much brutality, overstepped its mandate and was too severe (Isa. 47:6). Babylon is caught in a "no-win" situation, for it is judged by criteria about which it knew nothing. Babylon did not know that Yahweh, even in judgment on Judah ("my people, my heritage") sets limits on what is to be done as punishment. The very agent of punishment is in turn now to be punished. This new posture against Babylon gives new possibilities for Judah's future.

God's work is not ended in the destruction of Jerusalem. God continues to be at work, supervising the nations. Therein lies hope for Israel in exile. The two-stage philosophy of history—Babylonian mandate, Babylonian punishment—indicates that history is finally still governed by Yahweh's compassionate attention to Judah. The same two-stage structure of mandate-punishment is implemented against Assyria (Isa. 10:5-19) and, in a less direct way, against Gog (Ezek. 38–39). The practical effect is that Judah judged now becomes Judah with fresh historical possibility.

The great Babylonian Empire, which seemed eternal and beyond assault, is now to be utterly reduced and finally nullified (Jer. 25:12). Historical events implemented this verdict: in 537 Persia ended Babylonian imperialism. This text is not a historical comment, however. It is a theological assertion that no nation is finally autonomous and free of Yahweh's rule. Therein lies the source of Judah's judgment, and therein is the basis of Judah's hope. Yahweh rules.[37]

---

37. The general rubric for interpretation is Yahweh's sovereignty, a clue already presented in 1:10. For a critical analysis of such oracles, see Norman K. Gottwald, *All the Kingdoms of the Earth* (New York and London: Harper & Row, 1964).

Verse 13 contains an interesting editorial note. In the very text of Jeremiah we find an explicit reference to "the book of Jeremiah." This phraseology makes clear that v. 13 is a late redactional layer of the book, for the writer of this text has already had in hand some version of the book of Jeremiah. Moreover, this later redactional activity seems to complete the book with a denunciation of Babylon (cf. chs. 50–51).

Jeremiah 25:13-14 asserts God's judgment against the empire. In the end, Yahweh's solidarity is indeed with Judah and against Babylon. This occurs, however, only at the end, after "seventy years," after the land had been destroyed. It is most important for Israel (and for us) that Yahweh is not immutable but reverses policy in light of God's own compassion.[38] Israel's hope is precisely in Yahweh's freedom to limit what was "eternal." This is the source of hope offered in our text. It is a sure hope, but it is given voice only in the "second reading" made by the tradition of Jeremiah in the midst of exile.

25:15-29 This section constitutes a startling passage in Jeremiah, expressed in an idiom we have met nowhere else in the tradition. The governing metaphor is "the cup of wrath" which is given by Yahweh and which all the nations are forced to drink. Its content is a sentence of wrath, destruction, and devastation from God's hand, delivered by the prophet and inescapable for the nations. The idiom ("cup of wrath") is apocalyptic (cf. Mark 10:38-39; Rev. 14:10). The metaphor expresses the rhetoric of prophetic judgment writ large.[39] It asserts that the whole world of international order is coming unglued, as God has purposed. Every nation will suffer. It is a vision of God's majestic and sovereign power, from which no nation, kingdom, or empire is immune.

The prophet receives instruction to carry the cup to the nations (Jer. 25:15-16). Already in 1:10 Jeremiah had been sent to the na-

---

38. On God's capacity for change through suffering, see Terence E. Fretheim, *The Suffering of God* (Philadelphia: Fortress, 1984); Jörg Jeremias, *Die Reue Gottes: Aspekte alttestamentlicher Gottesvorstellung,* Biblische Studien 65 (Neukirchen-Vluyn: Neukirchener Verlag, 1975); and Walter Brueggemann, "A Shape for Old Testament Theology, II: Embrace of Pain," *Catholic Biblical Quarterly* 47 (1985): 395-415. Jonah 4:1-2 is the clearest articulation of this reality. It is precisely Yahweh's fidelity that requires that God not be immutable.

39. See William McKane, "Poison, Trial by Ordeal and the Cup of Wrath," *Vetus Testamentum* 30 (1980): 474-492. McKane seeks to go behind the metaphor "cup" to find its concrete usage in trial, judgment, and punishment. See 16:7 for a parallel metaphor, "cup of consolation."

tions. The Jeremiah tradition understands clearly that Judah's destiny in the ancient Near East is connected to that of the other nations. (See this theme explicitly in 29:7.) If Yahweh seriously presides over Judah's future, then Yahweh must also govern the nations. The nations are not autonomous. They finally must answer to Yahweh. They must answer to Yahweh's good news for Judah, whom Yahweh loves.

The command of 25:15-16 is implemented in vv. 17-26. Jeremiah is obedient and delivers the cup. These verses constitute a roll call of the nations of the ancient Near East. All nations are under judgment.[40] Three items are of special interest in this inventory of nations. First, consistent with what we have seen of the Jeremiah tradition, the list begins with Judah and Jerusalem. Judgment begins in God's people (1 Pet. 4:17). Judgment does not stop with God's people, however. It moves out in every direction. Second, the first nation named after Judah is Egypt. The Jeremiah tradition is particularly hostile toward Egypt and regards it as a formidable foil to Yahweh's purpose.[41] Third, last in the list is Babylon (Jer. 25:26). It is almost as if the list deliberately holds off this name for dramatic effect. No nation is immune, not even mighty Babylon. For Jews in exile, the inclusion of Babylon in the list for judgment is decisive. This nation which seemed beyond all accountability is judged. In that judgment Judah has a basis for future and hope. There are no limits to Yahweh's mighty sovereignty and Yahweh's terrible wrath. The claims of vv. 12-14 are now given full expression in the apocalyptic specificity of vv. 15-26.

The prophet is instructed on what to do with "the cup." The first imperative in v. 15 is "take." The prophet is to "make drink." That imperative is repeated in the imperatives of v. 27: "drink," followed by the series "be drunk, vomit, fall." The nations will be undone by the "cup" from which they cannot avoid drinking. The view of the

---

40. This large claim is already made for the Jeremiah tradition in 1:10. It is articulated in chs. 46–51, which in the Greek text (widely regarded as a preferred text) are placed in the midst of ch. 25. See J. Gerald Janzen, *Studies in the Text of Jeremiah*. Harvard Semitic Monograph 6 (Cambridge, Mass.: Harvard University Press, 1973), 115-116.

41. See Richard Elliott Friedman, "From Egypt to Egypt: Dtr[1] and Dtr[2]," in *Traditions in Transformation,* ed. Baruch Halpern and Jon D. Levenson (Winona Lake, Ind.: Eisenbrauns, 1981), 167-192. Friedman's analysis concerns the Deuteronomist, but his concluding comments note the related perspective of the Jeremiah tradition.

historical process expressed here presents a clear, coherent theory of punishment (vv. 28-29). Judgment begins with God's own people. That is not in doubt. But it moves from there beyond Judah.[42] That God judges Israel does not mean that God is indifferent to the other nations. All are accountable, and none escapes!

25:30-38 This section consists of a series of poetic fragments that have as a common theme the judgment of the nations. The first element (vv. 30-31) announces that God is about to work a judgment from his holy abode, which could be either Jerusalem or heaven (cf. 1 Kgs. 8:36,39; Amos 1:2). No nation is mentioned as the object of judgment. This is poetry that, unlike the prose of Jer. 25:17-26, lacks specificity. The language is partly juridical. Yahweh has an indictment and will punish wicked nations. Individuals are not sorted out for particular attention as in 5:1-5, but nations are treated under single verdicts. The poem asserts that there are moral criteria to which whole nations must answer. In 25:32, an isolated fragment, the evil will reach everywhere, and in v. 33 the corpses will be too many to grieve. No specifics are given, but the picture is surely the result of invasion (sword), famine, or an epidemic (pestilence). God's judgment is mediated through such disasters. The picture proposed partakes both of realism and fantasy.

The last poetic unit (vv. 34-38) asserts judgment once more, this time addressed specifically to "shepherds" (rulers). The ones who seem safest are now the ones assaulted. Even the royal class has no protection. It is usually the poor and marginal who cry in calamity, because they are more exposed to danger. Now, however, the cry comes from the center of society (cf. Exod. 11:6), because the judgment reaches into every protected place. No specific indictment is given beyond the reference to wickedness in Jer. 25:31. We surmise that the cause of judgment is that the nations do not practice the elemental requirements of justice, which apply in all regions of Yahweh's governance. The nations can never be strong enough or wise enough to avoid such a requirement.

The difficult and unusual text of ch. 25 suggests three conclusions. (1) This text is not really a statement of punishment, but of Yahweh's

---

42. The construction which moves from Judah to the nations contrasts with the pattern in Amos 1–2 which begins with the other nations and moves to Judah and finally to Israel. In both cases, the common theme of sovereignty and judgment is shown to pertain to both Israel-Judah and the nations.

sovereignty (cf. vv. 30-31). God has not abdicated God's governance. Finally, after a long, seeming indifference, God harshly calls all nations to accountability. All are found wanting and under heavy jeopardy.

(2) The countertheme to God's sovereignty is the denial of autonomy to the nation-states (v. 14). They seem to be autonomous and imagine themselves to be, but they are not. This is an exceedingly difficult theme in the face of modernity. The illusion of autonomy is powerful among us. Indeed, political powers in every time and place have imagined they were autonomous. The prophetic tradition relentlessly refutes such imagined autonomy.[43] The historical ordering of life among the nations has a moral coherence rooted in the reality of God's rule. God presides over the historical process and will not be mocked.

(3) There is no explicit hint of hope for Judah in ch. 25, except for the reference to a time limit (v. 11). Yahweh's sovereign rule over the nations has no instrumental purpose. It is not done for the sake of Judah. Nonetheless, insofar as the nations are called to accountability, and insofar as this includes Babylon, Yahweh's dreadful, inescapable sovereignty gives Judah its only possibility for the future. That Yahweh still rules the historical process and has not succumbed to Babylon or the gods of Babylon does indeed create a new chance for Judah. The Exile is not "forever" (v. 9). In the face of massive imperial power and cynical disregard of the moral dimension of human reality, God's sovereign rule is the only ground for historical possibility for God's people. Without the rule of Yahweh, Judah is at the disposal of the nations. Because of Yahweh's rule, however, Judah (and every vulnerable community) has a possibility in the historical process. This text asserts that the cynical, ruthless power of nations and empires is very real in the world, but such power is not the final reality. The final reality is in the One who "plucks up and tears down," who "plants and builds" (1:10). Yahweh is at work on both of these decisive, astonishing tasks which reshape life and evoke hope. There is a massive "cup of reeling," commensurate with massive human sin. The Jeremiah tradition shows God taking this sin with utmost seriousness. But there is, however, a second cup (Matt. 26:27; Mark 14:23) which is a cup of healing. It is then promised that the healing of God will overcome the reeling caused by God. In our text the second cup is held in abeyance. Here there is only reeling. God's people live in the midst of both cups. One is often bitter. The other is often held in abeyance. In the end the second cup is also "for all."

---

43. See Donald E. Gowan, *When Man Becomes God,* Pittsburgh Theological Monograph 6 (Pittsburgh: Pickwick, 1975).

SELECTED BIBLIOGRAPHY

Books

Bright, John. *Jeremiah,* 2nd ed. Anchor Bible 21 (Garden City, N.Y.: Doubleday, 1978).

Carroll, Robert P. *From Chaos to Covenant: Prophecy in the Book of Jeremiah* (London: SCM and New York: Crossroad, 1983).

Holladay, William L. *The Architecture of Jeremiah 1–20* (Lewisburg, Pa.: Bucknell University Press, 1976).

————. *Jeremiah: Spokesman Out of Time* (Philadelphia: United Church, 1974).

————. *Jeremiah 1.* Hermeneia (Philadelphia: Fortress and London: SCM, 1986).

Ittman, Norbert. *Die Konfessionen Jeremias: Ihre Bedeutung für die Verkündigung des Propheten.* Wissenschaftliche Monographien zum Alten und Neuen Testament 54 (Neukirchen-Vluyn: Neukirchener, 1981).

Janzen, J. Gerald. *Studies in the Text of Jeremiah.* Harvard Semitic Monograph 6 (Cambridge, Mass.: Harvard University Press, 1973).

McKane, William. *Jeremiah, 1.* International Critical Commentary (Edinburgh: T. & T. Clark, 1986.

Nicholson, Ernest W. *Preaching to the Exiles: A Study of the Prose Tradition in the Book of Jeremiah* (Oxford: Blackwell, 1970).

Perdue, Leo G., and Kovacs, Brian W., ed. *A Prophet to the Nations: Essays in Jeremiah Studies* (Winona Lake, Ind.: Eisenbrauns, 1984).

Polk, Timothy. *The Prophetic Persona: Jeremiah and the Language of the Self.* JSOT Supplement 32 (Sheffield: University of Sheffield Press, 1984).

Reventlow, Henning Graf. *Liturgie und prophetisches Ich bei Jeremia* (Gütersloh: Gerd Mohn, 1963).

Seitz, Christopher R. "Theology in Conflict: Reactions to the Exile in the Book of Jeremiah" (Ph.D. dissertation, Yale University, 1986).

Skinner, John. *Prophecy and Religion: Studies in the Life of Jeremiah* (1922; repr. Cambridge and New York: Cambridge University Press, 1955).

Welch, Adam C. *Jeremiah, His Time and His Work* (1928; repr. Oxford: Blackwell, 1951).

Articles

Ackroyd, Peter R. "The Book of Jeremiah—Some Recent Studies," *Journal for the Study of the Old Testament* 28 (1984): 47-59.

Brueggemann, Walter. "The Book of Jeremiah: Portrait of the Prophet," *Interpretation* 37 (1983): 130-145.

————. "Land, Fertility, and Justice," in *Theology of the Land,* ed. Bernard F. Evans and Gregory D. Cusack (Collegeville, Minn.: Liturgical Press, 1987), 41-68.

Gerstenberger, Erhard S. "Jeremiah's Complaints: Observations on Jer. 15:10-21," *Journal of Biblical Literature* 82 (1963): 393-408.

Holladay, William L. "The Covenant and the Patriarchs Overturned: Jeremiah's Intention in 'Terror on Every Side' (Jer. 20:1-6)," *Journal of Biblical Literature* 91 (1972): 305-320.

————. "The Years of Jeremiah's Preaching," *Interpretation* 37 (1983): 146-159.

Lemke, Werner E. "The Near and the Distant God: A Study of Jer. 23:23-24 in its Biblical Theological Context," *Journal of Biblical Literature* 100 (1981): 541-555.

McKane, William. " מצא in Jeremiah 23,33-40," in *Prophecy: Essays Presented to Georg Fohrer on His Sixty-Fifth Birthday,* ed. John A. Emerton. Beihefte zur Zeitschrift für alttestamentliche Wissenschaft 150 (1980): 35-54.

Overholt, Thomas W. "King Nebuchadnezzar in the Jeremiah Tradition," *Catholic Biblical Quarterly* 30 (1968): 39-48.

von Rad, Gerhard. "The Confessions of Jeremiah," in *A Prophet to the Nations,* ed. Perdue and Kovacs, 269-284.

Rowley, Harold H. "The Prophet Jeremiah and the Book of Deuteronomy," in *Studies in Old Testament Prophecy* (Edinburgh: Clark and New York: Scribners, 1950), 157-174.

Other Works

Ackroyd, Peter R. *Exile and Restoration: A Study of Hebrew Thought of the Sixth Century B.C.* Old Testament Library (Philadelphia: Westminster and London: SCM, 1968).

Alter, Robert. *The Art of Biblical Poetry* (New York: Basic Books, 1985).

Blank, Sheldon H. *"Of a Truth the Lord Hath Sent Me"* (Cincinnati: Hebrew Union College Press, 1955).

Bright, John. *Covenant and Promise: The Prophetic Understanding of the Future in Pre-Exilic Israel* (Philadelphia: Westminster, 1976).

Brueggemann, Walter. *Hopeful Imagination: Prophetic Voices in Exile* (Philadelphia: Fortress, 1986).

————. "A Shape for Old Testament Theology, II: Embrace of Pain," *Catholic Biblical Quarterly* 47 (1985): 395-415.

Childs, Brevard S. *Introduction to the Old Testament as Scripture* (Philadelphia: Fortress and London: SCM, 1979).

Cogan, Morton. *Imperialism and Religion: Assyria, Judah and Israel in the Eighth and Seventh Centuries B.C.E.* SBL Monograph 19 (Missoula, Mont.: Scholars Press, 1974).

Crenshaw, James L. *Prophetic Conflict: Its Effect upon Israelite Religion.*

Beihefte zur Zeitschrift für die alttestamentliche Wissenschaft 124 (1971).

Fretheim, Terence E. *The Suffering of God* (Philadelphia: Fortress, 1984).

Gottwald, Norman K. *All the Kingdoms of the Earth* (New York and London: Harper & Row, 1964).

Gowan, Donald E. *When Man Becomes God: Humanism and Hubris in the Old Testament*. Pittsburgh Theological Monograph 6 (Pittsburgh: Pickwick, 1975).

Greenberg, Moshe. *Biblical Prose Prayer* (Berkeley: University of California Press, 1983).

Hardy, Daniel W., and Ford, David F. *Praising and Knowing God* (Philadelphia: Westminster, 1985).

Heschel, Abraham J. *The Prophets* (New York and London: Harper & Row, 1962).

Kitamori, Kazō. *Theology of the Pain of God* (Richmond: John Knox and London: SCM, 1965).

Klein, Ralph W. *Israel in Exile: A Theological Interpretation*. Overtures to Biblical Theology 6 (Philadelphia: Fortress, 1979).

Koch, Klaus. *The Prophets*. Vol. 1: *The Assyrian Period* (Philadelphia: Fortress and London: SCM, 1983). Vol. 2: *The Babylonian and Persian Periods* (1984).

McKay, John W. *Religion in Judah under the Assyrians, 732-609 B.C.* Studies in Biblical Theology, 2nd series 26 (Naperville: Allenson and London: SCM, 1973).

Mendenhall, George E. "The 'Vengeance' of Yahweh," in *The Tenth Generation* (Baltimore: Johns Hopkins University Press, 1973), 69-104.

Miller, J. Maxwell, and Hayes, John H. *A History of Ancient Israel and Judah* (Philadelphia: Westminster and London: SCM, 1986).

Miller, Patrick D., Jr. "The Human Sabbath: A Study in Deuteronomic Theology," *Princeton Seminary Bulletin* New Series 6 (1985): 81-97.

―――. *Sin and Judgment in the Prophets*. SBL Monograph 27 (Chico, Calif.: Scholars Press, 1982).

Niditch, Susan. *The Symbolic Vision in Biblical Tradition*. Harvard Semitic Monograph 30 (Chico, Calif.: Scholars Press, 1983).

Oded, Bustenay. "Judah and the Exile," in *Israelite and Judean History*, ed. Hayes, John H., and Miller, J. Maxwell. Old Testament Library (Philadelphia: Westminster and London: SCM, 1977).

von Rad, Gerhard. *Old Testament Theology*. 2 vols. (New York: Harper & Row and Edinburgh: Oliver & Boyd, 1962-1965).

Trible, Phyllis. *God and the Rhetoric of Sexuality*. Overtures to Biblical Theology 2 (Philadelphia: Fortress, 1978).

Wilson, Robert R. *Prophecy and Society in Ancient Israel* (Philadelphia: Fortress, 1980).